THE FIRST FIVE HUNDRED

Library and Archives Canada Cataloguing in Publication

Cramm, Richard, author
The first five hundred : the Royal Newfoundland Regiment in Gallipoli
and on the Western Front during the Great War (1914-1918) / Richard Cramm;
introduction by Michael O'Brien.

Reprint of The first five hundred. Originally published: Albany, N.Y. : C.F.
Williams, 1921.
ISBN 978-1-927099-56-8 (bound)

1. Great Britain. Army. Newfoundland Regiment, 1st. 2. World War,
1914-1918–Regimental histories–Great Britain. 3. World War, 1914-1918–
Campaigns–Western Front. 4. World War, 1914-1918–Campaigns–Turkey–
Gallipoli Peninsula. 5. World War, 1914-1918–Newfoundland and Labrador.
6. Soldiers–Newfoundland and Labrador–Biography. I. O'Brien, Michael,
1959-, writer of introduction II. Title.

D547.N55C7 2015   940.4'12718   C2014-905150-6

This edition published by Boulder Publications 2015
Portugal Cove-St. Philip's, Newfoundland and Labrador
www.boulderpublications.ca

Printed in Canada

Cover design and interior layout by Sarah Hansen

We acknowledge the financial support of the Government of Newfoundland and Labrador through
the Department of Tourism, Culture and Rural Development.

We acknowledge the financial support for our publishing program by the Government of Canada and
the Department of Canadian Heritage through the Canada Book Fund.

THE FIRST FIVE HUNDRED

Being a historical sketch of the military operations

of the

Royal Newfoundland Regiment

in Gallipoli and on the Western Front
during the Great War (1914-1918)

Together with the individual military records and
photographs where obtainable of the men of
the first contingent, known as the "The First
Five Hundred," or "The Blue Puttees."

By
RICHARD CRAMM

Published by
C. F. WILLIAMS & SON, INC.
Albany, New York, U. S. A.

INTRODUCTION

A century has now passed since Newfoundland Governor Sir Walter Davidson issued a proclamation calling for 500 volunteers to form a Newfoundland Regiment for service in "the greatest War in the history of the World." With much of the country caught up in the patriotic enthusiasm that accompanied the outbreak of war, the goal of 500 men had been reached within a month, and the Regiment began training at Pleasantville camp, near St. John's. Over the next four years, the men of the Newfoundland Regiment would distinguish themselves on the battlefields of Europe as, in the words of Field Marshal Sir Douglas Haig, "better than the best."

Although by the war's end over 6,000 men would serve in the Newfoundland Regiment (the title "Royal" was granted in early 1918), pride of place has long been given to the "First Five Hundred," that is, the first contingent of volunteers who joined up in the early weeks of the war and were sent overseas on 3 October 1914. "First Five Hundred" is a slight misnomer, though, as the term has always been applied to all 537 officers and men of the first contingent.

The men of the first contingent also proudly carried the nickname "The Blue Puttees," after the improvised military garb in which they were sent overseas. The Patriotic Association, which administered the Regiment, had initially intended to outfit the men in British service dress uniforms, but this idea had to be scrapped when the requisite khaki serge material proved impossible to obtain. So instead, they created distinctive fatigue uniforms for the men, patterned after those of Brabant's Horse, an irregular colonial cavalry unit that fought in the Anglo-Boer War of 1899–1902. That unit's dark blue cloth leggings, or puttees, also became part of the Newfoundland Regiment's first uniforms. Hence, the men of the First Five Hundred came to be dubbed "The Blue Puttees," an appellation which stuck with them long after their switch to standard British service dress in late 1914.

While the early volunteers signed on to the Regiment for a period of one year, almost all of them agreed to re-enlist in 1915 for the duration of the war. Men of the First Five Hundred would go on to fight in numerous engagements, from the landings at Suvla Bay in September 1915 to the battle of Courtrai in October 1918. Over 150 of the Blue Puttees lost their lives during the war, with roughly half of those deaths coming in a single action: the ill-fated attack at Beaumont Hamel on the first day of the battle of the Somme. Those who remained until the end of the war returned to St. John's in the summer of 1919, where the Regiment was disbanded in late August.

While a majority of the First Five Hundred were from St. John's, other parts of the island were represented within their ranks, and many Newfoundlanders today have family connections to one or more of the Blue Puttees. In my own case, there was my great-uncle, Corporal Michael Vail of St. Mary's, who was a 21-year-old police constable in St. John's at the outbreak of war. He fought in the Gallipoli campaign, but was discharged in 1916 after suffering a severe case of dysentery. After leaving the military, he returned to service in the Constabulary, and later moved back to St. Mary's, where he owned and operated a tavern until his death in the early 1960s. This is but one case among hundreds of Newfoundland families who saw loved ones off to war in 1914, some lucky enough to see their soldier boy return, others left to mourn his passing.

It was as a tribute to these 537 volunteers that this book was written. Its author, Richard Cramm, was born in 1889 in Small Point, Conception Bay. The son of a merchant, he was educated at Wesleyan University in Middletown, Connecticut. On his return to Newfoundland, he took up a position as a student-at-law in the St. John's firm of Squires and Winter, of which the senior partner was soon-to-be Prime Minister Richard Squires. In 1923, Cramm entered politics as a member of Squires's Liberal Reform party, being elected as an MHA for Baie de Verde and later serving as Attorney General. He returned to the practice of law after losing his seat in the 1928 election. Immediately after confederation with Canada, Cramm briefly re-entered politics, running unsuccessfully as a Progressive Conservative in the 1949 provincial election. He practiced law until his death in 1958.

By early 1920, while still employed at Squires and Winter, Cramm had begun work on an illustrated history of the First Five Hundred to create a tribute to what he termed their "persistent gallantry and splendid achievements." Though it began as a private venture, the project soon obtained official sanction. To offset the high printing costs for a book with so many half-tone illustrations, Cramm received some financial support from the Newfoundland government, which agreed to purchase 500 copies from public funds at the price of $5.50 per copy. In April 1920, to expedite publication, the government provided Cramm with an advance of $1,000, drawn from the "War Expenses" account. The remaining $1,750 was paid to him on the book's publication in 1921. The government also agreed to exempt the book from customs duty and sales tax.

The government's willingness to subsidize Cramm's efforts was at least in part the result of its own difficulties in getting an official war history written. Though a War History Committee had been established by the Patriotic Association in 1917, and a year later British war correspondent F.A. Mackenzie was commissioned to write an official account, nothing had been forthcoming by 1920. So Cramm's *The First Five Hundred* provided the opportunity to at least have something in print. When Mackenzie finally came up with a manuscript in 1927, the government rejected it as inadequate, and subsequent efforts to create an official history came to naught. Thus Cramm's work remained the most extensive published account of the war service of the Royal Newfoundland Regiment until the appearance of *The Fighting Newfoundlander*, Colonel G.W.L. Nicholson's official history of the Regiment, in 1964.

While the strongly patriotic tone of his prose seems rather dated today, Cramm's account of the Newfoundlanders' exploits stands up fairly well almost a century later as an introductory chronicle of the wartime activities of the Regiment. The inclusion of the service records of every one of the First Five Hundred makes this book an essential reference work for anyone researching Newfoundland's military history in World War I.

In his preface, Cramm states that his purpose in writing is that "the young people of our country ... will not forget the heroes of their own country." That purpose holds true for this republication of *The First Five Hundred*: that subsequent generations will continue to remember those 537 brave young Newfoundlanders who went off to a faraway war a century ago.

Michael O'Brien
Department of History
Memorial University

Preface

THIS volume has a twofold purpose. The first is to chronicle briefly the military operations of the heroic, fighting battalion that represented Newfoundland among the gallant and victorious troops of the British Empire in the greatest war of history, and to illustrate its persistent gallantry and splendid achievements by reference in each chapter to conspicuous individual heroism. The second purpose is to put in compact form and within reach of the public the individual military records of the first contingent which embarked from Saint John's on the most solemn duty that has ever been thrust upon our country. The latter purpose has been greatly facilitated by the data available at the Militia Department. The task of procuring individual pictures of the men of the first contingent, which would add meaning and individuality to each record, has, however, been a most difficult one. Only slightly less difficult has been the task of getting proper information regarding the various engagements in which our Regiment took part. The work has necessitated scores of interviews, and a continual search for scraps of information wherever it could be found. This work does not profess, however, to be a detailed record of the whole of the movements and a complete description of every engagement of the Regiment. Many readers may be fortunate enough to be able to supplement some of the descriptions or movements with interesting information already in their possession. These, however, will be comparatively few. The hope is that the information contained herein will become general, especially among the young people of our country, who, when reading of heroes and heroic accomplishments, will not forget the heroes of their own country.

R. C.

SERGEANT RICKETTS, V. C.

PRIVATE T. RICKETTS

PRIVATE T. RICKETTS was awarded the VICTORIA CROSS for most conspicuous bravery and devotion to duty on October 14, 1918. During the advance from Ledgehem the attack was temporarily held up by heavy hostile fire, and the platoon to which he belonged suffered severe casualties from the fire of a battery at point blank range. Private Ricketts at once volunteered to go forward with his Section Commander and a Lewis Gun to attempt to outflank the battery. They advanced by short rushes while subject to severe fire from enemy machine guns. When 300 yards away, their ammunition gave out. The enemy, seeing an opportunity to get their field guns away, began to bring up their gun teams. Private Ricketts at once realized the situation. He doubled back 100 yards, procured some ammunition and dashed back to the Lewis gun, and by very accurate fire drove the enemy and their gun teams into a farm. His platoon then advanced without casualties, and captured four field guns, four machine guns and eight prisoners. A fifth field gun was subsequently intercepted by fire and captured. By his presence of mind in anticipating the enemy intention and his utter disregard for personal safety, Private Ricketts secured the further supplies of ammunition which directly resulted in these important captures and undoubtedly saved many lives.

SIR RICHARD ANDERSON SQUIRES, K. C. M. G., PRIME MINISTER

HON. W. R. WARREN, K.C.
Minister of Justice

HON. W. F. COAKER
Minister of Marine & Fisheries

NEWFOUNDLAND

HON. H. J. BROWNRIGG
Minister of Finance & Customs

HON. ALEX CAMPBELL, M.D.
Minister of Agriculture & Mines

HON. W. W. HALFYARD
Minister of Posts & Telegraphs

HON. S.J. FOOTE, K.C.

HON. ARTHUR BARNES, Ph.D.
Minister of Education

NEWFOUNDLAND

HON. GEORGE SHEA

W.H. CAVE, ESQ.
Minister of Shipping

W.B. JENNINGS, ESQ.
Minister of Public Works

SIR E. P. MORRIS (NOW LORD MORRIS)
Who was Prime Minister of Newfoundland at the outbreak of the great war and quickly rallied Newfoundland
to the aid of The Empire.

JOHN R. BENNETT, ESQ.
Who was Colonial Secretary of Newfoundland at the outbreak of the war. He later became the first Minister of Militia.

LIEUTENANT-COLONEL (REV.) THOMAS NANGLE
Newfoundland's Representative on the Imperial War
Graves' Commission.

PART I

Historical Sketch of the Military Operations of the
Royal Newfoundland Regiment

CHAPTER I

From Saint John's Through Gallipoli

When the great war-cloud burst over the world in August, 1914, Newfoundland was engrossed in her peaceful occupations. From a military standpoint no country could be in a state of greater unpreparedness. Such various Church organizations as the Methodist Guards, the Highlanders, the Church Lads' Brigade and the Roman Catholic Cadets had very little resemblance to a modern military organization, though their ranks became rapidly depleted by the enlistment of the Regiment. And even those organizations were confined to Saint John's. In the outports there was no group or body of men either in the nature of a military or social organization that could render any assistance as a unit in preparing to fight an enemy.

Newfoundland unprepared for a military emergency.

From the standpoint of immediately available untrained men the country was scarcely more prepared than in military organization. It was the time of every year when almost the entire country is engrossed in the prosecution of the cod fishery. Large numbers of men were scattered along the Labrador coast, far from the excitement and anxiety caused by the international cloudburst. And others, a greater number, were engaged in the same work at their homes around the entire Island. They were engrossed in a means of livelihood that could not be put off for a month, or even a week, but a kind of work upon the success of one brief week of which the happiness of the family for the entire year might depend. At any time of the year from October to May the response to a national call would have been many times as great.

The Government, however, lost no time in taking suitable action to meet the emergency. On the eighth of August Governor Davidson wired the Secretary of State as follows: "Ministers desire authority to enlist special men service abroad by land and sea. Ministers undertake to raise force of Naval Reserve by October 31st to 1000 efficient men available for naval service abroad for one year and are willing to meet all local expense. Several hundred with efficient local brigade training offer for enlistment

Government action.

for land service abroad. Believe that 500 could be enlisted within one month. Propose to induce serviceable men between 18 and 35 years to enroll themselves in training for home defense wherever corps instructors are available. These will form material for further drafts." On the following day the Secretary of State replied to Governor Davidson: "Your telegram of August 8th. His Majesty's Government gladly avail themselves of offer of your Government to raise troops for land service abroad. Will telegraph later as to Naval Reserve." For the purpose of making good our offer, a preliminary meeting was held on the afternoon of the tenth of August in the Executive Council Chamber, and was presided over by the Prime Minister, Sir E. P. Morris. Besides the Prime Minister there were present at that meeting the Colonial Secretary, Mr. J. R. Bennett; Lieutenant-Commander MacDermott of the H. M. S. Calypso; Inspector General Sullivan; Captain Wakefield, M. D., of the Legion of Frontiersmen; Major Hutchings of the Methodist Guards' Brigade; Lieutenant-Colonel Rendell of the Church Lads' Brigade; Lieutenant-Colonel Patterson of the Highlanders; Major Carty of the Catholic Cadet Corps; Captain Goodridge and Captain J. W. Morris of the Rifle Club. On Wednesday night, August 12, a public patriotic meeting was held in the C. L. B. Armory, the purpose of which, as stated by Sir E. P. Morris (now Lord Morris), was to endorse what the Government had already decided on. The enthusiasm of the meeting left no doubt that the public endorsation of the Government's action was unanimous.

During the following week patriotic meetings were held for the purpose of getting together an efficient organization that would be responsible for the immediate development of a military force. The public spirit ran high. While public excitement, and, in consequence, confusion, would have been more pronounced, the spirit of unselfish patriotism and of resistance of a brutal and militaristic enemy could not have been greater if the enemy were at the entrance of Saint John's harbor. On August 21, a proclamation was issued by the Governor-in-Council calling for 500 volunteers. If the patriotic meeting of the twelfth lacked anything in the way of demonstrating the public endorsation of the Government's action that was unquestionably supplied by the public response during the days immediately following the issuing of the proclamation. By the thirty-first of August over 500 had offered their services, mostly from the stores and offices of the Capital City. It is significant that considerably more than half of these hailed from the city brigades. On September 3, the second day of the Legislative Session, Governor David-

son informed the Prime Minister that in response to a telegraphic message he (Governor Davidson) had replied saying that "the Newfoundland Regiment is now 800 strong and going under canvas. Contingent of 500 will be ready to start on the first of October."

No. 1 TENT AT PLEASANTVILLE, 1914
Being the first ten men to take the oath.
Standing, left to right: W. H. Janes, J. Thompson, N. Patrick, M. Sears, J. Long.
Sitting, left to right: J. Irvine, R. Andrews, G. Langmead, J. Carter, R. Williams.
This tent produced 4 Commissioned Officers, 1 Warrant Officer (1st class), 1 Warrant Officer (2nd class), 3 Sergeants, 1 Private.

The action which had already been taken by the Governor-in-Council received the necessary legislative sanction by the enactment on September 4 by the General Assembly, which met on September the second, and was again prorogued on the seventh of "AN ACT RESPECTING

A VOLUNTEER FORCE IN THIS COLONY." Section 1 of the Act provided, that: "The Governor may accept the services of any persons desirous of being formed under this Act into a volunteer corps and offering their services, and upon such acceptance the proposed corps shall be deemed to be lawfully formed."

First War Legislation.

Section 5 provided that: "Volunteers shall be enlisted for service abroad and for home defence against the alien enemies of the King. Every volunteer shall sign a roll in which the conditions

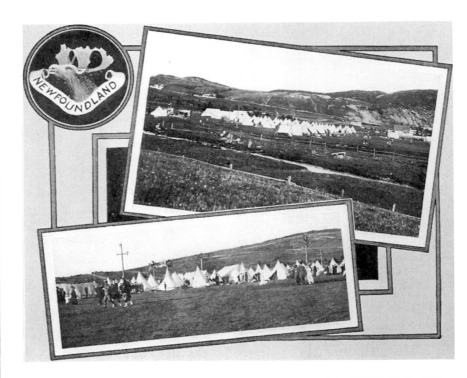

TWO VIEWS OF PLEASANTVILLE MILITARY CAMPS, SEPTEMBER, 1914

of his service shall be stated. No person shall be enlisted for a longer period than the duration of the war, but not exceeding one year." It was the general opinion at that time that one year would cover the period for which military service would be required, but we shall later see that re-enlistment became necessary while the volunteer force was still in training in England and at a time when men of the type of the Newfoundland force were badly needed to reinforce the troops that were operating against the Turks on the Gallipoli Peninsula.

IN TRAINING AT PLEASANTVILLE, SEPTEMBER, 1914.

The month of September was spent in the rudiments of military training in Saint John's. The scene created by the hastily constructed military camps at Pleasantville will for many years remain fresh in the memories of the people of the Capital City. It was an entirely new scene, and one

LIEUTENANT-COLONEL W. H. FRANKLIN, D. S. O., AND HIS SON.

of immense importance. The uniforms worn by the first volunteers speak adequately of Newfoundland's military preparedness in peace times. They remind one of a famous utterance by an American states-man when he was opposing any increase in the military forces of the United States. "If a foreign foe should invade our shores," he said,

"a million of us would rush to the shore and push them into the sea." Fortunately it was not the uniforms that counted, but the same high spirit of patriotism and courage that carried the Newfoundland Regiment through a glorious record. No small amount of credit is due Lieutenant-Colonel Franklin whose untiring efforts contributed so largely to the success of the initial steps in the formation of the Newfoundland Battalion. He gave up his successful business, and devoted his entire energy and attention to the training of the first contingent.

On the fourth of October, the first contingent of the land force that was to represent Newfoundland in the Allies' struggle against Central Europe set out for England on the H. M. S. Florizel. The event was one which, in point of military importance and demonstrated national patriotism, was without parallel in Newfoundland history. In answer to the call of the Mother Country her Oldest Colony had spoken in no uncertain terms. The voice of the country was loud and clear, and at no time during the struggle, not even when the hardest blow was met at Beaumont Hamel, can there be said

First Contingent embarked for England.

H. M. S. FLORIZEL WITH THE BLUE PUTTEES.

to have been a note of uncertainty or faintheartedness. Whatever doubt there may have been as to the wisdom of the method of raising men, the fact that men were to be raised was practically unquestioned, even in the more isolated parts where the supreme importance of the situation

OFFICERS OF THE FIRST NEWFOUNDLAND REGIMENT, 1915

Top row, left to right: Tait, Ledingham, Nunns, Wighton, Summers, Rowsell, Goodridge, Butler, Wakefield.

Bottom, left to right: Ayre, Raley, O'Brien, Alexander, Rendell, De-Burton, Carty, Bernard, March.

was not fully realized and hence the spirit of national patriotism not so fully aroused. Voluntary enlistment may have been regarded as a plausible method during the first months of the war when it was almost unanimously believed that the war would be of short duration, but after Lord Kitchener's famous prediction it must have been apparent to the enlightened legislators of that time that the only democratic, fair and systematic method, though more difficult to operate and less tasteful to the politician, would have been selective conscription. No sentimental argument should stand in the way of efficiency and fairness. The United States did not for one moment question the loyalty and patriotism of her subjects, though she had scarcely declared war on the Central Powers before she announced a plan of selective conscription. Political expediency, especially when international or intercolonial questions are involved, is a menace to the right conduct of any country. At the moment that this chapter is being written the United States are placing their own sincerity, and, indeed, their whole national reputation, at stake by declining to support or make any pronouncement on the League of Nations, though they themselves brought in the plan to forever prevent the horribleness and inhumanity of modern wars. Political expediency versus national and international interests, and in all such cases the former generally wins. The point is worthy of notice here only because it involves a very important principle affecting the conduct of our own Government while the question of maintaining a battalion in the field was persistently asking for a non-political solution.

Our concern here, however, is not the particular method adopted for raising and maintaining a battalion, but to chronicle briefly the military operations of our Battalion with its splendid record of heroism and ability. More than ten months were spent at Salisbury Plain, Fort George near Inverness, Stobs Camp near Hawick and finally at Aldershot in intensive military training, during which time several other drafts were sent over seas which brought the Regiment up to full battalion strength. It will be remembered that volunteers were first accepted for a period of one year, but at Aldershot, where the last days of training were spent, upon being given the alternatives, when reviewed by His Majesty the King and Lord Kitchener, of returning home or enlisting for the period of the war practically every man accepted the latter alternative.

It was on the same day, in the early part of August, that Lord Kitchener made the pronouncement that the Newfoundlanders were just the men he wanted for Gallipoli, and a week later, on the seventeenth

Selected for Gallipoli. of August, they were informed that on that same night they would embark for the Dardanelles. The order went into effect, and early next morning the Regiment detrained at Devonport and marched on board the converted cruiser, "Megantic,"*

* See Extracts from the diary of the late Lieut. O. W. Steele at the end of this chapter for details.

A COMPANY, 1st NEWFOUNDLAND REGIMENT, BEFORE EMBARKING FOR GALLIPOLI.

NEWFOUNDLAND

ROYAL

NEWFOUNDLAND

REGIMENT

which was to take them to Alexandria. At Alexandria the Regiment entrained for Cairo, and on arrival there marched into camp at Heliopolis, on the desert about a mile from Cairo. The stay at Cairo was brief, only a few days, and the Regiment proceeded to Mudros (Mudros had been selected as a subsidiary base of the Allies), in Lemnos, from which port it arrived at Suvla shortly after 9 o'clock in the evening of September 19.

Before continuing to trace the operations of the Newfoundland Regiment it is necessary that we understand something of the stage of the Gallipoli campaign when our Battalion arrived there, and the conditions under which it was fought by the Allied troops. As stated above, the port of Mudros, in the historic Island of Lemnos, about fifty miles from Gallipoli, was selected as a necessary subsidiary base. Mudros, as far as facilitating the campaign or being in any way beneficial to the Allied forces was concerned, was scarcely more than a safe anchorage. Quantities of stores, such as ammunition and fuel for the ships engaged, could with great difficulty be stored there, but no supplies for the troops or the battleships could be purchased there. The Island produces comparatively little of what is consumed by its own small population. Neither did it offer any facilities for loading or discharging, so that the work of storing supplies of anything like the quantity required involved an enormous amount of incessant and strenuous toil. At Gallipoli this situation was aggravated and intensified by the fact that the work had to be done under the fire of the enemy's guns. When a large British transport crossed the English Channel with a load of shells and big guns she pulled alongside a commodious pier in a French port, and her cargo was rapidly discharged by the use of powerful cranes, with comparatively little manual labor and out of the reach and sound of enemy guns. At Gallipoli ships' derricks were used for taking the cargoes from the decks and the holes of ships, but there the labor-saving devices of scientific invention ended and incessant, arduous toil began. Only the troops who actually did the work can fully understand the difficulties and the hardships. Probably, however, the greatest difficulty, failure in which caused the greatest demoralization and enervation among the troops, was in keeping on hand an adequate supply of fresh water to relieve the scorching thirst of a whole army. The strip of land occupied by the Allied troops offered no fresh water that could with safety be utilized. This meant that all the water used by our entire army had to be brought

Stage of the Gallipoli Campaign.

Inspection by Sir William MacGregor, Representing the "Army Council" at the historic event of the Newfoundland Regiment receiving its colors, the gift of the "Daughters of the Empire."

Officiating Clergy representing three denominations, and Lady MacGregor representing the "Daughters of the Empire."

Lady MacGregor presenting the colors and Lieutenant Fox receiving them on behalf of the Regiment, June 11, 1915, at Stobs Camp.

Battalion "at ease" after receiving its colors.

W. & N. C. Os. ROYAL NEWFOUNDLAND REGIMENT—STOBS CAMP, 1915.

Back Row: W. Chancey, S. James, A. Canham, C. Rendell.

2nd from back: S. Goodyear, A. Penny, A. S. Newman, W. Manstan, W. Ryall, N. MacLeod, J. Williams, J. Robinson, W. Clare, J. Gardner, C. Duley, E. Butcher, C. James, G. Hicks, J. Bethune, S. Smith, W. Ayre.

3rd from back: S. Ferguson, C. Oke, G. Taylor, C. Strong, W. Edwards, B. Dicks, E. Ebsary, M. McKay, G. Paver, H. McNeill, H. Ross, R. Ferguson, W. Miles, L. Murphy, C. Melville, L. Stick, H. Peckham, D. Eaton.

Front row: M. Nugent, E. Barnes, R. Kershaw, G. Byrne, J. Snow, E. Churchill, G. Langmead, E. Edwards, R. Stick.

500 miles. The quantity needed was 80 tons a day. Without fresh water in the scorching heat of a Gallipoli summer's day, living on a salt meat diet, while engaged in the most strenuous labor,—carrying heavy packs and getting large pieces of machinery up trackless hills,—and all under the fire of the enemy's guns, created a hardship and mental strain which only the men who actually did it can ever fully appreciate.

It was in the face of these difficulties and others of scarcely less magnitude that the Gallipoli campaign was carried on from April 25, 1915, when the first landing was effected, until the first days of 1916. The fighting during May, June, July and the first part of August was very severe, and costly in human life. Not only, however, was the German boast that the Allied troops would not land settled for all time, but great successes were achieved and possession taken of a considerable portion of the Peninsula. The record is one of glorious sacrifice and unsurpassable courage. The Allied offensive terminated with the failure of the thrust at Sari Bair, August 6th–10th. It failed through lack of sufficient men and water. The five days' battle on a front of twelve miles had cost the Allies almost a quarter of their entire Gallipoli army. Fifty thousand men, with large quantities of food and ammunition supplies would be required for another attack. It was decided that these should not be sent, and after several thrusts during the latter days of August the fighting on both sides settled down into trench warfare.

This, then, is the situation both as regards the nature and the stage of the Gallipoli campaign, when, in the early morning of September 20, the Newfoundland Regiment landed on the beach **Regiment Landed at Suvla.** at Suvla, and was shelled for the first time by the enemy. The beach was piled high with ammunition, sand bags, large and small guns and innumerable other things that go to make up the equipment of an army. The ground inland was very hilly and in some places set with steep clifts, and as our men moved off in this direction in small platoons the Turkish shell fire became heavier. One officer and eight men of other ranks were wounded during the first day. As night came on, under cover of darkness, our Regiment marched toward the trenches, about four miles distant, A Company taking a position in the support trenches. Each day a new company went into the support trenches, and on the 24th A and B Companies relieved the Worcester and Hampshire Regiments respectively. These two regiments with the King's Own Scottish Borderers and now the Newfoundlanders constituted the 88th Brigade, and formed part of Sir

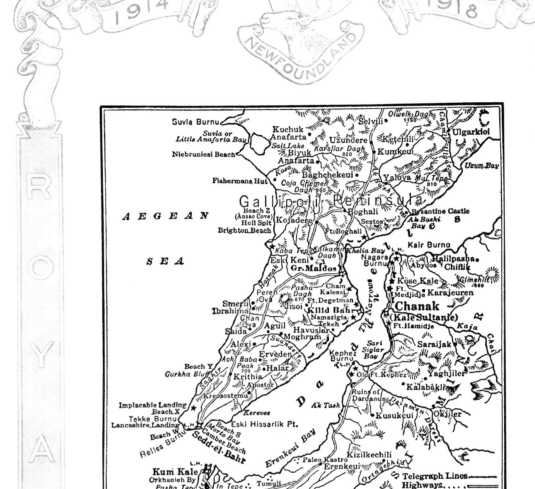

THE LAND OPERATIONS ON GALLIPOLI

The various beaches where British, Australian and Newfoundland troops
made landings on the west coast of the peninsula, are indicated as
"Beach W," "Beach X," etc., running north to "Beach Z."
Points where some of the severest fighting took place,
after the cliff on the shore had been surmounted
were Krithia, Achi Baba, Gaba Tepe, and
Anafarta. In the earlier operations
with ships the Dardanelles were
penetrated almost through
the Narrows.

The beach where numerous troops landed.

Mule Gully, a scene familiar to our men who fought at Gallipoli,
and typical of the inland approach.

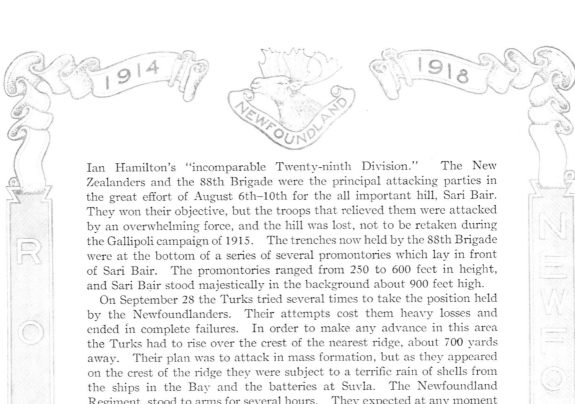

Ian Hamilton's "incomparable Twenty-ninth Division." The New Zealanders and the 88th Brigade were the principal attacking parties in the great effort of August 6th–10th for the all important hill, Sari Bair. They won their objective, but the troops that relieved them were attacked by an overwhelming force, and the hill was lost, not to be retaken during the Gallipoli campaign of 1915. The trenches now held by the 88th Brigade were at the bottom of a series of several promontories which lay in front of Sari Bair. The promontories ranged from 250 to 600 feet in height, and Sari Bair stood majestically in the background about 900 feet high.

On September 28 the Turks tried several times to take the position held by the Newfoundlanders. Their attempts cost them heavy losses and ended in complete failures. In order to make any advance in this area the Turks had to rise over the crest of the nearest ridge, about 700 yards away. Their plan was to attack in mass formation, but as they appeared on the crest of the ridge they were subject to a terrific rain of shells from the ships in the Bay and the batteries at Suvla. The Newfoundland Regiment stood to arms for several hours. They expected at any moment the order to advance and engage the enemy, or to have to ward off a strong enemy attack. Although the Turks did make an attempt to advance, and in great strength, so accurate and destructive was the work of our ships and artillery that comparatively few of the enemy were left to be held up by rifle fire. No casualties were suffered by our men.

Practically no attempt was made by the enemy after this time to take the position held by the Newfoundland Regiment, and life at Gallipoli became monotonous and full of routine. The whole experience was a complete disappointment to our men. They went to fight the Turks, but, as we have seen, the Allied offensive at Gallipoli was over more than a month before the Newfoundland Regiment arrived there. But it must not be concluded that the soldier's life at Gallipoli from this time until evacuation was mere play. Quite to the contrary; conditions brought about by other enemies were far worse than the Turks were capable of creating by military activity. Dysentery and enteric **Dysentery and** spread with amazing rapidity and played havoc with the **Enteric.** entire forces. In front of the trenches held by our men were the corpses of hundreds of the enemy. Clouds of flies swarmed over these as they decayed in the sweltering heat of the day. The same flies preyed on the food and the drink, carrying disease and death in their trail. High winds blew the Peninsula sandy soil, which was thickly inhabited with disease germs, into the food and the water. The

very fine sand, apart from any disease germs carried by it, was claimed to be responsible for much of the dysentery. Available hospitals at Alexandria, Cairo, and other places were filled with men suffering from dysentery and enteric, and, as will be seen from the records of the "FIRST FIVE HUNDRED," many of our men were invalided to hospitals, some going to England. The vitality of the entire army was lowered. Few escaped the disease entirely, and many died from its effects.

Apart from the haunts of disease and extreme thirst, life was scarcely more than a daily routine. There was some shelling every day and every night, especially when either side showed unusual activity. Machine gun and rifle fire formed part of the daily and nightly program; but the most effective activity on the part of the enemy was sniping. Every possible nook or place of any kind in which they could conceal themselves was inhabited by Turkish snipers. Specially did they watch with great vigilance any place where drinking water could be obtained, so that any of our men who attempted to relieve their maddening thirst was shot down by cleverly hidden snipers. One writer, referring to the Newfoundland Regiment, says: "The soldiers had come expecting to find war a life of excitement. They found it, on the contrary, duller than the most dreary spells of lonely life in the back woods of their own island. * * * The heat, the hard work, the flies, the thirst, and the intermittent shelling combined to tax the nerves and temper of the men to the full." Dullness, however, in the outport settlements of Newfoundland, has no resemblance, not even in the matter of degree, to the experience of our men at Gallipoli. It was dull only in the sense that there was no severe fighting. Disease and deprivations created hardships that were too great for human strength.

Sickness Caused Many Casualties. As an indication of how the ranks became depleted, although the Regiment sustained comparatively few casualties from the activities of the Turks, up to October 11 only half of the Regiment was in the front line at one time, and its place was taken after six or seven days by the other half. From that date it was no longer possible to make such a division. The whole Regiment went in together, with the time of relief always very uncertain. Usually, however, the period during which they were in the front line trenches was double what it had previously been. Relief depended upon Imperial troops being available. The only diversion from digging new trenches and making those already occupied more comfortable was in hunting enemy snipers. For this purpose, and also for the purpose of finding out what the Turks were doing, patrol parties would go out into No Man's Land every night.

One of these patrols had a trying experience. On the night of November 4, a patrol sent out under Lieutenant J. J. Donnelly occupied a ridge midway between the trenches occupied by the enemy and those held by our men. From this ridge the Turks had been giving trouble every night for some time. The patrol had scarcely reached the ridge before it was opposed by the enemy who outnumbered our men by about seven to one. The sound of the firing from the ridge indicated to the Commanding Officer that our patrol was being attacked, and, suspecting that it was greatly outnumbered by the enemy, he immediately despatched six men under Lieutenant Ross and Sergeant Greene to reinforce the patrol. As this small party was slowly making its way across No Man's Land it encountered a large party of Turks who were rapidly surrounding our men who were holding the ridge.

CAPTAIN DONNELLY.

In the skirmish that followed only Sergeant Greene and Private Hynes escaped without being wounded. The coolness, resourcefulness and courage with which these two men **Two Heroic Parties.** managed the situation could not be surpassed by soldiers of many years active warfare experience. By their rapid fire at close range they completely deceived the Turks who greatly exceeded them in numbers. The enemy finally retired to his own trenches, and the attempt to surround our original patrol was

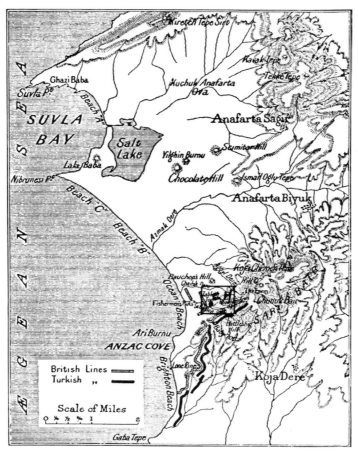

Caribou Hill, position of the *Royal Newfoundland Regiment*
is indicated by square and " C. H."

completely foiled.   This timely aid enabled Lieutenant Donnelly and his men to hold the ridge all night, although every man in the party had been wounded, some several times.   On the following day the Regiment advanced its front line to the ridge that had been so nobly held by the two small patrols, and placed machine guns in commanding positions.   This ridge was afterward most appropriately called Caribou Hill.   The name will for many years linger in the minds of Newfoundlanders, and will recall the true soldierly qualities of the Newfoundland troops who fought at Gallipoli.

Of these two patrols, three men were awarded decorations for their skill, coolness and courage in extreme danger.   The official statement of the London Gazette is as follows: "The Military Cross was awarded to Lieutenant J. J. Donnelly for conspicuous gallantry and determination on the night of the fourth–fifth of November, 1915, on the Gallipoli Peninsula.   He occupied with eight men a knoll to which our firing line was extended the next day.   By his coolness and skill in handling his small party, which was reduced to five by casualties, he repelled several determined Turkish bomb and rifle attacks on his front and flanks, and held his own during the night."

LIEUTENANT W. M. GREENE.

"The Distinguished Conduct Medal was awarded to Sergeant Greene and Private Hynes under the following circumstances: 266 Sergeant W. M. Greene, First Newfoundland Regiment.   For conspicuous gallantry on the night of the fourth–fifth of November, 1915, on the Gallipoli Peninsula. With an Officer and six men he led the way in front of our advanced line in order to sup-

port a party of his Regiment which was being heavily attacked and likely to be surrounded. The enemy were encountered at close range, and, when the Officer and two men had been wounded, Sergeant Greene took command, drove off the Turks and brought in the wounded."

"807 Private R. E. Hynes, First Newfoundland Regiment. For conspicuous gallantry on the night of the fourth–fifth of November, 1915, on the Gallipoli Peninsula. With an Officer and six men he attacked superior numbers of Turks, who were attempting to surround a small post. In spite of heavy casualties on our side, Private Hynes kept up rapid fire at close range, which resulted in the Turks abandoning their enterprise, and enabled his party to bring in the wounded."

The following three weeks were spent in comparative quiet along the section of the line held by the Newfoundland Regiment. The Turks were unable to carry out their nightly sniping raids as formerly, and there was a marked diminution in the casualties sustained by our men. Soon, however, the Turks were to be temporarily replaced by a much more powerful and destructive enemy. From November 26th to 28th, following on the heels of the decision to evacuate the Gallipoli Peninsula, an indescribable blizzard swept the entire Peninsula, falling with its cruelest violence in the Suvla region. The 26th, when the Newfoundlanders had already been in the trenches twelve days without relief, began as a bitter cold day, with a northeasterly wind augmenting

A Disastrous Storm. its severity. In the afternoon the wind grew much stronger, assuming the proportions of a gale, with heavy sleet. The wind continued to strengthen, and in the evening was accompanied by thunder and a violent downpour of rain. It is impossible to describe adequately the conditions caused by the rain. The Suvla area is thickly set with abrupt slopes, and in a few hours the water was rushing over these with a force that threatened to carry everything before it. So suddenly were the trenches turned into rushing rivers that the men had to jump from them, leaving food, trench coats and rifles behind them. In trenches that were at all tenable men were standing waist high in water. Parapets caved in and whole trench systems were wiped out. During the night of the 26th–27th the rain turned into sleet, which came down with a cutting force. The mud became frozen, and the biting, northerly wind increased, striking with a vicious force the drenched troops, who were without overcoats or food. All through the 27th this dreadful condition continued. Efforts were made to keep the men moving, but it was impossible to keep the men from becoming severely frost-bitten. On the 28th the storm reached its climax. The northerly wind became colder, and a blinding snow storm prevailed the greater part of the day. To the men in the trenches it seemed as though the storm would never cease, and that the whole army would be wiped out. As is very often the case, the storm was at its worst just before the calm. When, on the 29th, the storm abated, the ever famous Twenty-ninth Division, of which the Newfoundland Regiment formed a part, had lost two-thirds of its strength. The British had suffered 30,000 casualties, of whom 10,000 were unfit for further service. It must be placed to the credit of the Newfoundland Regiment that it stood the terrible ordeal with a physical resourcefulness and courage that was without parallel in the whole army. The severe winter weather of our own climate had provided our men with a physical adaptability that could hardly be expected of office clerks from the city of London, and only when they were so frost-bitten that they were unable to walk did they give themselves over to the field hospital. The Regiment had suffered heavily, but not so heavily as most other units. Reinforcements which arrived from England on the first of December brought the strength of the Regiment up to 400.

Newfoundlanders Stood the Test Well.

It is almost impossible to imagine that such a disastrous storm, which had caused so much suffering and so many deaths, could have any good result. But one effect of the storm was welcomed by the entire army. The dysentery, which, for several months, had taken close on a thousand victims a day, stopped immediately, and was no longer a cause of casualties.

One Good Result of Storm.

There can be little doubt that the storm also hastened the evacuation. The season was getting late, and there was grave danger that severe weather would continue for several months. The coast is very rugged and unsheltered, and if the weather continued stormy the ships would be prevented from landing supplies and the troops would be unable to leave the Peninsula. It was a strong warning, and the warning was taken seriously. Preparations for the evacuation were immediately started, and were rushed with all possible speed. Numerous devices were rigged up to deceive the Turks, and evidently the devices were entirely successful. At 7 o'clock on the night of December 19, in slightly hazy weather, but with a full moon illuminating the entire region, the Regiment proceeded

Evacuation Hastened.

to the beach, except two Officers, Captain Herbert Rendell and Lieutenant Cecil B. Clift, and 30 men. These were left behind for the purpose of keeping up a desultory rifle fire during the night and doing final necessary work in connection with the plans for preventing the Turks from learning of the evacuation. The position that they held was an exceedingly dangerous one. It meant that these two Officers and 30 men stood for six hours and a half, from 7 p. m. until 1:30 a. m. when they also started for the beach, between the main body of the Regiment and the Turks. If they had been attacked by the Turks during the first hour or two they would have had to hold them up until the last man of the 32 was killed. It was a position of tremendous responsibility, and reflects great credit upon the high esteem in which the two Officers and the 30 men of the News foundland Regiment were held.

Before midnight the whole Regiment had been transferred to the ship except the men who formed the rearguard who were taken off just before daylight the following morning. It is indicative of how well the plans had been laid and how well they were carried out that not a single casualty occurred amongst the entire Regiment. On the morning of the 20th, Battalion Headquarters and most of the Regiment, about 480 altogether, were landed at Imbros, and the remainder were landed at Mudros.

It was the general hope that Christmas would be spent in peace, but the Gallipoli campaign was not over for the Newfoundland Regiment. On **Cape Helles.** the evening of December 22, those who had been landed at Imbros again found themselves on the way to the Gallipoli Peninsula, this time to Cape Helles. They landed at Helles early the following morning, and were joined on the 24th by those who had landed at Mudros. The Newfoundland Regiment took over the work of a Greek Labour Corps, which numbered about twice as many as the Regiment contained at this time. Their work consisted chiefly of building roads and bridges, and later of building piers and loading lighters with the war material which was being transferred to the ships in preparation for the evacuation of Cape Helles. The quarters which the Regiment had to occupy were those vacated by the Greeks only the previous day, and were both cramped and filthy. The stay at Helles, though at all times exceedingly dangerous, the position being shelled day and night, was destined not to be a long one. On January 4, a party consisting of one Officer and 30 men of other ranks, most of whom were sick or had been wounded, were taken from the Peninsula. Another party, numbering about 90 of all ranks left on the 6th,

PREPARING FOR A BIG FEED

ROYAL   NEWFOUNDLAND

REGIMENT

and during the night of the 8th and the early morning of the 9th, the remainder of the Newfoundland Regiment acted as the rearguard to the last troops to leave Cape Helles, and saw the last of the unfortunate Gallipoli campaign. Captain Herbert Rendell and Captain Joe Nunns with four men of other ranks of the Newfoundland Regiment were the last of the Allied troops to push away from the side of the old "River Clyde," which had been beached there on the first day of the landing on the Peninsula to serve as a sort of pier.

Our Regiment consisted of 1050 Officers and men of other ranks when it left England for the Gallipoli Peninsula. Of these, 933 reached Suvla. Of the remaining 127, some had been taken for other duties but most of them had become unfit for military service because of sickness. The Regiment sustained 39 deaths in action and from disease, and 76 casualties from wounds. The casualties brought about by disease and the storm of November 26–28 were so great that less than half of the Regiment was left to take part in the evacuation of Suvla.

No unit which took part in the Gallipoli campaign was more appreciated or received greater praise than the New-**Commander Praised** foundland Regiment. In this connection, **Newfoundland Battalion.** a letter written to Governor Davidson by Brigadier-General Cayley, who commanded the 88th Brigade, is a fitting conclusion to this chapter.

"I feel sure that you and the people of Newfoundland will be anxious to hear of the doings of their contingent since they have been on active service. As you doubtless know, the Regiment landed at Suvla in the Gallipoli Peninsula in September, and were attached to the 88th Brigade of the 29th Division, which Brigade I have the honor to command.

"The Brigade was holding trenches very close to the Turks on the left centre of the line. The Newfoundland Regiment was at first in reserve. Whilst in reserve all officers and the different companies were sent up to the trenches and attached to the regiments in warfare. All ranks were remarkably quick in picking up all there was to be learnt, and their keenness was very noticeable. The result was that after a very short time they took over part of the firing line as a separate unit. There was no big operation, but small enterprises were frequently on foot, and in all they had to do, the Regiment continually showed a splendid spirit of readiness and resource. I especially recall incidents of the nights of November 4 and 5, when we advanced a part of our line. I detailed them for this work, and it was admirably carried out, all who took part showing the highest courage and determination in face of very severe opposition. The results of the operations were entirely successful.

"Another occasion I should wish to recall is the storm of November 26 and the following days. A very violent rainfall, which flooded the trenches more than waist deep, was followed up by three days of northerly blizzard with intense frost. The conditions were such that the most veteran troops might have been excused for losing heart, but, in spite of very heavy casualties from exposure, the Regiment never for a moment gave in, but maintained their spirit and cheerfulness in a most wonderful manner.

"Then again, in the evacuation of Suvla and Helles operations, of which the success depended entirely upon the steadiness and discipline of the troops taking part, their share in these extremely anxious movements was most admirably performed.

"It has been the greatest honor and pleasure to me to have these gallant fellows in my brigade, whose traditions they have most worthily upheld. Their fellow-countrymen have every reason to be proud of them on their doings. Their casualties have been many from bullets and sickness.

Extracts from the diary of the late Lieutenant Owen W. Steele of the First Newfoundland Regiment. These extracts cover the period from August 20, 1915, the date of leaving England for the Gallipoli Peninsula, to March 22, 1916, when the Regiment disembarked at Marseilles.

August 20, 1915. On board train, 6 a. m. From 6 a. m. to 5 p. m. (men's tea time), the officers have been constantly busy, getting their men fitted out with dozens of various necessities for the front. They have been issued with new boots (better quality than previously), new uniforms (Khaki Drill, light in weight and color), and helmets. Their stocks of the following were also completed:—socks, shirts, underclothing, housewives, canteens, water bottles,—in fact, twenty-five or thirty other items. Sometimes we were compelled to work after tea. Then what spare time I had I endeavored to get the mess books done up. However, I finished and got clear of them yesterday at lunch time—and am not sorry.

We "fell in" last night at 9 o'clock, marched to the station and left Aldershot at 11:20 p. m.; that is, C and D Companies, for A and B left an hour before.

The new uniforms, boots and helmets are not being worn just yet, but have been all packed in boxes. The officers have had to get a lot of new equipment also, but have had to pay for it themselves. Our new uniforms

cost us about £4-15 /-, helmets 21 /-, boots 20 /-to 40 /-, binoculars and compass £5 and £3-10 /- respectively, I think.

August 20, 1915. On board S. S. "Megantic" 5 p. m. This is just a final word before we go. We are on board the White Star Liner "Megantic" (15,000 tons) and are all ready to go, and may do so any minute, but expect she will leave about 6 p. m. We are having a warship go with us and two destroyers for a period of twelve hours. I think we shall be about a fortnight on the water, but will be a thousand times more comfortable than on the "Florizel." The "Arabic," which was torpedoed yesterday, is of the same line.

Thursday, August 26, 1915. Arrived off Malta at 11.30 a. m. and had to stand by and await orders but keep moving. At noon we commenced to go into Valetta (capital of Malta), and got to our berth at 1 p. m.

At 4 p. m. officers were allowed to go on shore until 6 p. m. I went ashore with Gerald Harvey, and, on meeting Butler and Windeler, we hired a carriage and went for an hour and a half's ride. Saw the Governor's house and walked through the Marine Gardens. Malta is of very Eastern style.

Went aboard at 6 p. m. and found that we could remain until 11 p. m., so went ashore again. Had dinner and then went to a small theatre and was on board at 11 p. m. Weather, fine and warm.

Friday, August 27, 1915. Left Malta for Island of Lemnos at 7 a. m.

Sunday, August 29, 1915. Arrived at Mudros, Island of Lemnos, at 7.30 a. m. and anchored. Moved into one of the very small harbors at 10.30 a. m. and anchored again to await orders. Having received orders we left for Alexandria at 6.30 p. m. Through some bungling at Malta we had been sent to Lemnos by mistake.

Tuesday, August 31, 1915. Arrived at Alexandria at 2 p. m. * * *

Monday, September 13, 1915. Parade at 6 a. m. for inspection by General and his Staff, which lasted two hours.

All the men's equipment, and what not required of officers, is taken by the Transport to Abbassia Siding, ready for shipment to Alexandria, as the Battalion is under orders to embark from there tomorrow for an unknown destination.

Tuesday, September 14, 1915. Reveille was at 4 a. m., for we had to prepare for two companies to leave at 6.30. Remaining two companies left at 7.30 a. m. My company was in the latter two, and we left Abbassia Siding at 9.30 a. m., arriving at Alexandria about 3 p. m. My platoon did not get on board steamer until about 5 p. m.

Page Forty-seven

Our steamer was a very poor one—the "Ansonia," a four years old purchase of the Cunard Line. Our camp neighbors—the London Regiment—(Reserves) were also on board. We left Alexandria at 6.30 p. m.

Saturday, September 18, 1915. We are going to Suvla and shall land on the beach. We shall then probably march about a mile and a half to the Reserve Trenches, and after a few days shall watch our chance to get up to the firing line.

We have had a very good time all along so far, but we all know that the hardest part has now to come. The place where we are to land is shelled all day long, and the last Division which was sent there lost 1200 men and 36 officers the first day, and that without having fired a shot or seen a single Turk, so we have heard.

Sunday, September 19, 1915. This morning was spent in continuing disembarking preparations.

At 3 p. m. we transferred to the small steamer "Prince Abbas" (about the size of the "Fiona"), and left for Suvla Bay at 3.30 p. m., where we arrived at 9.30 p. m. After an hour or more landing, by means of lighters, was commenced. I was in the last load which left the ship about 12.30 (midnight).

Monday, September 20, 1915. Left the "Prince Abbas" and boarded a lighter at 12.30 a. m. After reaching the landing stage, owing to the unhandiness of the lighters, it took two hours to berth us.

Landed about 3 a. m. and after forming up were led by the Landing Officer to our "Dug Outs" for the night, amid clouds of sand, just like a Newfoundland snow storm.

Our "Dug Outs" are simply holes dug into the ground and have no covering. We rolled ourselves in our blankets and slept as well as we could, for it was bitterly cold.

Got up at 6 a. m., having had two hours sleep. We were shelled by the Turks for an hour, from 8 to 9 a. m., from a distance of seven or eight miles. We had some fourteen casualties, including the Adjutant, Capt. Rendell, who was, during the day, sent back to Mudros. Fortunately no one was killed. Harvey, Knight and I had narrow escapes when having breakfast; a shell burst not ten yards from us, shrapnel falling all around us.

During the day we moved behind a hill to be sheltered from the enemy's guns, as we were on the side of a hill facing them.

At night A Company went into the trenches.

Thursday, November 4, 1915. It was decided today to take possession of a sniper's post midway between our firing line and the firing line of the Turks. Capt. Butler was acting O. C. Firing Line, so it naturally followed that C Company was given this to do. Lieutenant Donnelly with six men and an N. C. O. went out about 4 p. m. and occupied, or rather took up their position in this post, which could be easily occupied in the daylight unseen by the enemy. About 7.30 p. m. Lieutenant Ross went out with another six men and an N. C. O. as the N. C. O. of the first party had come in wounded, and was asked by Lieutenant Donnelly to ask for reinforcements to be sent out. It seems that just at dusk three Turkish snipers came stalking up to this post, as unconcerned as could be, and when quite close were challenged by Lieutenant Donnelly's N. C. O. The only answer they got was a babble of Turkish. The order to fire was then given to our men. They immediately got the first two men, but the third retaliated and succeeded in getting Lieutenant Donnelly's N. C. O. in the side of the neck—not seriously though. They claim they eventually got him, too.

When Lieutenant Ross went out with his men, whilst going along a small gulley, he came in contact with a small party who challenged them, saying "Who goes there?" to which Lieut. Ross replied "Newfoundlanders." The Turking party, for such it was, then said "Newfoundlanders; Allah, Allah il Allah!" (or something similar which they use as a battle cry), and then commenced firing. Our party, of course, returned the firing which continued for quite a while. Our party then returned, for Lieut. Ross and three of his men were wounded. Lieut. Ross was wounded in the arm, but the most serious was Joe Murphy of Mundy's Pond. He got struck by a couple of bullets and a hand-bomb. Lieut. Ross said large reinforcements would be needed to hold the post, in case the Turks endeavored to obtain it. No reinforcements were sent out that night, for no one knew exactly where to locate the post, nor did they know whether the first party, Lieutenant Donnelly's party, was O. K. or not. After midnight everything was normal again.

Friday, November 5, 1915. Early this morning Lieut. Donnelly returned with the information that he and his party were O. K., excepting for two men who were slightly wounded. It was then decided to place about thirty men with N. C. Os. in the post. This was done later in the day, Captain Rowsell, accompanied by Lieut Rendell, going in charge.

Saturday, December 4, 1915. Well, today is just a week after the "Flood," and things are now almost normal again. There is still a lot of work to be done in the way of clearing and cleaning up the trenches and making repairs.

Our Regiment is stated to have come out of the affair the most satisfactorily by far. Of course, some Regiments or Battalions were not very inconvenienced by the storm, such as the Essex, who were on our left for they were higher up on the hill. We got it very badly indeed, as did also the rest of the 88th Brigade who were on our right, that is, the Worcesters, the Hants, and the Londons. The latter three lost some hundred men by death from exposure during the couple days frost that followed the flood. They had several hundred sent to hospital with frost-burnt feet, sickness, etc. One of the Worcester Officers told me four days after the storm that he had, the previous day, been down to the Block House (about a mile to our right) in the lines held by the 86th Brigade, where he had seen many men lying dead in the trenches and being walked over. He also saw fully thirty men sitting up on the firing steps, exactly as they were at the time of the storm, frozen to death. There was so much to do in clearing away and burying the dead that these bodies had not yet been attended to. He said it was a very gruesome sight indeed, as was another sight he had seen. We had recently built some winter Dug-Outs, made to hold about eight men lying down. Well, an Officer of one of the 86th Brigade Battalions had evidently gone into one of these and taken some men with him to the number of about thirty. These Dug-Outs are without roofs, being unfinished, so the result was that the Officer and every man froze to death. Another Officer told me he was standing in the doorway of his Dug-Out, when he saw in the river of water flowing just outside the trench, two dead mules, one live mule, two dead Turks and many boxes and large pieces of debris pass down together.

On the night of the flood, the water in our support trenches and in the firing line was three feet deep nearly everywhere, and in many places men had to walk in water up to their waists. Everyone, of course was wet to the skin, and a means of drying one's clothes was out of the question. Then when the frost came it tried us all to the limit and all suffered severely, but thanks to the general hardiness of Newfoundlanders not one death resulted in our Battalion, and I know there were very few Battalions, indeed, around here which could say that. Of course, sleeping for the majority was out of the question, for many of the men had lost their blankets and rubber sheets, and quite a few had even lost their great

coats. Fires were made without any thought being given to the fact that we were showing our exact position to the Turks; but the Officers were worse off than we, and they also had fires burning everywhere. All these big fires were just in the rear of the support line, and men on both sides wandered around and stood around the fires with a wanton and utter disregard of the other side. Neither side bothered about the other in the least, until the severity of the frost began to lessen. Our firing line then got many wandering Turks, and they got a few of ours. Owing to the communication trench being from two to three feet deep with water in most places, our ration parties had got into the habit of walking in the open, with the result that the Turks noticed it and eventually got a machine gun onto the track, followed and also sent in a few shells. We lost rather heavily in this for two days, for about a half dozen of ours were killed and a dozen wounded. Most of the Officers, too, lost the greater part of their kit.

I shall never forget the look of most of our men after the first and second night's frost. It reminded one of the "Greenland Disaster." The men's faces were nearly all as black as niggers, where they had been getting as close as possible to the smoking fires all night, and what with their eyes and woe-begone looks, they presented a really terrible sight. One was fully expecting to find some lying dead from exposure, but wonderful to relate, there was not a single fatality, which speaks well for the physique of our men, for those were really terrible nights. * * *

After the flood we were very short of rations for a while and had to do without some meals because food and drinking water were so scarce. It was with the latter that we had the greatest difficulty, for all the wells were spoilt, the water they contained being the same as the trench water. The doctor condemned the water for drinking purposes, and consequently, the first day we had nothing to drink, and on the second day, one lot of water for making tea was issued, but the drinking of unboiled water was absolutely forbidden, for there were so many dead bodies and rubbish of all kinds around that an epidemic of some kind would have resulted. Even the water that we then had was really only muddy trench water in which we would not have attempted even to wash our hands under normal conditions. * * *

We have sent about 150 men to hospital, most of them suffering from frost-burnt feet. We have heard that the 86th Brigade lost 200 men by drowning and exposure, and nearly two thousand were sent to hospital.

Monday, December 20, 1915. (Evacuation of Suvla.) My party went on board the Isle of Man paddle boat "Barry" at 12.15 a. m., and left for "we know not where" at 1 a. m. We arrived at the Island of Imbros at 2.15 a. m., but by the time we got inside the two lines of torpedo nets, reported, etc., it was 2.45 a. m. We had then to go on shore on lighters, and I landed at 3.30 a. m. We then had to walk about three miles to our allotted area, where we found many other Regiments' or Battalions' details. Everyone was then supplied with a good supper.

This morning was spent in getting the Battalions and Companies together.

About 1 p. m. Lieuts. Rendell and Clift with their party arrived. Everything up to the last went off without a hitch. The Turks were apparently under the same impression they have been under for some time, viz., that we were preparing to attack them for they had been continually strengthening, improving and renewing their barbed wire, etc. I would certainly like to be overhead in an aeroplane when the Turks find out that they are shelling empty trenches. Then when they move forward they will have all kinds of plots to contend with, for the R. E. have various kinds of mines laid, such as "trip-wires," and those which will explode when one walks on them. Then in many Dug-Outs mines have been laid, attached by a wire to a table leg, which will be exploded by a movement of the table. * * *

Wednesday, December 22, 1915. There were rumors this morning that we were moving; some rumors said to Mudros and some to Cape Helles. However, at noon we got orders to be ready to leave camp at 1.15 p. m. at which time we left and arrived at the beach at 2 p. m. We then went on board a lighter and were taken off to a small steamer, the "Redbreast." In about an hour they had the various portions of units of the 88th Brigade on board, to the number of about 1300. * * * At nine o'clock the anchor was taken up and preparation for starting was made. By this time we had heard almost definitely that we were going to Helles. At 10.40 p. m., just an hour and a half after we left Imbros, we arrived at Cape Helles. We had to go ashore on lighters in two or three parties, and by midnight were all ashore, except three officers and about thirty men, who were kept back for the purpose of landing some stores. * * *

Thursday, December 30, 1915. Having received orders from the Brigade last night, we went out to W. beach this morning where we were to take

up our quarters, for we were now to do some fatigue work, as the Greek Corps had refused to work on account of so many shells coming to the beach; they were beginning to lose quite a lot of men and were, therefore, afraid to work there.

Friday, December 31, 1915. This morning we commenced work on various jobs in preparation for the evacuation of Cape Helles, or, in other words, the remaining portion of the Gallipoli Peninsula now held by us.

It looks as if the 88th Brigade, 'our Brigade' of the Twenty-Ninth Division, will be in the final stages of this evacuation, as well as that of Suvla, which everyone says is a great compliment and honor. Am afraid this one will not be so successful as Suvla, for conditions are not nearly so favorable here. However, we hope for the best.

Some of our men were building piers, others quarrying rocks, others carting the stone by means of trucks on rails to the piers, and others doing fatigue work of various sorts. * * *

Saturday, January 1, 1916. We continued work as yesterday and had the same inconvenience regarding the Turkish shells. The one we fear most is a 5.9 Naval Gun fired from Asia Minor at 9000 yards, and is a gun from the "Goeben." Being on the beach with sloping high clifts on all sides, and as the shells come over the clift on the left side, we do not hear it until it is quite upon us and have not time even to wink an eyelid, so have no time to seek cover. However, as the Turks generally send four or five, we have time to get under cover before the second one comes. The Turks can enfilade our beaches from the other side, so they become very hot sometimes. This Asiatic Gun is known by the men as "Asiatic Annie"; there is also another known as "Louise Loue."

Sunday, January 16, 1916. (At Alexandria.) Some of the troops on board received orders to go last night at 9 o'clock, others this morning at 7 o'clock, and we, that is the Newfoundland Regiment, at 12.45 p. m.

We left Alexandria at 1 p. m. The weather was quite fine and warm, and as we got farther in the country, it got much warmer and we could feel much more power in the sun.

We had an uneventful trip and enjoyed the ever-changing country scenery until darkness came. About 7 or 8 o'clock we went asleep. At 2 a. m. we were awakened and told that we had arrived at Suez, so went to see about "falling in" our men.

Page Fifty-three

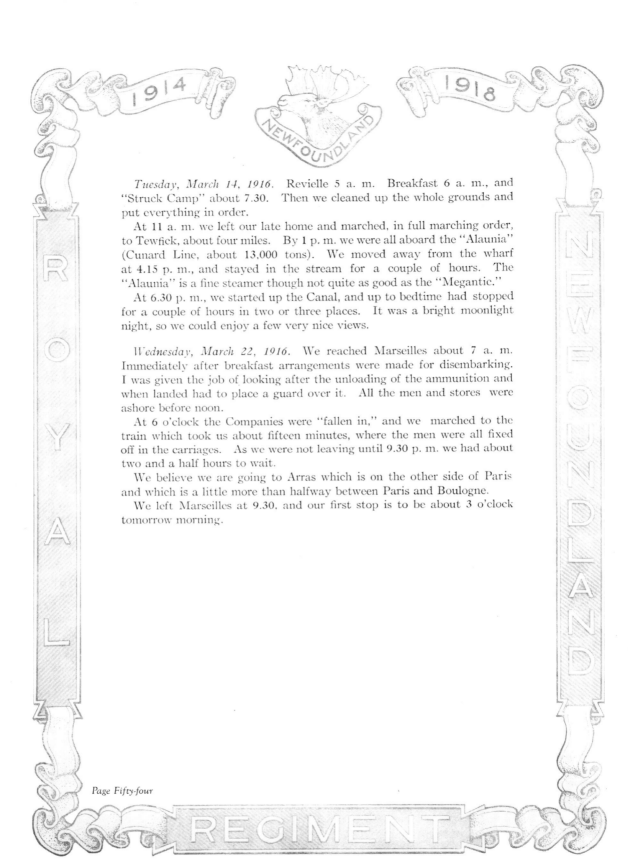

Tuesday, March 14, 1916. Revielle 5 a. m. Breakfast 6 a. m., and "Struck Camp" about 7.30. Then we cleaned up the whole grounds and put everything in order.

At 11 a. m. we left our late home and marched, in full marching order, to Tewfick, about four miles. By 1 p. m. we were all aboard the "Alaunia" (Cunard Line, about 13,000 tons). We moved away from the wharf at 4.15 p. m., and stayed in the stream for a couple of hours. The "Alaunia" is a fine steamer though not quite as good as the "Megantic."

At 6.30 p. m., we started up the Canal, and up to bedtime had stopped for a couple of hours in two or three places. It was a bright moonlight night, so we could enjoy a few very nice views.

Wednesday, March 22, 1916. We reached Marseilles about 7 a. m. Immediately after breakfast arrangements were made for disembarking. I was given the job of looking after the unloading of the ammunition and when landed had to place a guard over it. All the men and stores were ashore before noon.

At 6 o'clock the Companies were "fallen in," and we marched to the train which took us about fifteen minutes, where the men were all fixed off in the carriages. As we were not leaving until 9.30 p. m. we had about two and a half hours to wait.

We believe we are going to Arras which is on the other side of Paris and which is a little more than halfway between Paris and Boulogne.

We left Marseilles at 9.30, and our first stop is to be about 3 o'clock tomorrow morning.

CHAPTER II

Nineteen-sixteen In France

Unlike the Gallipoli campaign, the campaign of the Western front was far from being over when on March 22, our Regiment reached Marseilles and became part of the rapidly increasing **The Western Front.** Allied Armies which were determined to drive the Hun forces out of France and Belgium. The fiercest battles, those that were to use up the largest amount of ammunition, take the greatest toll of human life, and bring sorrow and grief to the largest number of homes had yet to be fought. It must also be said that the battles that were to record the greatest successes for the Allies on the Western Front were fought after this time; and it is to the glory of the Newfoundland Regiment that no unit of the British Armies has received more favorable comment from its commanding officer than has our Regiment. Plans were already in preparation when the Regiment reached France for a strong British attack in the Somme section, and efforts were being made to strengthen the British positions around Ypres. The Germans showed great activity in the Ypres salient, partly, no doubt, for the purpose of holding the British armies to their ground while they dealt with the French at Verdun, and partly for the purpose of bringing about a premature offensive or entirely dispersing the gathering storm in the Somme Valley. The fighting in the Ypres salient continued severe for four months, during which time both sides suffered heavy losses. The Canadians alone lost about 7000 men.

Our Regiment still formed part of the Twenty-Ninth Division, which was soon to add new laurels to its already enviable distinction. Since its arrival in France the Twenty-Ninth had not taken part in any big attack, but, for the most part, was being kept in reserve and preparing for the monstrous attack on the **Preliminary Preparations.** Germans in the Somme Valley. In the latter days of June our Regiment made several raids on the German trenches for the purpose of clearing the ground of the wire entanglements. On the 27th a party under the command of Captain Bertram Butler got up to the German wire defenses, but found

that their wire-cutters were unable to sever the very heavy wire which the Germans had recently put in. They were obliged to retire as soon as they were detected by the enemy. Again the following night they went forward, and this time succeeded in making several gaps in the wire defenses and getting through to the enemy trenches. They were subject

ROUEN

Where the base depot of the *Royal Newfoundland Regiment* was established while the Regiment was in France.

to heavy fire and bombing from the enemy, but they held their ground until every available hand grenade had been used. In this action several men displayed unusual courage and ability. Private T. M.

O'NEIL. O'Neil, seeing an enemy bomb thrown in the midst of his party and realizing the danger to the entire party, picked up the bomb and threw it back. It exploded on leaving his hands and

severely wounded him, but his quick and brave act undoubtedly saved several of his company. Captain Butler was awarded the

BUTLER. Military Cross because of the great ability and daring courage that he displayed on this occasion. A glance at Captain Butler's military record, contained in the second part of this volume will show that he carried the same soldierly qualities in

PHILIPS. every action. Without any assistance Private G. Philips attacked several Germans, some of whom he killed and others severely wounded. He later received the Military Medal and the Russian Order of St. George for his conspicuously courageous conduct.

These two minor actions constitute the prelude to an action by the entire Regiment, which, in its almost reckless courage in the face of unsurpassed and obvious dangers, was probably

Beaumont Hamel. not excelled by any circumstance or instance of the entire war. For several months General Haig had been amassing a strong army north of the Somme. Preparations had been completed during the month of June in spite of the continuous and severe enemy attacks in the Ypres sector.

On the night of June 29, instructions were given as to the particular part of the German line to be stormed by the Twenty-Ninth Division.

Newfoundlanders' Objective. The Newfoundland Regiment was to start from St. John's Road, a new trench built by the Regiment, south of Beaumont Hamel. They were to cross two support trenches and our firing line, from which they would pass through the gaps in our wire and across to No Man's Land. They were then to cross the first and second German systems, which were supposed to have been taken by the 86th and 87th Brigades, and halt near Pursieux Road while our artillery weakened the third enemy system, which was the objective that our Regiment was to take possession of. On the following night, when, to use the words of one of the First Five Hundred who took part in this battle, "the sun had hidden its face from the horrors of the battle front" and conditions were favorable for the secret movement of troops, our Regiment was ordered to take its position as supports to the 86th and the 87th Brigades, which were to attack the first and second line of the German trenches, south of Beaumont Hamel.

The Twenty-Ninth Division now consisted of the 86th, 87th, and 88th brigades. The 1st South Wales Borderers and the 1st Inniskilling Fusiliers of the 87th Brigade formed the van of the attack upon the right of the

Page Fifty-seven

THE ANGLO-FRENCH OFFENSIVE
ON THE SOMME

Allies front until July in 1916....
Allies front on Sept. 18th, 1916....
Allies front on Oct. 18th, 1916....
Allied front after Nov. 15, 1916....

PERMISSION FUNK & WGNALLS CO. (THE LITERARY DIGEST)

The position of *Royal Newfoundland Regiment* indicated by squares

division, and the 2nd Royal Fusiliers and the 1st Lancashire Fusiliers of the 86th Brigade formed the van of the attack upon the left of the division.

The ground over which they had to advance could scarcely be more difficult. It formed a gradual descent, which rendered our troops completely exposed. It contained enormous quarries **Impossible Frontal** and excavations in which large numbers of the **Advance.** enemy could remain concealed, almost immune from shell-fire, and ready to rush out and attack our men in the rear. Although the bombardment from the British guns was terrific it had comparatively little effect in lessening this danger. There was another condition which tended to minimize the success of the Twenty-Ninth Division. It was found that the artillery fire had thoroughly cut the German wire, but our own wire had not been cut to the same extent and proved a serious menace to the advance of the troops. Some gaps were cut, but they were not sufficient and they were quickly discovered by the Germans who played their guns on them with terrible results.

At 7:30 on the morning of July 1, the whistles blew, and the men, determined to force the lines of Beaumont Hamel or show the absolute impossibility of the task, sprang from their trenches and advanced in successive waves of assault against the enemy trenches. The entire 86th and 87th Brigades were drawn into the fight and suffered tremendous losses, and about 8:40, scarcely more than an hour after the opening of the "Battle of the Somme", the Newfoundland Regiment and the 1st Essex were ordered forward to take the first line of the enemy trenches. Like the other battalions, our Regiment and the Essex were held up by the murderous machine-gun fire in front of Beaumont Hamel. They were also subject to the fire of flanking machine guns. The whole action was so rapid, the positions occupied by the enemy machine guns so advantageous and commanding, and the fire from those guns so destructive that by 10:20 the assault had to be given up, and only a defensive line could be held.

Our Regiment suffered very heavily, but only in proportion to the indomitable courage and fortitude displayed under most adverse conditions, and even in the face of death itself. It is said that no other unit suffered so heavily in proportion to the number of men engaged. One hundred men were reported killed, 210 missing, and 374 wounded. No action could be more fitting than that this field should be bought by the

voluntary subscriptions of the people of Newfoundland and forever held in memory of the men who sacrificed their lives that day. July 1, 1916, will be remembered in the history of our country as at once glorious and tragic. Regarding the conduct of the Regiment, Sir Douglas Haig telegraphed: "The heroism and devotion to duty they displayed on the 1st July has never been surpassed." In a letter to Sir E. P. Morris (now Lord Morris) the Lieutenant-General who commanded the corps said:

"That battalion covered itself with glory on July 1 by the magnificent way in which it carried out the attack entrusted to it. It went forward to the attack when two other attacks on that same part of the line had failed, and by its behavior on that occasion it showed itself worthy of the highest traditions of the British race, and proved itself to be a fit representative of the population of the oldest British colony. When the order to attack was given every man moved forward to his appointed objective in his appointed place as if on parade. There were no waverers, no stragglers, and not a man looked back. It was a magnificent display of trained and disciplined valour, and its assault only failed of success because dead men can advance no farther. They were shot down by machine guns brought up by a very gallant foe under our intense artillery fire. Against any foe less well entrenched, less well organized, and above all, less gallant, their attack must have succeeded. As it was the action of the Newfoundland Battalion and the other units of the British left contributed largely to the victory achieved by the British and French farther south by pinning to their ground the best of the German troops and by occupying the best of their artillery, both heavy and field. The gallantry and devotion of this battalion, therefore, was not in vain, and the credit of victory belongs to them as much as to those troops farther south who actually succeeded in breaking the German line. An attacking army is like a football team; there is but one who kicks the goal, yet the credit of success belongs not alone to that individual but to the whole team whose concerted action led to the desired result.

"I should like you to let my fellow citizens of the Empire in the Oldest Overseas portion of the British Realm know how well their lads have done, both officers, non-commissioned officers and men, and how proud I, as their Corps Commander, am to have such a battalion under my command, and to be a comrade-in-arms of each and all of them."

It would be an injustice to the whole Regiment to single out any one man or half a dozen men because of conspicuous gallantry on this occasion. On other occasions if two or three men were to perform deeds of fear-

less gallantry such as were performed by every man that day, they would receive the highest distinction of the British Army. Every man distinguished himself. Sergeant Thomas Carroll is

Whole Regiment Distinguished Itself. credited with having got farther than any other man before he was detected by the enemy and killed. There is abundant evidence that the heavy casualties suffered by their comrades did not shake the courage of those who remained. After the severest fighting had died down, although still subject to heavy machine-gun fire, Private J. Cox and Private S. Dewling distinguished themselves in a determined effort to relieve the suffering, and, if possible save the lives, of some of their comrades-in-arms. Because of their splendid services in this connection, and the absolute contempt for danger under such circumstances, which these men displayed, they were both awarded the Military Medal.

The efforts of the British forces at the Southern end of the line produced much more favorable results. From Fricourt to Montauban, a stretch of seven miles, the German first line was broken

Success at Southern End of Line. on the memorable first of July. General Haig adopted the plan of rolling up the German line from this point. The plan was entirely successful. On July 14, the second line was broken from Great Bazentin to Longueval, and on September 15, the third line was broken at Martinpuich.

The tremendous losses suffered by our Regiment, and, indeed, by the whole Twenty-Ninth Division, necessitated a long recuperation and a complete reorganization. The 2nd Hants and the 4th Worcesters were the only battalions that were not drawn into the fight at Beaumont Hamel, and around these the Twenty-Ninth Division had to be rebuilt. Three months were spent in rest camps, during which time several drafts were sent over from England, and the Regiment was again brought up to fighting strength. A short period was spent behind the lines in the Ypres salient during the first part of October, and from there the Regiment proceeded to the Somme where it was to make its second great effort in the First Battle of the Somme, this time at Gueudecourt. While the

Conditions at Gueudecourt. natural topographical condition did not present so serious a difficulty as that at Beaumont Hamel, other conditions were more serious. For more than three months severe fighting had been going on in the Somme area. The ground had become torn up, and was covered with large shell

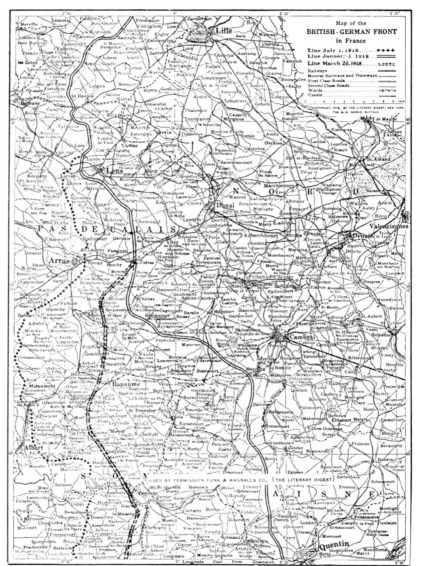

holes. Added to this was the fact that for weeks previous torrentia rains had flooded the whole area, and the mud had become so deep and soft that the ground was almost impassable.

The 88th Brigade was lent to the much weakened Twelfth Division to advance and capture the position held by the enemy at Gueudecourt under these conditions. It was the first chance for revenge since the reverse and losses at Beaumont Hamel, and the Regiment did not fail to take advantage of it. Heavy casualties were suffered by our men from the preliminary shelling by the enemy on October 11, but on the following day, when the attack was to be made, the vigor and courage of those who remained were found undiminished and unshaken. Our

The Advance at Gueudecourt. Regiment, led by Captains March, Butler and Bartlett, and Lieutenants Clouston and Edens, advanced in two waves on a front of two platoons each. Their advance was covered by a creeping barrage of machine-gun fire which kept pace in front of the advancing troops. Every foot of Rainbow trench had to be fought for. The enemy held on stubbornly and tenaciously, but was finally dislodged with heavy losses. Not only did the Newfoundland Regiment take its objective, but it also took the objective which the Essex Regiment was supposed to have taken on the left. The fighting was severe and costly, but our men were driven by a determination that knew no defeat. The success which they achieved was the only success for the day, and it was won under most unfavorable conditions and against a foe far superior in numbers.

The day was marked by heroic and daring conduct, and by the loss of some of the very finest of the Regiment. Among those who fell were Captain Donnelly, whose steady nerve and heroism at Gallipoli have already been mentioned; Captain O'Brien, Lieutenants Ebsary, Clift and Norris. These men and many others displayed a courage, fearlessness and defiance of danger that were fatal. They could not be stopped except by death itself. There were numerous individual distinctions, some of which should be specially noted. Captain March, who was senior officer,

MARCH. displayed great ability and calm resourcefulness in the face of very great danger. He took a leading part in the first attack, and is credited with having bayoneted three Germans. In the work of organizing the defence after the position had been taken he showed an ability for initiative and thoroughness that would be highly praiseworthy in one of higher rank. His gallantry and ability won for him great honor, and for his Regiment and Country,

respect and admiration. He was subsequently awarded the Military Cross and the Croix de Guerre for his noble and efficient conduct in this engagement. Captain Bertram Butler has already been **BUTLER.** mentioned in connection with his initiative and daring enterprises at Beaumont Hamel. It would be impossible to relate the numerous stories told about Captain Butler all of which illustrate his fearlessness, initiative and determination. On one occasion, in the early dawning, a corporal's attention was drawn to the fact that a man was crawling under our wire. A private pointed his gun, but the

MAJOR J. W. MARCH   MAJOR BERTRAM BUTLER

corporal, fearing it was one of our men, requested him not to fire until he could determine whether the man was an enemy or a friend. The corporal called out "Who goes there?" and back came the reply "Butler." It turned out that Captain Butler had been in close proximity to the enemy trenches all night, and was returning only when it became obvious that

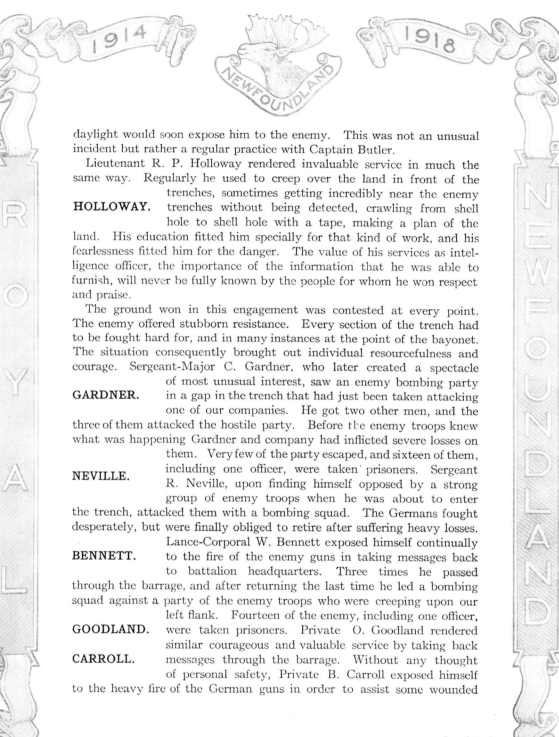

daylight would soon expose him to the enemy. This was not an unusual incident but rather a regular practice with Captain Butler.

Lieutenant R. P. Holloway rendered invaluable service in much the same way. Regularly he used to creep over the land in front of the trenches, sometimes getting incredibly near the enemy **HOLLOWAY.** trenches without being detected, crawling from shell hole to shell hole with a tape, making a plan of the land. His education fitted him specially for that kind of work, and his fearlessness fitted him for the danger. The value of his services as intelligence officer, the importance of the information that he was able to furnish, will never be fully known by the people for whom he won respect and praise.

The ground won in this engagement was contested at every point. The enemy offered stubborn resistance. Every section of the trench had to be fought hard for, and in many instances at the point of the bayonet. The situation consequently brought out individual resourcefulness and courage. Sergeant-Major C. Gardner, who later created a spectacle of most unusual interest, saw an enemy bombing party **GARDNER.** in a gap in the trench that had just been taken attacking one of our companies. He got two other men, and the three of them attacked the hostile party. Before the enemy troops knew what was happening Gardner and company had inflicted severe losses on them. Very few of the party escaped, and sixteen of them, including one officer, were taken prisoners. Sergeant **NEVILLE.** R. Neville, upon finding himself opposed by a strong group of enemy troops when he was about to enter the trench, attacked them with a bombing squad. The Germans fought desperately, but were finally obliged to retire after suffering heavy losses. Lance-Corporal W. Bennett exposed himself continually **BENNETT.** to the fire of the enemy guns in taking messages back to battalion headquarters. Three times he passed through the barrage, and after returning the last time he led a bombing squad against a party of the enemy troops who were creeping upon our left flank. Fourteen of the enemy, including one officer, **GOODLAND.** were taken prisoners. Private O. Goodland rendered similar courageous and valuable service by taking back **CARROLL.** messages through the barrage. Without any thought of personal safety, Private B. Carroll exposed himself to the heavy fire of the German guns in order to assist some wounded

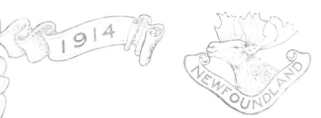

comrades. He saved a number of lives by his heroic and unselfish conduct. Lieutenant Clift attempted to advance beyond Rainbow trench, but his party was practically wiped out.

At Beaumont Hamel, the strength of the Regiment was approximately 900 of all ranks. In the engagements at Gueudecourt it was less than half that number, and the casualties were in about the same proportion. Forty-five men were killed, 119 wounded, and 75 missing. The engaagement was fought with many individual distinctions, praise to the entire Regiment and honor to Newfoundland.

In an action north of Gueudecourt on the eighteenth of October, in which the 2nd Hants and the 4th Worcesters were successful, 250 of the Newfoundland Regiment acted as stretcher-bearers.

These two actions, July 1 at Beaumont Hamel and October 12 at Gueudecourt, constitute the actual fighting in which the Regiment was engaged

Beaumont Hamel and Gueudecourt Contrasted.

during 1916. The names will ever be familiar to the ears of Newfoundlanders. They will carry with them a mixed feeling of joy and sorrow; sorrow because of the tremendous loss to the finest manhood of our little country, and joy because of the splendid heroism and fearless courage which those men displayed and the never dying honor and fame that they won for Newfoundland. The results of Beaumont Hamel remain as a tragic and glorious memory. The engagement at Gueudecourt, from the standpoint of Military achievement, was more victorious; from the standpoint of human sacrifice, less tragic, and from the standpoint of individual initiative and distinction more productive. The results present a great contrast, due entirely to the fact that the conditions under which the two actions were fought were so very different. Had the German machine-gun fire been no more advantageous and no more severe at Beaumont Hamel than at Gueudecourt, the story of Beaumont Hamel would be quite different.

The following decorations were awarded at Beaumont Hamel and at Gueudecourt.

BEAUMONT HAMEL

Captain B. Butler	Military Cross
Private J. Cox	Military Medal
Private T. M. McGrath	Military Medal
Private S. Wedling	Military Medal
Private G. Phillips	Military Medal

Captain A. O'Brien, Second Lieutenant W. J. Clare, Private Cahill, Mentioned in despatches of Sir Douglas Haig, Commander-in-Chief

Gueudecourt

Captain J. W. March
Military Cross and French Croix de Guerre

Sergeant P. Samson	Distinguished Conduct Medal
Corporal C. Gardner	Distinguished Conduct Medal
Captain B. Butler	Bar to Military Cross
Corporal S. Webber	Military Medal
Lance-Corporal S. Manuel	Military Medal
Lance-Corporal W. Bennett	Distinguished Conduct Medal
Private D. Brown	Military Medal
Private B. Carroll	Military Medal
Private O. Goodland	Military Medal

CHAPTER III

From Gueudecourt through Monchy-le-Preux

In the last chapter we have followed the operations of the Regiment up to October, 1916. The remaining days of 1916, and practically all the first month of 1917 were spent in rest camp. That was the period of reconstruction, and of preparation for the severe battles of the following spring. The British campaign of 1916 ended with

Capture of Beaumont Hamel. the brilliant victory on November 13, at Beaumont Hamel. which resulted in the capture of that very important position. The name has a special significance for Newfoundlanders. but let no one think that its final capture casts any reflection on the courage and ability of our own Regiment. Its capture was the outcome of practically five months' flanking operations in which upwards of fifty divisions took part, most of them more than once. The position was approached from a different and less difficult direction, and was defended by a less efficient foe. The period of comparative quiet during the winter months was welcomed as a reconstruction period. Our Regiment had taken part in two important actions of the "First Battle of the Somme," and had incurred heavy casualties. The task of reconstructing was not a light

Regiment rebuilt. one, but it was begun with unshaken courage and carried out with great enthusiasm, and when the Kaiser's birthday came along the Newfoundland Regiment was prepared to give him the kind of present that, from the standpoint of humanity and democracy, he most needed.

The Regiment had spent an enjoyable Christmas in a quiet French village and was in splendid shape, when in the latter

LesBoeufs. part of January it moved into the line at LesBoeufs. The roads were frozen and in many places covered with ice. and on the morning of the twenty-seventh, when the Kaiser's birthday box was to be presented, the ground was covered with snow. The action was timed for half past five in the morning. Our Regiment was in reserve, but, when to the second, every gun was fired and the thunderous noise seemed to shake the whole battlefield, the Newfoundland Regiment

insisted on taking part in the greeting. The terrific bombardment lasted for more than an hour, and the enemy became nervously excited. All kinds of distress signals were sent up from the German lines. The whole area, for miles along the enemy front line, was lit up with large flares, and the advance of our troops as well as the activities of the enemy could be seen as clearly as in broad daylight. Without any orders some companies of our Regiment followed close on the heels of the attacking troops, and soon found themselves up to the enemy trenches.

It happened that our attacking troops had advanced so quickly over the enemy front line of trenches, and probably at a time when the flares were not being sent up, that many enemy troops had escaped their notice and had organized themselves into a strong party when some of our Regiment came up to the trench. Had their plans no been forestalled these would have been a serious menace to our troops which had gone betndy the trench. Lieutenant C.eantdner (then Company Serg-Gra Major), who was one of those who went over unofficially, found himself face to face with a whole company of enemy troops. Lieutenant Gardner had gone out without even a revolver, and when he saw the first German pop his head above the trench he called upon him to surrender. The German did so, and Lieutenant Gardner took his revolver and captured the whole company of enemy troops. The incident is probably without parallel in the whole war. The enemy troops were not disarmed, they were not of a poor type, but Gardner's invincible will and courage defeated them. He got his 68 Germans together and made them march back to the Newfoundland trenches. Not many British or French soldiers can boast of receiving an enemy decoration because of the faithful performance of duty

LIEUTENANT C. GARDNER

but Lieutenant Gardner received the highest military decoration of the German army that day. As he was marching his capture back to our lines a British officer charged down on them. The officer was about to fire on the prisoners when Gardner stopped him, and it is said, told him that if he shot one of the Germans he would get shot himself. When a German officer, who was among the captured soldiers, saw Gardner's action he took the Iron Cross from his own breast and pinned it on Gardner's.

In this engagement a number of the Newfoundlanders acted as stretcher-bearers. Their capacity for this work was not surpassed by any unit in the British army, and whenever they were available they were sought for this duty. It required faithfulness when subject to the severest shell-fire. In this action they rendered invaluable services and suffered some losses. Seven men were killed and 179 were wounded.

Our Regiment was not again brought into conflict with the enemy until shortly after their general retreat in the latter days of February and the early part of March. The positions held by the **German Retreat.** Germans became untenable after the splendid victories of the British armies in the First Battle of the Somme. On February 25, the whole German front both north and south of the Ancre caved in for a depth of over three miles. The enemy retreat to their great permanent second line was orderly and skilful, and the most unfavorable weather conditions prevented the pursuit by the British armies being anything but slow and tedious. In many places also the advance of the troops was strongly opposed, and all kinds of devices were used to obstruct their onward flow. Gradually the enemy retreat spread south, and on March 3, after scarcely more than a month of usual periodic trench duty and rest camp life, our Regiment was drawn into an important action at Saill-Saillisel, better known to the Regiment as "Silly, Silly, Sal," just south of Gueudecourt.

The action was preceded by a terrific bombardment by the enemy of the position occupied by the Newfoundland Regiment. The bombardment started at 7 o'clock on the morning of March 3, **Saill-Saillisel.** and continued with increasing intensity for more than an hour. It is to the honor and glory of the famous Twenty-Ninth Division that they never lost a trench, but on this occasion the record was nearly broken. The Regiment was faced with some very active enemy brigades whose movements were concealed by a heavy mist and the use of smoke bombs. A party of about 50 enemy troops advanced on each side of the trench occupied by our men and were within about 700 yards before they were discovered. The situation called for quick action. Quite a number of our men, including the platoon commander at that point, were so severely wounded during the bombardment that they were put out of action. A non-commissioned officer, who attempted to fire rockets as signals for aid, was severely wounded before he could send up more than two rockets. Fortunately a S. O. S. was telephoned to headquarters before communication by telephone was cut off. Every Lewis gun except one was put out of action. Bombs were used effectively by our men, and three more Lewis guns were quickly brought up, but the enemy troops succeeded in getting into the trench and drove our men out for a distance of 40 yards, to the head of the communication trench.

The situation was saved by two well arranged incidents. The British guns opened a heavy barrage about midway between our front line and the enemy front line. The barrage was highly successful in its purpose, in that it prevented more enemy troops from coming up. Lieutenant Gerald Byrne, who commanded a platoon farther to the left, took advantage of this situation. He quickly organized a bombing squad, and secured a supply of bombs. He personally led the attack up the trench, and with the aid of his party inflicted severe losses on the enemy and drove him out. The party then followed the enemy troops into their own territory, and drove them out of 60 yards of their front trench. The whole 100 yards were consolidated and held by the small party under Lieutenant Byrne despite heavy

CAPTAIN G. G. BRYNE

shell fire and bombing by the enemy. The prompt and courageous conduct of Lieutenant Byrne turned the part-enemy victory into a complete

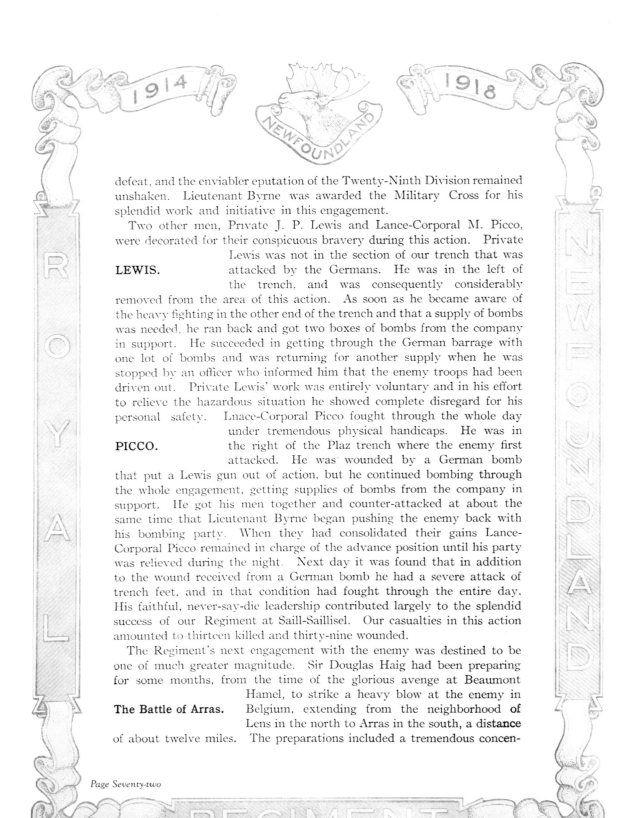

defeat, and the enviabler eputation of the Twenty-Ninth Division remained unshaken. Lieutenant Byrne was awarded the Military Cross for his splendid work and initiative in this engagement.

Two other men, Private J. P. Lewis and Lance-Corporal M. Picco, were decorated for their conspicuous bravery during this action. Private Lewis was not in the section of our trench that was attacked by the Germans. He was in the left of the trench, and was consequently considerably removed from the area of this action. As soon as he became aware of the heavy fighting in the other end of the trench and that a supply of bombs was needed, he ran back and got two boxes of bombs from the company in support. He succeeded in getting through the German barrage with one lot of bombs and was returning for another supply when he was stopped by an officer who informed him that the enemy troops had been driven out. Private Lewis' work was entirely voluntary and in his effort to relieve the hazardous situation he showed complete disregard for his personal safety.

LEWIS.

Lnace-Corporal Picco fought through the whole day under tremendous physical handicaps. He was in the right of the Plaz trench where the enemy first attacked. He was wounded by a German bomb that put a Lewis gun out of action, but he continued bombing through the whole engagement, getting supplies of bombs from the company in support. He got his men together and counter-attacked at about the same time that Lieutenant Byrne began pushing the enemy back with his bombing party. When they had consolidated their gains Lance-Corporal Picco remained in charge of the advance position until his party was relieved during the night. Next day it was found that in addition to the wound received from a German bomb he had a severe attack of trench feet, and in that condition had fought through the entire day. His faithful, never-say-die leadership contributed largely to the splendid success of our Regiment at Saill-Saillisel. Our casualties in this action amounted to thirteen killed and thirty-nine wounded.

PICCO.

The Regiment's next engagement with the enemy was destined to be one of much greater magnitude. Sir Douglas Haig had been preparing for some months, from the time of the glorious avenge at Beaumont Hamel, to strike a heavy blow at the enemy in Belgium, extending from the neighborhood of Lens in the north to Arras in the south, a distance of about twelve miles. The preparations included a tremendous concen-

The Battle of Arras.

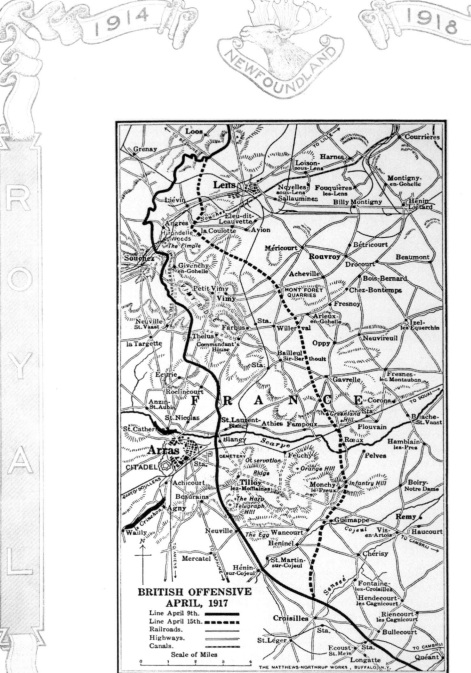

BRITISH OFFENSIVE
APRIL, 1917

Line April 9th.
Line April 15th.
Railroads.
Highways.
Canals.

Scale of Miles

THE MATTHEWS-NORTHRUP WORKS, BUFFALO, N.Y.

tration of artillery, and roughly, 120,000 men in the storming line and 40,000 in support. The first blow was to be delivered on April 9. The attack was preceded by a very intense bombardment of the German first and second line of trenches, and at 5:30, in the first dim grey of a rainy, misty, sleety morning—that kind of mixed, miserable, spiritless weather which we sometimes experience in Newfoundland during the latter part of March and the first of April—the infantry dashed forward to the attack. The engagement was a monstrous display of military genius and power, and was fought with wonderful success for the British armies.

The Newfoundland Regiment reached Arras on Easter Monday. It was not until the night of the twelfth, however, when the Battle of Arras had reached the end of its fourth day of desperate fighting, that the Twenty-Ninth Division took its turn in the front line of attackers in front of the village of Monchy-le-Preux. This village was captured by the Thirty-Seventh Division on the eleventh. The thirteenth was a comparatively quiet day for our men. No large forward movement was planned in this section, and the whole area from north of the Cojeul River to the south of the Scarpe was held by the Twenty-Ninth and the Seventeenth Divisions, the Twenty-Ninth to the south and the Seventeenth to the north. At about 5:30, on the morning of the fourteenth, both divisions advanced for the purpose of testing the enemy strength, and, if possible, to push them farther back from Monchy. Their efforts were unsuccessful, but the Newfoundland Regiment added new honors to its already splendid records at Beaumont Hamel and Gueudecourt.

The plan of the attack was that the 88th Brigade, which consisted of the Newfoundland Regiment, the 1st Essex, the 2nd Hants, and the 4th Worcesters should advance in a direction about east from Monchy, on a front of about 500 yards. Another brigade of the Twenty-Ninth Division was to advance at their right and the Seventeenth Division at their left. The attacking troops had not gone far before they were subject to a strong German counter-attack and a murderous shell fire from the enemy guns.

The Advance. As they advanced, enemy machine guns were turned on them with terrible results. Despite the heavy shell and machine-gun fire, however, our Regiment reached part of its objective, though heavy losses were sustained in so doing. The brigades which were supposed to advance on the right and on the left of the 88th suffered severely from the German barrage and before they could advance far were held up by the on-rush of enemy troops. Some

of our men reached the enemy trench, but no sooner had they done so than they saw strong parties of enemy troops advancing on both sides. Before they had time to realize the situation two whole companies of our Regiment were hemmed in and were being fired on from all sides. Escape was impossible. Small parties of our men fought against whole companies of the enemy until many of them were severely wounded and they were obliged to give themselves up. All communication by telephone had been cut, but at about half past nine, a private of the Essex Regiment ran into headquarters and reported that the Newfoundland Regiment had been wiped out. Lieutenant Keegan was immediately sent out to find out what the exact situation was and bring back a report. He saw the Germans coming along victorious, only about 250 yards away. Every man available at headquarters was quickly collected together, and, led by Lieutenant-Colonel Forbes-Robertson, the little party of sixteen men rushed out, collecting weapons and ammunition from dead or wounded soldiers as they went, determined, if possible, to hold up the Germans until reinforcements arrived. A company of the 2nd Hants, which had been brought up by a lieutenant of the Essex Regiment, defended the northern flank and prevented the enemy troops from getting around in that quarter. The small headquarter's party, which had been reduced to nine when they reached the edge of the village, established themselves in a grove of trees just outside the village, and every German who came up was shot. The nine men held the grove from 10 o'clock in the morning until 4 in the afternoon, and at times they were obliged to keep up a rapid fire in order to ward off the enemy and keep information as to the number by which the important position of Monchy was defended concealed from them. German scouts which were sent out never returned; and it is obvious that had one scout returned with information as to the exact situation Monchy would have been lost, and quite probably the victories of the previous four days together with the months of preparation that made the victories possible would have been in vain.

Regarding this engagement Sir Arthur Conan Doyle says: "It was an unsuccessful day, and yet it was one of those failures which will be remembered where facile successes have been forgotten, for it brought with it one episode which elicited in the highest degree the historical qualities of British Infantry." It was later discovered that our Regiment and the Essex Regiment had held up the advance of a strong German counter-attack by a whole Bavarian Division with the intention of retaking Monchy. The Newfoundland Regiment simply declined to be beaten.

Its courage, stubborn resistance and willing sacrifice undoubtedly saved Monchy, and probably the whole splendid success of the Battle of Arras. Regarding the Headquarter's Staff Captain (Reverend) Nangle said in his lecture on the work of the Regiment: "Lieutenant-Colonel Forbes-

"THE BOYS WHO SAVED MONCHY AND THE BRITISH LINES"

Top row, left to right: Lieut. Albert Rose, Pte. Walter Pitcher, Lieut-Col. J. Forbes-Robertson, Capt. Kevin Keegan, Sergt. Charles Parsons, Sergt. Ross Waterfield
Bottom row, left to right: Pte. Fred Curran, Staff Sergt. John J. Hillier, Lance-Corpl. Japheth Hounsell.

Robertson and his eight men are the men who saved Monchy. They won fame for themselves; they won fame for the Regiment. The whole British army in France honors the names of these nine men for their heroic conduct."

Our Regiment suffered heavily in this action. The casualties included Sergeant-Major Gardner, whose splendid achievement at LesBouefs has

already been mentioned; Captain Rowsell, and Lieutenants Stevenson, Smith and Outerbridge. Fortunately most of the losses were in prisoners who were rehabilitated after the armistice. Forty-nine men were reported killed, 142 wounded, and 296 missing. A number of decorations were awarded for heroic and valuable services, but one can well imagineath t many of those who advanced to the German trench earned decoration, but because their heroic sacrifice and gallant resistance were not witnessed, except by the enemy who were held up and suffered severe losses in consequence, the distinguished conduct could not be reported.

As in the First Battle of the Somme, so in the Battle of Arras, our Regiment was destined to take part **Les Fosses Farm.** in two important engagements. Only nine days after the action at Monchy-le-Preux, the advance along the British line was renewed, and the Regiment was brought into conflict with the enemy at Les Fosses Farm, a short distance to the south-east of Monchy. Other battalions of the 88th Brigade formed the van of the attack, but during the day, when a severe counter-attack was launched by the enemy against the positions taken by

CAPTAIN R. W. BARTLETT

the 88th and 87th Brigades, our men were drawn into the fight. They held on to their positions all day, though subject to severe blows from the enemy. On the following days the two brigades made small gains, but they were unable to hold them, and fell back upon their old line. Captain R. W. Bartlett was awarded the Military Cross for his conspicuous gallantry and devotion to duty at a critical moment when our Regiment was being hard pushed by the Germans.

During the two engagements the whole Twenty-Ninth Division gave a

splendid account of itself, and suffered severe losses. Our Regiment lost in killed, wounded and missing, 550 men of all ranks.

It will be seen that from the standpoint of numbers, the Regiment was too weak to take its position in the front line as a unit until it could be built up with fresh drafts from England. During the first part of 1917, which was occupied with the four engagements that we have reviewed in this chapter, the record of the Regiment was a splendid exhibition of true soldierly fighting qualities. Never did a unit display greater valor and more persistent resourcefulness than did the Newfoundland Regiment at Monchy. In every engagement the men showed such initiative and ability as could be expected only from soldiers of much longer experience, and an eagerness and cheerfulness that were admired by all with whom they came in contact. Their record in each action stands out as unquestionable testimony of the real fight-to-conquer spirit by which they were impelled, and the courageous, resourceful manner in which they handled the most trying and difficult situations. The severe losses which they had suffered almost 800 in killed, wounded and missing, indicate the willingness with which they were prepared to sacrifice themselves in order that victory be obtained, and the honor of the Regiment and the fame of their country increased.

The following decorations were awarded for conspicuous bravery and devotion to duty during the period reviewed in this chapter:

Les Boeufs

Company Sergeant-Major C. Gardner	Bar to D. C. M.

Saill-Sallisl

Lieutenant G. G. Byrne	Military Cross
Private J. P. Lewis	Military Medal
Lance-Corporal M. Picco	Distinguished Conduct Medal

Monchy-le-Preux

Captain K. Keegan	Military Cross
Captain J. W. Tocher	Military Cross
Lieutenant-Colonel Forbes-Robertson	Distinguished Service Order
Sergeant J. R. Waterfield	Military Medal
Corporal J. Hillier	Military Medal
Corporal C. Parsons	Military Medal
Lance-Corporal W. Pitcher	Military Medal
Private F. Curran	Military Medal
Private J. Hounsell	Military Medal
Private A. S. Rose	Military Medal
Sergeant A. Gooby	Military Medal

Les Fosses Farm

Captain R. W. Bartlett	Military Cross

CHAPTER IV

Three Important Engagements in the Latter Part of 1917

It will be remembered that the operations upon the Somme in the autumn of 1916 gave the British armies command of the high ground in the Somme district. The Battle of Arras was a continuation of these operations, and we have seen how, in the initial days of the battle, our Regiment added new laurels to its already brilliant record. The operations, covering a period of almost two months from April 9, gave the British armies command of the high ground between Arras and Lens. Sir Douglas Haig's plan was to continue to attack the prolongation of the same ridge in the direction of Ypres. On June the 7th, this plan was carried out with notable success in the Battle of Messines. In spite of the command of the German Chief that "the enemy must not get Messines Ridge at any price," nine miles of commanding country were captured and permanently held. Vast preparations were then made for a severe blow to the north of Ypres, and on July 31 the Third Battle of Ypres began.

General Position of the British Armies.

It should be noted in passing that from this time until the end of 1917 the Allied armies on the Western Front were faced by rapidly increasing German armies. The Russian army ceased to exist as a serious force, and the German armies that had fought on the Eastern Front were transferred to France and Belgium.

Our Regiment did not take an important part in any engagement for four months after the severe fighting at Monchy-le-Preux. Several times it was in the support trenches or in reserve without being brought into conflict with the enemy. On the night of July 12, when the Regiment was in the front line on the eastern bank of the Ypres Canal, it was subject to a heavy bombardment by the enemy. Several parties of our men were out placing wire entanglements some distance in front of the trenches while parties of the Essex Regiment were digging new trenches farther back. While the latter worked on the top of the ridge they could be seen against the horizon, and presented the spectacle of much larger numbers. Evidently the Germans thought that a big attack was being prepared,

Ypres Canal.

and at about 9 o'clock they opened a terrific bombardment and kept it up until 4 o'clock the following morning. Our Regiment suffered slight casualties, but the Essex men came under the full effect of the bombardment.

It was not until August 16, two weeks after the Third Battle of Ypres had begun, however, that our Regiment took its turn in the front line of attackers. On July 31, when the Guards Division undertook to capture those ridges which girt in Ypres and dominated it from the north and north-east, the only high ground along the line which up to that time had not fallen into British hands, our Regiment formed part of the supports. The situation was now reversed, and those divisions which had borne the brunt of July 31, were now in support, while the old supporting divisions were in the line. The Twenty-Ninth Division went into the line on the western bank of the Steenbeek River the

Steenbeek River. night of August 15. On the 14th and 15th both sides were bombarding heavily, and about 11 o'clock on the night of the 15th the Twenty-Ninth began to lay bridges across the river. The advance started from the line of the stream, and necessitated a big swing by the left flank, while the right advanced comparatively slowly but assisted the left by an effective flank fire on the enemy troops. The left had to advance about 1400 yards to reach its objective, while the right had to advance about 800 yards. The first objective was Passerelle Farm, the second, Martin's Mill and the final meant a straightening up of the line with our Battalion's left at Wydendrift and its right at Langemark.

The advance started from the bank of the Steenbeek River in the early dawning. For the first 500 yards progress was necessarily slow, and made under most difficult circumstances. The ground has

The Advance' been characterized as a "floating swamp," and the term will probably convey as accurate an idea as can be given of the actual conditions of the ground. As the men waded through the swamp some sank to their waist and others deeper, in many cases having to remain there until pulled out by more fortunate ones. Unfortunately there was little or no time in which to aid a comrade who had sunk into the swamp. The advance was preceded by a sweeping barrage, and those who could keep themselves above the surface had to keep pace with the barrage, otherwise its effectiveness would be lost. One favorable circumstance of the advance, however, was the lack of fighting spirit in the German troops who defended the position. In many instances they

offered no resistance whatever, but either gave themselves up or made their escape. They displayed a cowardice and enervation which our men had not previously seen so conspicuous among the enemy troops. Th first objective was therefore reached with remarkably few casualties from the activities of the enemy. The most difficult ground was passed, but new obstacles presented themselves. The heavy bombardment by the British guns caused the ground for a distance of about 500 yards beyond the first objective to be converted into large mud heaps, and huge shell holes which in many cases were filled with water. Added to this was the fact that some distance beyond there was a large number of enemy machine guns in a commanding position and protected by the famous pill-boxes, and until they were reached by our men and put out of business they did considerable damage. The condition of the ground, which seemed to be the greatest obstacle, was not so serious, however, as in the first part of the attack, and the advance to the second objective was carried out much more rapidly. In less than an hour after the capture of the second objective, the Newfoundland Regiment was digging in on the top of the ridge, which extended from Langemark on the right to Wyden-drift on the left. The village of Langemark itself was taken by the Twentieth Division, which operated on the right of our Regiment.

The whole advance by the Newfoundland Regiment was carried out with admirable regularity and efficiency, and with comparatively few casualties. Trouble given by the enemy **Splendid Advance by** Mebus, or pill-boxes, was overcome by **Newfoundland Regiment.** parties which worked around them and trapped the occupants. The guns in these concrete emplacements could swing through an angle of about twenty degrees, and sometimes a party of three or four men would work around to the right or the left and once out of range of the guns would rush up to the pill-boxes and throw bombs in through the loop-holes. In this way whole garrisons of from twenty to fifty enemy troops were instantly put to death. In this particular engagement, however, the Germans showed no disposition to fight the Newfoundlanders. Only in a few cases did the garrisons stick to their batteries and fight until captured or overcome by our advancing troops. In many instances the Germans ran from the batteries and gave themselves up. In one instance it was found that all the enemy troops had fled except an old man whose feet were chained to the base of the gun that he was supposed to operate. There were many evidences of demoralization among the German troops, and where they did attempt to put up a fight they were quickly disposed of by our men Great credit is due the Commanders of the different companies for the thorough and courageous manner in which the various obstacles were overcome, and the new positions organized with minimum losses to the Regiment.

The engagement brought out a number of high individual qualities. At several points of the advance, and after the Regiment had taken its final objective, great courage and ability were shown by our men. Captain R. G. Paterson was awarded the Military Cross because of the conspicuously cool and thorough manner in which he handled several difficult situations. He showed great skill and coolness in laying a tape in front of the position of our Battalion just before the attack for the companies leading the attack to form upon. This was of the greatest importance, and in doing it Captain Paterson exposed himself to very great danger. He then led his company with conspicuous courage and judgment and captured his objective, killing many of the enemy and capturing a machine gun.

CAPTAIN R. G. PATERSON

Corporal H. Raynes received the Distinguished Conduct Medal and the French Croix de Guerre for the great ability and cool courage which he displayed at one point during the advance. His company was held up by the rapid rifle fire of the enemy. He took two of his company, Privates J. J. **RAYNES.** Peddle and G. Lacey, and crept around from shell hole to shell hole until they got to the rear of the Germans who were holding up the advance. They quickly bombed out the four or five dug-outs, each one of which contained six or seven Germans, and signaled to their company to advance. Their splendid initiative and courage enabled their company to carry on at this point without a single casualty. Privates Peddle and Lacey were both deco-

PEDDLE and LACEY. rated for the magnificent way in which they helped Corporal Hynes to carry out the daring and successful attack on the enemy. Private Murray was awarded the Military Medal for his noble endurance

MURRAY. and courage in keeping a machine gun, which he was in charge of, continuously in operation against the Germans for upwards of 24 hours under most adverse conditions of mud and enemy fire. Privates F. Dawe, J. H. Simms and E. G. Wiseman rendered similar

DAWE, SIMMS and valuable service with Lewis guns. At
WISEMAN. various points of the advance these men crept around to the flank or rear of parties of enemy troops and operated their guns with admirable success. The importance of these individual undertakings cannot be lightly regarded. In many instances they meant a complete disregard of personal safety in order that the objectives of the Regiment might be reached.

Alongside these, must be placed the courageous and self-sacrificing spirit of such men as Privates T. Meaney and R. Spurrell. These men were acting as stretcher-bearers, and during

MEANEY AND the most intense German bombardment
SPURRELL. crossed through the mud and water of the "floating swamp" several times in an effort to save some of their comrades. The work was done under most difficult conditions and with great personal risk.

The advance was a splendid achievement for the Newfoundland Regiment. It was skillfully conducted by the officers, and every man fought his way through mud and water and against German machine gun and rifle fire, overcoming all resistance until the final objective was reached. The gains were consolidated and held against strong and repeated enemy counter-attacks, and with remarkably low casualties for such an achievement. The losses to the Regiment included 9 killed, 93 wounded and 1 missing.

Only nine days after this engagement, when the Regiment was billeted at Elverdinghe, the village was subject to a very heavy

Elverdinghe. bombardment by enemy guns. The Germans had brought up guns that far outdistanced any that had previously been used. They shelled areas that were considered entirely

outside the theatre of action. On August 25, the village of Elverdinghe was practically blown to pieces by these long range guns, and a considerable number of casualties were sustained by the troops that were billeted there. The Newfoundland Regiment had 38 casualties, and 7 of these were instant deaths.

Our Battalion spent considerable time in the line and in support trenches during the following weeks, but saw no other big engagement until in the early days of October, when it moved to Canal Bank, **Canal Bank.** near Ypres. The weather conditions could not be more unfavorable for an advance in this sector. For weeks past the whole area had been flooded with heavy rains, and the ground was a mass of deep soft mud, together with numerous shell holes filled with water. It has been described by one writer as a "desolate, shell-ploughed landscape, half-liquid in substance, brown as a fresh turned field, with no movement upon its hideous expanse, although every crevice and pit was swarming with life, and the constant snap of the sniper's bullet told of watchful, unseen eyes." So terrible were the conditions that for three days there was no connection between the right of the Twenty-Ninth Division and the left of the Fourth.

With these conditions to meet and conquer before getting to the real enemy, the Newfoundland Battalion left Yypes at 8:30 o'clock on the night of October 8. It took four and a half hours to **Broembeek.** cover six miles. With their usual resourcefulness and invincible courage the men struggled on through the mud, the swamps and the small gullies until they reached the starting off point, a line astride the Staden Railway about 300 yards south of the Broembeek River, about 1 o'clock the following morning. They were ordered to take the third objective, and were lined up on assembly behind the 4th Worcester Regiment. At 5:30 our artillery opened fire. The bombardment of the enemy positions lasted for about half an hour when it took a line about 50 yards in front of our troops and began creeping towards the enemy line. The infantry was supposed to keep pace with the creeping barrage, but at the outset our Battalion was confronted with an unexpected difficulty. The 4th Worcester Regiment was supposed to have bridged the Broembeek and to have continued in the front wave until the first two objectives were taken, but owing to the dense fog and the difficulties of the ground, direction was lost somewhat, and the battalions became intermingled. From the first objective onward, the Newfoundland Battalion found itself in the front wave of attackers.

In the front line were D Company on the right commanded by 2nd Lieutenant G. Hicks, and A Company on the left, commanded by Captain J. A. Ledingham; and in the second line were C Company on the right, commanded by Captain K. Keegan, and B Company on the left, commanded by Captain J. Nunns. Captain Ledingham was fatally wounded early in the advance, and his place was taken by Lieutenant A. L. Summers. At many points during the advance, the Regiment was held up by enemy machine-gun fire and sniping from pill-boxes, but by the capable leadership of the officers and the daring courage of small parties who worked around the pill-boxes and machine guns and put them out of action, the advance was carried out successfully. By about 11 o'clock, all objectives were taken, and the new position was quickly fortified. The Germans continued sniping heavily during the remainder of the forenoon, and large numbers of enemy troops collected around Taube Farm for the purpose of retaking the ground that they had lost. The first counter-attack took place at about noon, but it was beaten off with severe losses to the enemy. All through the afternoon the enemy could be seen collecting in great force and making preparations for a much stronger attack. At 6:30 they opened a heavy machine gun fire on the position occupied by the Newfoundland Battalion and the battalion on the left, and began to advance in great numbers. The Battalion on the left was driven back, after putting up a stubborn fight, and the Newfoundland Regiment was obliged to fall back about 200 yards because of its left flank being exposed. This position it held until it was relieved by the 2nd Hampshire Regiment during the night.

In this engagement our Regiment lost 50 men of all ranks in killed, 130 in wounded and 14 in missing. Among those who were killed was Lieutenant Stanley Goodyear, Transport Officer. The importance of the work of a transport officer cannot be over-estimated. Upon him more than upon any other person depended the well-being of the Regiment. Lieutenant Goodyear never disappointed the men who looked to him to get their rations to them on time. There were numerous ways in which a transport could become lost or get temporarily astray, but Goodyear knew of these ways only the better to be able to avoid them. He always saw to it that the Regiment's supplies were delivered as close to the line as possible and with clockwork regularity. No man was better appreciated and better liked by the Regiment than was Lieutenant Goodyear, and there can be no doubt that his attention to duty and the capable manner in which he

GOODYEAR.

always carried it out were deserving of the greatest praise. His death was a severe loss to the Regiment, and was deeply regretted by every man whose happiness and comfort he had worked untiringly and willingly to insure.

There were many instances of conspicuous bravery and ability during the engagement. Second Lieutenant G. Hicks took charge of a section of the line after several of the officers had become casual-

HICKS. ties, and by his splendid leadership and ability held the position against a severe counter-attack when a unit of his flank was forced back. The situation called for the highest qualities of skill and courage, and Lieutenant Hicks met the demand in an admirable way. Captain R. H. Tait was awarded

TAIT. the Military Cross because of the resourceful and entirely successful manner in which he organized the forming up of the Battalion on its assembly position under the most difficult circumstances. After reaching the final objective, though the position was being shelled heavily and enemy snipers were very plentiful, he made a reconnaissance of the whole line, and brought back valuable information.

Captain J. Nunns did splendid work during the rapid

NUNNS. advance and all through the severe counter-attacks of the enemy. He led his company with great skill in the first attack and captured all his objectives. Later in the engagement, when in an exposed part of the line, he held his ground for many hours against repeated counter-attacks. Second Lieutenant

CHAFE. E. R. A. Chafe was awarded the Military Cross for the highly commendable way in which he measured up to a difficult situation. After his company commander was killed he took charge, and by his personal energy and courage instilled the greatest vigor into the attack, and, in spite of heavy losses, carried the attack through with marked success.

Several other men were decorated because of their great courage and valuable services, and among them were some who acted as runners and others as stretcher-bearers, work which called for the highest degree of endurance and self-sacrifice. The whole engagement was a splendid success for the Newfoundland Regiment. Its usual fighting qualities were upheld in every difficult part of the action. One more unit of the German army had learnt to its sorrow that when it was faced by the Newfoundland Battalion it was in for a hard time.

After the severe fighting in the Broembeek engagement our Regiment

saw no further action until the closing days of 1917. By this time the Germans had transferred all their best troops from the Eastern Front, where they were no longer needed, to the Western Front, and could oppose the British with greatly superior numbers. The

Allied Reverses. Russian debacle was a military disaster of the first order. It completely checked for more than six months the victorious career of the Allies on the Western Front. Along with this came the disaffection and sudden collapse of the Italian Second Army, and the capture of upwards of 200,000 Italian troops with large stores of ammunition and nearly 2000 guns. Five British Divisions were taken from Flanders and sent to relieve the Italian situation. No greater proof of Great Britian's loyalty to her Allies could be given. The severe fighting in the Paschendaele sector had, however, thinned the German ranks farther south, and a surprise blow was prepared by the Field-Marshall for the Cambrai area. No part of the famous Hindenburgh line was more strongly fortified than was the area around Cambrai, but there were big advantages to be considered also.

It was clear to all who were familiar with the conditions on the British front that the success of the undertaking depended entirely upon the swiftness with which it was carried out. It was well known that in 48 hours the Germans could bring up a sufficiently strong force to prevent any further advance unless a most advan-

The Battle of Cambrai. tageous position was gained during that time. Shortly after 6 o'clock on the morning of November 20, the advance began. The British operations were favored by a thick haze which lowered the visibility considerably, and an effective smoke-barrage was used to screen the initial steps of the advance. When the signal for the advance was given the British guns opened a terrific bombardment of the enemy position, and the long line of tanks moved majestically forward, breaking down the heavy wire entanglements without the least difficulty and crawling invincibly upon the German concrete emplacements, the infantry following their lead. Approximately 400 tanks were lined up to clear the way for the infantry.

The Newfoundland Regiment had been billeted at Sorel-le-Grand, which place it left at 2:30 on the morning of the 20th and marched up to assembly by way of Gauzeaucourt. At 6:20, when the whole line moved forward, the Newfoundland Battalion formed the centre of the 88th Brigade; the Worcesters were on the left and the Essex on the right. The whole Twenty-Ninth Division dashed swiftly forward,

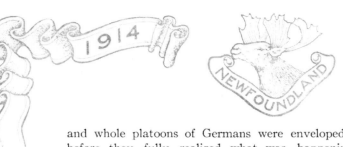

and whole platoons of Germans were enveloped and taken prisoners before they fully realized what was happening. The 87th Brigade seized the village of Marcoing, and the 86th, Neuf Wood, while the 88th pushed resolutely on and captured Les Rues Vertes and part of Mesnieres. The bridge crossing the Canal de l'Escaut at Marcoing was reached and successfully crossed before the fleeing Germans could make any progress in their attempt to destroy it. At Mesnieres, however, they had succeeded in considerably weakening the bridge and when a tank attempted to cross, both the tank and the bridge crashed into the Canal. The Newfoundlanders were the first to secure a foot-hold on the opposite bank. They crossed by means of a foot bridge which they had secured whilst a more permanent structure was being built. They were quickly followed by other units. The advance was continued at this point without the aid of the tanks, and the Germans were rapidly driven out of the whole of Mesnieres. The whole advance was so methodical, determined, and forceful, declining to be halted at any point, that numerous gallant deeds and heroic sacrifices must have gone unnoticed, but the splendid success represented the courage and ability of all. The position held by the Twenty-Ninth Division was a very serious one for the enemy. It was a commanding position, and if the advance from this point on the 21st could be conducted with the success that attended the previous day's operations, the town of Cambrai with all its important net-work of railways would be in British possession. For this reason the Germans threw all their force against this point, and on the 21st, and, in fact, from the 21st until the 27th, the enemy made ceaseless desperate attempts to drive the Twenty-Ninth Division across the Canal so as to regain possession of Mesnieres and Marcoing.

Advance by the Newfoundland Battalion.

The Twenty-Ninth in Pivotal Position.

Meanwhile the Germans had brought up a strong force of reserves and were preparing to strike back at the British with the full weight of their advantageous position and the full strength of their reserves. The 28th and 29th were quiet on both sides. It was a case of a calm before a great storm. Our Regiment was out of the line, enjoying a short rest in the village of Mesnieres, when on the morning of the 30th, the German great counter-attack burst forth in all its fury. Two companies of the Newfoundland Battalion went to the assistance

Germans Brought up Reserves.

ROYAL   NEWFOUNDLAND

CAMBRAI OFFENSIVE

Battle Line Nov. 20th 1917 ▬▬▬
Battle Line Nov. 27th 1917 ▬ ▬ ▬
Railroads:
Tramways:
Canals:
Highways:
Woods:

Scale of Miles
0   1   2   3

FRANCE

Cambrai

Marquion, Cooset Wood, Haynecourt, Tilloy, Cantimpré, Sailly, Neuville-St.Remy, Baralle, Sta., Sains-les-Marquion, Raillencourt, Ste. Olle, Fbg. Cantimpré, Inchy en Artois, Sta. Bourlon, Petit Fontaine, Fbg. St. Sepulcre, Bourlon Wood, Fontaine-Notre Dame, Proville, Fbg. St. Druon, Mœuvres, Anneux Inn, Fbg. de Paris, Marlière, Anneux, Cantaing, Niergnies, la Justice, Graincourt-les-Havrincourt, Noyelles sur l'Escaut, Demicourt, Orival Wood, Neuf Wood, Rumilly, Flesquières, Marcoing, Canal del' Escaut, Masnières, Hermies, Havrincourt, Ribecourt, les Rues Vertes, Crevecœur, Grand Ravine, Highland Ridge, Couillet Wood, les Rues des Vignes, Bilhem, Welsh Ridge, High Woods, Havrincourt Wood, Trescault, Beaucamp, la Vacquerie, Lateau Wood, Cheneaux Wood, Vaucelles, Metz en Couture, Beaucamp Ridge, Villers-Plouich, Gonnelieu Ridge, Banteux, Bantouzelle Wood, Vaucelles Wood, Dessart Ridge, Gouzeaucourt Wood, Gouzeaucourt, Sta. Gonnelieu, Noble Ville, Terriere Wood, Gauche Wood, Villers Guislain, Honnecourt, la Terrière, Basket Wood, Villers, Ossus, De la l'Eau, Lark Spur, Epehy, Vendhuille, le Catelet, St. Quentin, Canal

TO DOUAI
TO BAPAUME 3 MILES

THE MATTHEWS-NORTHRUP WORKS, BUFFALO, N.Y.

USED BY PERMISSION FUNK & WAGNALLS CO. (THE LITERARY DIGEST)

ROYAL   REGIMENT

of the Twentieth Division, which was being severely pressed by the Germans, and the other two companies took a position in their old trenches on the left of the Twentieth.

The fighting during the following four days was terrific. Both the Twentieth Division on the right and the Sixth on the left were driven back, and our men were obliged to take a position at the south-western outskirts of Mesnieres. The whole Twenty-Ninth Division was in for a trying experience. Both flanks were being rapidly exposed by the supporting divisions, being forced back, and there was great danger that the enemy would force their way around the south and cut off the withdrawal of the Twenty-Ninth. The Germans pushed their way into the village of Gouzaecourt, Headquarters of the Twenty-Ninth Division, and came alarmingly near to capturing General de Lisle. He grabbed his papers and a revolver, and made his escape on horseback after the German infantry had entered the village. For two whole days the Newfoundland Battalion with other units of the Twenty-Ninth fought desperately against repeated German attacks, without giving an inch. Every machine gun, except one, which had been supporting the advance post held by the Division, had been captured. On the night of December 1, when it became clear that the position could not be held except at very great sacrifice, orders were given for a general readjustment of the line by the evacuation of Mesnieres sector. Two units, however, the Newfoundlanders and the South Wales Borderers, were left on the north side of the Canal. No greater compliment could be paid these two battalions. The position was one of extreme danger and difficulty, and required the greatest courage and ability on the part of the defending troops. They were practically unsupported by artillery or machine gun fire, while they were incessantly subject to a most destructive enemy machine gun fire. This part of the engagement proved beyond doubt that "the mechanical side of modern warfare can never quite eliminate the brave pushing heart and the strong arm."

Newfoundlanders Fell Back.

It was a cruel experience for the most seasoned soldiers, but the Newfoundland Battalion fought through it with a courage and determination that would not give in. All through the 2nd and until the evening of the 3rd of December they held the northern bank of the Canal. When it was decided that a withdrawal was advisable, because the position was not worth the sacrifice necessary to hold it, the two battalions got back to their new position on the southern bank with splendid discipline and

with remarkably few losses.   Our Regiment occupied a trench which ran from the Canal to a road that runs about south-west from Les Rues Vertes, about midway between Marcoing and Mesnieres.   This position it held, except a stretch of about 100 yards, until the morning of December 4, when it was relieved by another battalion.

The magnificent work of the Newfoundland Regiment in this battle won

CAPTAIN G. J. WHITTY

CAPTAIN H. RENDELL

for it the title "ROYAL."   When relief came the survivors of the Battalion could look back over their work as a unit with entire satisfaction.

Previous engagements in which the Regiment had taken part lasted generally one day.   But in many respects the Marcoing-Mesnieres engagement, lasting as it did over a period of two weeks, and, except for two days' intermission, at maximum strength and exertion, was an endurance test of the highest order.   It was a test, however, to which the Newfoundland Regiment stood up with unabated courage and perseverance, and many

of the men were decorated for deeds of conspicuous valor and untiring devotion to duty. Captain Bertram Butler again dis-

BUTLER. tinguished himself. After two attacks were held up, on his own initiative he organized and led another attack and captured the position. It was a magnificient display of resourcefulness and determination. Lieutenant G. J. Whitty was a

WHITTY. Signalling Officer. When several of the officers had been knocked out, he went forward on his own initiative and assisted in organizing an attack. He personally led a charge in an able manner and with entirely successful results. Captain H.

RENDELL. Rendell was in command of a strong point that was very heavily bombarded. When his trench was blown in, he withdrew his survivors in an orderly manner to a neighboring trench. He got a supply of bombs together, and as soon as the shelling ceased, he led a bombing party, drove out the Germans and re-established the position. By his initiative and determination he saved a vital point. Many other men were decorated for their courageous and valuable services in various capacities. As would be expected from such a long and severe engagement, in which the Regiment had put forth its bravest and most determined effort, heavy casualties were sustained. Seventy-nine men were reported killed, 340 wounded and 43 missing.

The following is a list of the decorations awarded for conspicuous bravery and devotion to duty in the three actions reviewed in this chapter:

STEENBEEK.

Captain R. G. Paterson	Military Cross
Sergeant T. Dunphy	Distinguished Conduct Medal
Corporal R. Raynes	Distinguished Conduct Medal
Captain R. W. Bartlett	Bar to Military Cross
Sergeant A. Hammond	Military Medal
Private J. H. Simms	Military Medal
Lance-Corporal J. Rose	Military Medal
Private P. O'Neil	Military Medal
Private G. Mullett	Military Medal
Private A. Murray	Military Medal
Private J. J. Peddle	Military Medal
Private E. G. Wiseman	Military Medal
Private T. J. Meaney	Military Medal

Private H. Spurrell	Military Medal
Private G. Lacey	Military Medal
Private F. Dawe	Military Medal

BROEMBEEK

Captain R. H. Tait	Military Cross
Captain J. Nunns	Military Cross
Second Lieutenant G. Hicks	Military Cross
Second Lieutenant E. Chafe	Military Cross
C. S. M., A. Taylor	Military Cross
Captain K. Keegan	Bar to Military Cross
Sergeant C. Spurrell	Distinguished Conduct Medal
Sergeant R. Purcell	Distinguished Conduct Medal
Sergeant J. J. Murphy	Distinguished Conduct Medal
Sergeant A. Davis	Distinguished Conduct Medal
Corporal L. Hollett	Distinguished Conduct Medal
Private W. Sutton	Distinguished Conduct Medal
Private T. J. Meaney	Bar to Military Medal
Sergeant E. Boutcher	Military Medal
Sergeant E. Aitken	Military Medal
Corporal H. Butler	Military Medal
Corporal L. Fitzpatrick	Military Medal
Corporal H. Tansley	Military Medal
Corporal E. Nichol	Military Medal
Lance-Corporal J. Dunn	Military Medal
Lance-Corporal C. Pafford	Military Medal
Private J. Abbott,	Military Medal
Private A. Hennebury	Military Medal
Private P. McDonald	Military Medal
Private H. Bowden	Military Medal
Private J. Davis	Military Medal
Private A. Adams	Military Medal
Private A. Bulgin	Military Medal
Private W. Jewer	Military Medal
Private A. Goudie	Military Medal
Private A. Paddick	Military Medal
Private F. Rees	Military Medal
Private W. Moore	Military Medal

Mercoing–Mesnieres

Captain Bertram Butler	Distinguished Service Order
Captain R. G. Paterson	Bar to Military Cross
Captain H. Rendell	Military Cross
Lieutenant G. Whitty	Military Cross
R. S. M., A. Taylor	Distinguished Conduct Medal
Sergeant L. Fitzpatrick	Distinguished Conduct Medal
C. S. M., A. J. Janes	Distinguished Conduct Medal
Sergeant M. G. Winter	Military Medal
Corporal E. Cheeseman	Military Medal
Corporal E. Joy	Military Medal and Bar
Lance-Corporal T. Cook	Military Medal
Private L. Moore	Military Medal
Private J. Loveless	Military Medal
Private J. Hennebury	Military Medal
Private H. Dibbon	Military Medal
Private W. Fowlow	Military Medal
Private T. A. Pittman	Military Medal
Private P. Power	Military Medal
Private A. J. Stacey	Military Medal
Sergeant A. Davis	Military Medal
Private M. Bennett	Military Medal
Corporal J. J. Collins	Military Medal
Corporal R. LeDrew	Military Medal
Lance-Corporal J. G. W. Hagen	Military Medal
Private H. Knee	Military Medal
Private E. Goodie	Military Medal and Bar
Corporal C. Parsons	Bar to Military Medal

The severe fighting that the Regiment had gone through in the Marcoing-Mesnieres engagement and the heavy losses sustained, necessitated a long period for recuperation and rebuilding. **Back to Rest Camp.** Fortunately the need came at a time when the severe fighting of 1917 was over, and preparations were being made all through the British Armies for the unpleasant outlook of the following spring. The journey back to winter quarters was made over roads, which, in many places, were blocked with deep banks of snow. It was typical Newfoundland winter weather; but the thought of spending

Christmas and enjoying a rest in a French town took the edge off all hard-ships and gave them a tinge of cheerful anticipation. Many good stories could be told and are told in other places, of experiences in French towns. A special Christmas dinner was given to the Newfoundlanders at Fressen, and a Battalion mess dinner was held during the night. It was a much enjoyed day, "the other side of a soldier's life."

CHAPTER V

The Closing Year of the War

When the campaign opened on the Western Front in the spring of 1918, the outlook for the Allies was anything but bright. The Germans had completed their preparations for a last desperate **General Situation** effort to defeat the British and French armies. Their **in Spring of 1918.** plan was to separate the British from the French. The Russian exit had almost doubled the number of German infantry available for the west, and from November, 1917, until March, 1918, when the whole German military genius and power were let loose, an endless succession of troop trains bore the divisions which had extended from the Baltic to the southern boundary of Russia to swell the formidable array already marshalled across France and Belgium. By the middle of March, when the German preparations were completed, there were pitted against the British from the Scarpe to the Oise about five German troops to every two British. The outlook was most pessimistic, but the situation was handled by the Commander-in-Chief and his Generals in a way that reflects great credit on their almost unlimited resourcefulness. It was obvious from the outset that much ground would have to be given up, but it was sold at such an enormous price that before many months the British and French could begin an offensive that knew no let-up until victory was proclaimed, and the Central Powers were obliged to accept an inglorious defeat.

The British and French Commanders were determined that the inevitable onslaught would be met with the same invincible spirit that had impelled their forces for almost four years. Along with the numerous other units that went to make up the British armies, the Newfoundland Regiment was rebuilt during the winter months. After spending 25 days in the Paschendaele sector, it left for the Somme on April 10, but when news of the Armentieres reverses were received it was diverted to that area. A position was taken about midway **Bailleul-Nieppe.** between Bailleul and Nieppe, a short distance to the south of Armentieres. On the morning of the 13th, A Company, under Lieutenant E. Chafe, went into the line between the

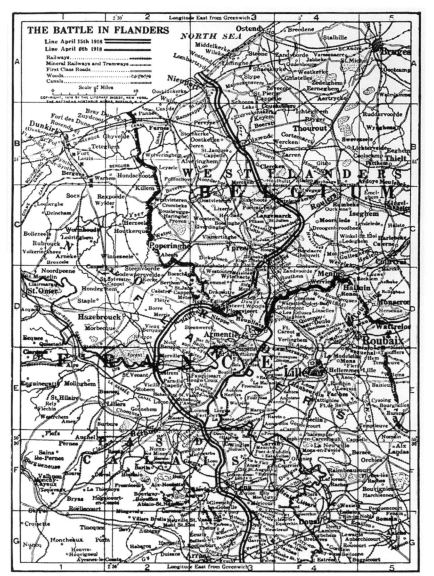

THE BATTLE IN FLANDERS

USED BY PERMISSION FUNK & WAGNALLS CO. (THE LITERARY DIGEST)

Hampshires and the Monmouths, and about noon, C Company was sent up in support of A Company. B and D Companies were in reserve. Everything went well until about 4:30 when the battalion on the left fell back, and exposed the left flank to a strong enemy attack. Lieutenant Moore and his platoon faced the enemy onrush and put up a gallant and stubborn fight until they were surrounded and taken prisoners. Their sacrifice, however, was not in vain. Their heroic resistance completely took the edge off the German attack, and the remainder of C Company and Headquarters were able to hold their position along a light railway line. Practically the same situation existed on the right flank. A Company lost its left wing, and for a time nothing could be heard of it. Later, however, it formed up, and with the assistance of Headquarters, stopped the enemy advance and formed a junction with C Company on the right. Both Companies put up a gallant fight, and too much credit cannot be given the heroic troops and the commanders for the high soldier-like spirit which they displayed in defending their position. B and D Companies, under command of Captain C. S. Strong, came up to the line about 6 o'clock in the evening and were assigned to a position on the left where the enemy showed signs of working around. They successfully counter attacked a small wood close to our line in which the enemy had penetrated. On the following day, owing to a dangerous situation developing on the

CAPTAIN CHARLES ST. CLAIR STRONG,

Whose capable leadership coupled with his genial spirit of comradeship made him one of the best liked officers of the Regiment.

high ground at Neuve Eglise, a general withdrawal to the Ravelsburg Heights was decided on, and was successfully carried out. The Newfoundland Battalion, in its position near DeBroeken, was entrusted with covering this withdrawal. The day passed quietly until 5 p. m., when the enemy attacked with great force and penetrated the British line near LeSeau. Their advance continued until about 6:30, when they were stopped by D Company. Captain J. Clift, who commanded D Company showed great judgment and ability in meeting the enemy onrush. He caught them in mass in the open, and had so arranged his men with Lewis guns that very few of the Germans escaped. More German infantry rushed up, however, and for a time it looked as though part of the Battalion would be surrounded. A Company and half of B Company were deployed to the right, the other half of B Company being sent to fill a gap between A and D Companies. The left wing of D Company was being hard pressed, and showed signs of being turned, but again Captain Clift showed great presence of mind and initiative in handling a dangerous situation. He immediately extended his left, and as soon as C Company could be escheloned

CAPTAIN JOHN CLIFT

on the left flank, Captain Clift personally collected some remnants of the Northumberland Fusillieres and filled a gap between C and D Companies. By Captain Clift's great energy and ability, and the invincible courage of the men under him, the situation was saved. The Germans were only 25 yards from our line when they were stopped.

Under cover of darkness the remainder of the 88th Brigade withdrew to the Ravelsburg Heights along a previously laid tape line. The order was then given for the Newfoundland Battalion to fall back, which was

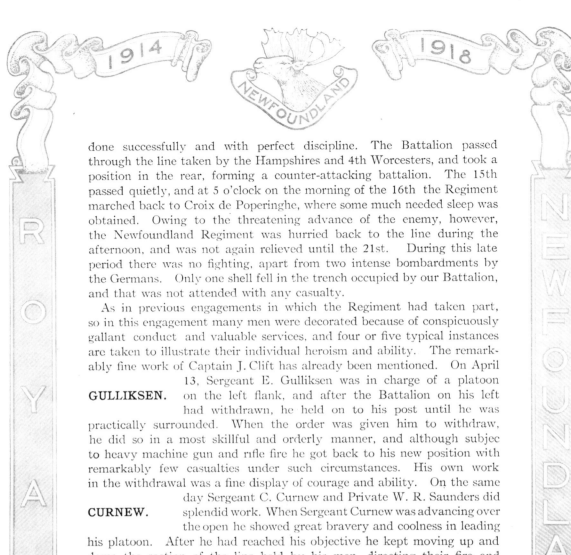

done successfully and with perfect discipline. The Battalion passed through the line taken by the Hampshires and 4th Worcesters, and took a position in the rear, forming a counter-attacking battalion. The 15th passed quietly, and at 5 o'clock on the morning of the 16th the Regiment marched back to Croix de Poperinghe, where some much needed sleep was obtained. Owing to the threatening advance of the enemy, however, the Newfoundland Regiment was hurried back to the line during the afternoon, and was not again relieved until the 21st. During this late period there was no fighting, apart from two intense bombardments by the Germans. Only one shell fell in the trench occupied by our Battalion, and that was not attended with any casualty.

As in previous engagements in which the Regiment had taken part, so in this engagement many men were decorated because of conspicuously gallant conduct and valuable services, and four or five typical instances are taken to illustrate their individual heroism and ability. The remarkably fine work of Captain J. Clift has already been mentioned. On April 13, Sergeant E. Gulliksen was in charge of a platoon **GULLIKSEN.** on the left flank, and after the Battalion on his left had withdrawn, he held on to his post until he was practically surrounded. When the order was given him to withdraw, he did so in a most skillful and orderly manner, and although subjec to heavy machine gun and rifle fire he got back to his new position with remarkably few casualties under such circumstances. His own work in the withdrawal was a fine display of courage and ability. On the same day Sergeant C. Curnew and Private W. R. Saunders did **CURNEW.** splendid work. When Sergeant Curnew was advancing over the open he showed great bravery and coolness in leading his platoon. After he had reached his objective he kept moving up and down the section of the line held by his men, directing their fire and watching the movements of the enemy. Private Saunders was wounded during the advance, but he wouldn't give in. He was **SAUNDERS.** determined to carry on, and he did so until he brought his Lewis gun carriers to their objective. Private Saunders, apparently, gave no thought to his personal safety, but thought only of carrying out the work that was assigned to him, **BENDALL and** however great the danger and the hardships involved, in **YETMAN.** order that the operations of his platoon might be successful. After an intense bombardment on the 18th, Privates F. Bendall and N. Yetman volunteered to reconnoitre forward

positions which were supposed to be occupied by the enemy. Both men carried out their work coolly and successfully, though with extreme danger to themselves, and returned with valuable information to their commander. Private S. White showed great resource-

WHITE. fulness when occasion demanded it of him. The Non-Commissioned Officer in charge of his party was wounded and Private White took charge, and with great courage and initiative successfully defeated several enemy attacks on his position. He held his ground until the order was given to withdraw to another position. During the whole engagement, the Regiment maintained its high reputation as a fighting unit, and made the Germans pay heavily for every foot of ground given up.

In this action our Regiment suffered in casualties, 50 killed, 133 wounded, and 16 missing. The loss of 200 men was a severe blow to the Regiment

Regiment Taken Out of Line. at this time. The trained men available were not sufficient to bring it up to fighting strength for some time. Also there was the fact that a number of the men of the first contingent, The Blue Puttees, those who had survived the strain and hardships of three years' severe fighting, should be given leave to return home, at least, for a brief holiday. This course was decided on. The result of the two circumstances was that our Battalion had to be taken out of the famous Twenty-Ninth Division, and replaced by another unit. No greater tribute could be

High Tribute to Regiment. paid any unit than that contained in the words of Major-General D. E. Cayley, commanding the Twenty-Ninth Division: "In bidding goodbye to the Royal Newfoundland Regiment on their departure from the Twenty-Ninth Division, I wish to place on record my very great regret at their withdrawal from a Division in which they have served so long and so brilliantly. The whole of their active service since September, 1915, has been performed in this Division, and during all that time the Battalion has shown itself to be under all circumstances of good and bad fortune, a splendid fighting unit. At Suvla, Beaumont Hamel, Gueudecourt, Monchy, Ypres, Cambrai, and during the last fighting near Bailleul, they have consistently maintained the highest standard of fighting efficiency and determination. They can look back on a record of which they and their fellow-countrymen have every right to be proud.

"I wish Lieutenant-Colonel Woodruffe and all ranks the best of luck in the future."

The Regiment went back to rest, and became rebuilt with small drafts that were slowly arriving from England. It was more than four months, however, before it went back to the line again, and during that time it was given the honor and privilege of being guards to the Commander-in-Chief.

It should be noted in passing that on May 11, 1918, the Newfoundland Government passed a "Military Service Act," which was a form of selective conscription. The measure was adopted too late to be of any benefit, a fact, of course, which was not known at that time. It was long realized that sufficient volunteers were not forthcoming to maintain the Regiment as a separate fighting unit, but it remained for our legislators to cast the one dark blot on the enviable military record of our Battalion, that of having to be taken out of the line because sufficient trained troops were not available to bring the Battalion up to fighting strength.

Meanwhile, the tide had turned. The mighty avalanche of infantry, guns and ammunition that was let loose at the junction of the British and the French armies on March 20 had been brought to a complete stand-still, and when our Regiment again entered the line in September, the Allied avalanche had started a counter-sweep, which was destined to culminate in victory.

On September 20, the Newfoundland Regiment took over a line of trenches in front of Ypres, about 2000 yards behind the line occupied by our Battalion in the Steenbeek engagement, 1917. The Regi-

Ypres. ment now formed part of the 28th Brigade of the Ninth Division. No actual fighting took place until the 28th, when, in conjunction with a Belgian unit on the left and the Twenty-Ninth Division on the right, the Ninth Division was ordered to attack and capture a line running from Zonnebeke through Polygon. At 5.30 on the morning of the 28th, the British guns opened a terrific bombardment, and half an hour after, the Newfoundland Battalion went over, D Company moving in artillery formation with its centre on Plank Road and B Company in the direction of Rifle Farm. A and C Companies were in support. The advance progressed steadily, and, except for a short duel with a machine gun in Chateau Wood, was uninterrupted during its early stages. By noon the first objecitve was captured and organized for defense. During the evening an enemy counter-attack was expected from Keiberg, and the front line platoons were ordered to put up a single line of trip wire. The attack did not materialize, however, and the evening passed quietly.

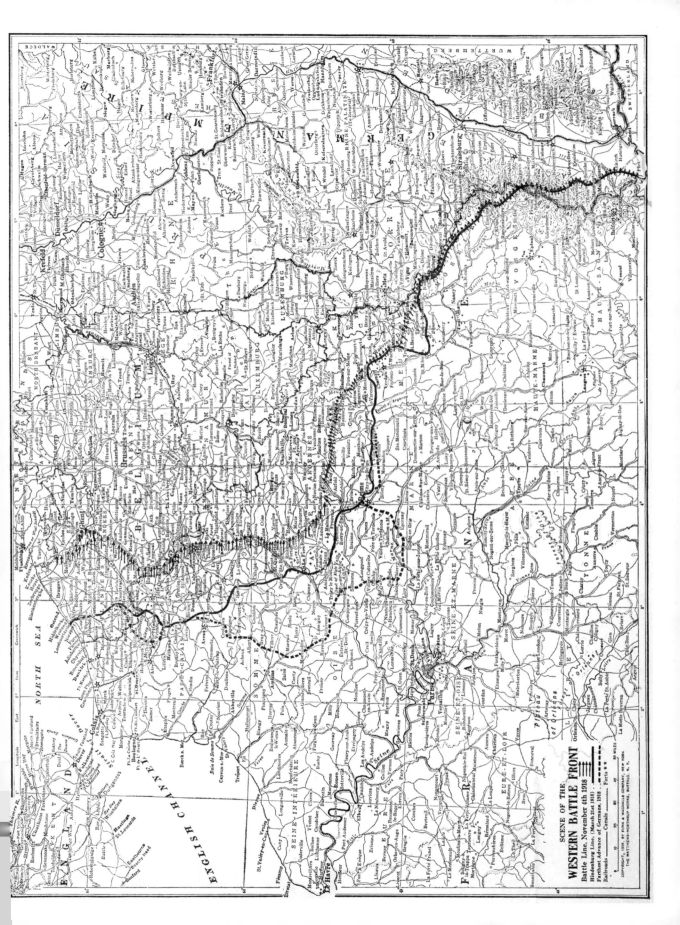

SCENE OF THE
WESTERN BATTLE FRONT

Battle Line, November 4th 1918 ▬▬▬
Hindenburg Line, (March 21st 1918) ┄┄┄┄
Farthest Advance of Germans, 1918 ┄┄┄┄
Railroads ━━━ Canals ━━━ Forts ★ ★

10   5   0   10   20   30   40   50 MILES

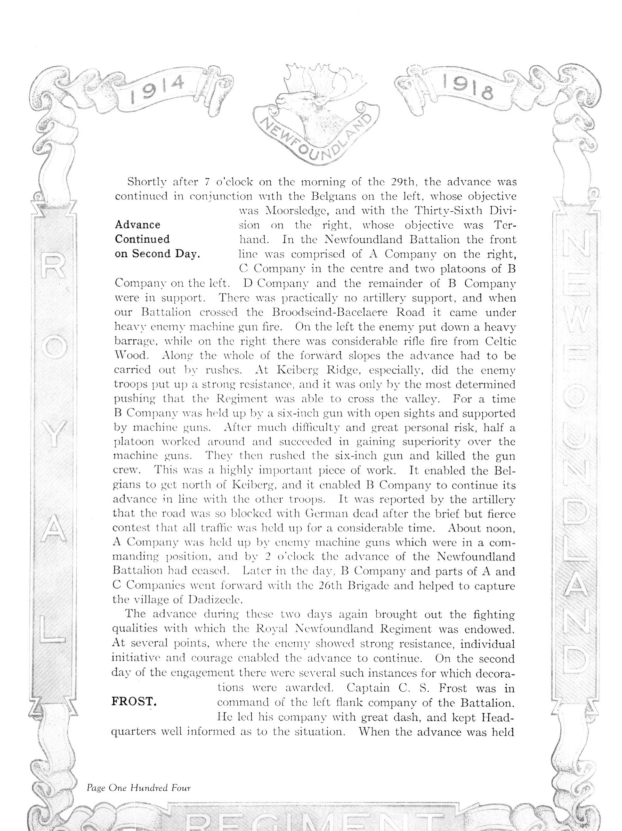

Shortly after 7 o'clock on the morning of the 29th, the advance was continued in conjunction with the Belgians on the left, whose objective was Moorsledge, and with the Thirty-Sixth Division on the right, whose objective was Terhand. In the Newfoundland Battalion the front line was comprised of A Company on the right, C Company in the centre and two platoons of B Company on the left. D Company and the remainder of B Company were in support. There was practically no artillery support, and when our Battalion crossed the Broodseind-Bacelaere Road it came under heavy enemy machine gun fire. On the left the enemy put down a heavy barrage, while on the right there was considerable rifle fire from Celtic Wood. Along the whole of the forward slopes the advance had to be carried out by rushes. At Keiberg Ridge, especially, did the enemy troops put up a strong resistance, and it was only by the most determined pushing that the Regiment was able to cross the valley. For a time B Company was held up by a six-inch gun with open sights and supported by machine guns. After much difficulty and great personal risk, half a platoon worked around and succeeded in gaining superiority over the machine guns. They then rushed the six-inch gun and killed the gun crew. This was a highly important piece of work. It enabled the Belgians to get north of Keiberg, and it enabled B Company to continue its advance in line with the other troops. It was reported by the artillery that the road was so blocked with German dead after the brief but fierce contest that all traffic was held up for a considerable time. About noon, A Company was held up by enemy machine guns which were in a commanding position, and by 2 o'clock the advance of the Newfoundland Battalion had ceased. Later in the day, B Company and parts of A and C Companies went forward with the 26th Brigade and helped to capture the village of Dadizeele.

The advance during these two days again brought out the fighting qualities with which the Royal Newfoundland Regiment was endowed. At several points, where the enemy showed strong resistance, individual initiative and courage enabled the advance to continue. On the second day of the engagement there were several such instances for which decorations were awarded. Captain C. S. Frost was in command of the left flank company of the Battalion. He led his company with great dash, and kept Headquarters well informed as to the situation. When the advance was held

Advance Continued on Second Day.

FROST.

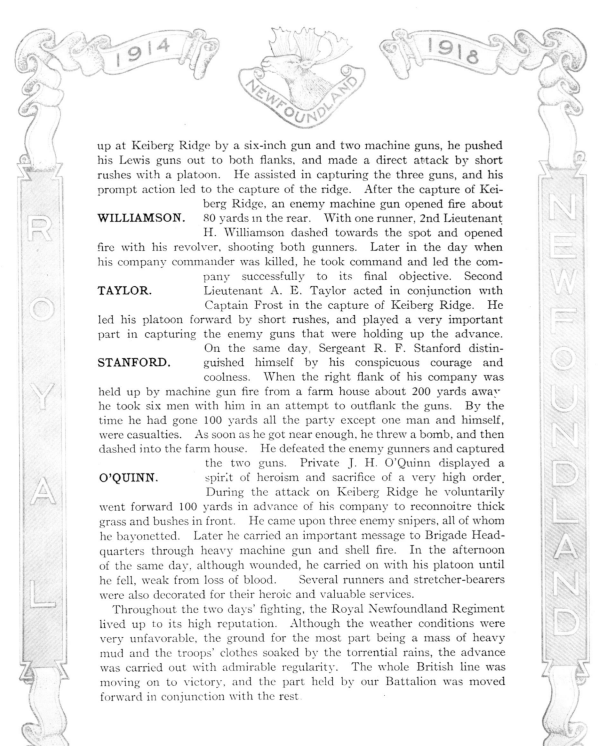

up at Keiberg Ridge by a six-inch gun and two machine guns, he pushed his Lewis guns out to both flanks, and made a direct attack by short rushes with a platoon. He assisted in capturing the three guns, and his prompt action led to the capture of the ridge. After the capture of Keiberg Ridge, an enemy machine gun opened fire about

WILLIAMSON. 80 yards in the rear. With one runner, 2nd Lieutenant H. Williamson dashed towards the spot and opened fire with his revolver, shooting both gunners. Later in the day when his company commander was killed, he took command and led the company successfully to its final objective. Second

TAYLOR. Lieutenant A. E. Taylor acted in conjunction with Captain Frost in the capture of Keiberg Ridge. He led his platoon forward by short rushes, and played a very important part in capturing the enemy guns that were holding up the advance. On the same day, Sergeant R. F. Stanford distin-

STANFORD. guished himself by his conspicuous courage and coolness. When the right flank of his company was held up by machine gun fire from a farm house about 200 yards away he took six men with him in an attempt to outflank the guns. By the time he had gone 100 yards all the party except one man and himself, were casualties. As soon as he got near enough, he threw a bomb, and then dashed into the farm house. He defeated the enemy gunners and captured the two guns. Private J. H. O'Quinn displayed a

O'QUINN. spirit of heroism and sacrifice of a very high order. During the attack on Keiberg Ridge he voluntarily went forward 100 yards in advance of his company to reconnoitre thick grass and bushes in front. He came upon three enemy snipers, all of whom he bayonetted. Later he carried an important message to Brigade Headquarters through heavy machine gun and shell fire. In the afternoon of the same day, although wounded, he carried on with his platoon until he fell, weak from loss of blood. Several runners and stretcher-bearers were also decorated for their heroic and valuable services.

Throughout the two days' fighting, the Royal Newfoundland Regiment lived up to its high reputation. Although the weather conditions were very unfavorable, the ground for the most part being a mass of heavy mud and the troops' clothes soaked by the torrential rains, the advance was carried out with admirable regularity. The whole British line was moving on to victory, and the part held by our Battalion was moved forward in conjunction with the rest.

During the following two weeks, the Regiment was in the line continually, except for short relief periods, but saw no close fighting until October 14, when an advance from the north of Ledgehem was begun. On the night of October 13, the Battalion marched from Keiberg to the front line, along a railway just north of Ledgehem. The attack started at 5.30 on the following morning, with B Company on the right and D Company on the left in the front wave, and A and C Companies in the second wave. The advance, for a considerable distance, was carried out under the most extraordinary circumstances. The smoke and high explosive barrage, together with the very thick mist which was rising from the ground, made it impossible to see more than a few yards distance, and the advance had to be carried out by compass bearing. Owing to this condition a large number of prisoners were captured in cellars and pill-boxes without putting up any fight whatever. At this stage of the advance one platoon alone captured 34 machine guns. As the Battalion neared the village of Neerhof, however, a light breeze sprang up and dispersed the fog and smoke. The whole Brigade was immediately reorganized on a line running north and south in front of Neerhof, and the advance was continued. All through the Regiment's advance to the high ground its operations were hampered and at points severely contested by heavy artillery fire. This was greatly intensified when the high ground was reached. A platoon of B Company undertook to outflank the hostile artillery, and after many daring and difficult undertakings succeeded in putting it out of commission and inflicting heavy casualties on the enemy troops who operated it. During the day, the Newfoundland Battalion captured over 500 prisoners and 100 machine guns.

At 9 o'clock on the 15th, the advance was continued with the whole 28th Brigade in reserve, and very little opposition was met until the Lys River was reached. The Newfoundland Battalion did **Lys River.** not again go into the front line until the night of the 19th, when it took a position near the west bank of the Lys. At 5.30, on the morning of the 20th, the Lys was crossed, and half an hour afterwards the advance was continued under a sweeping barrage. During the day the Regiment was subject to machine gun fire almost continually, and, although the front line was steadily pushed forward with great courage and determination, it was not without heavy casualties. At 4 p. m., the railway at Vichte was crossed, but owing to advantageous positions being held by enemy guns and the left flank of our Battalion

The marginal terms **Ledgehem.** and **Lys River.** appear in the left margin.

being exposed to a very heavy enfilade fire from machine guns, the advance was temporarily halted. For a whole day the left of the Battalion was out of touch with any other unit, being about 600 yards from the 26th Brigade, the nearest unit. Shortly after a connection was effected with a unit of the Thirty-Sixth Division, the Newfoundland Regiment was relieved by the 12th Royal Scots, and marched back to Harlebeke, at which place it arrived about 2 o'clock on the morning of the 22nd.

After a short rest, the Regiment again marched up to the front line on the 24th, and prepared for its last full day's conflict with the enemy, which took place on the following day. The Battalion, except B Company, was in reserve until about noon, when A and C Companies were ordered up for the purpose of taking a strong position held by the enemy southeast of Scheldt. To capture the position by a direct attack, however, was deemed to be too costly an undertaking, and about 5 o'clock it was decided to hold the line then occupied. After dark the Regiment withdrew to the support trenches. On the following day, after a patrol of the front line, the Regiment marched back to billets at Harlebeke, and when next it started to move toward Berlin it was with unqualified victory stamped indelibly on its gallant and determined efforts.

Regarding this last engagement in which the Newfoundlanders took part it must be said that although the Regiment was considerably weakened by the long period of severe fighting, individual courage and initiative were at no time more persistently conspicuous. It was in this engagement that Sergeant Ricketts won his V. C., the only V. C. awarded to the Newfoundland Battalion. Alongside the record of Sergeant Ricketts must be placed the great courage and ability of Lance-Corporal M. Brazil, the gallantry and quick resourcefulness of Lieutenant A. S. Newman and Lieutenant F. H. Hopson, the self-abnegation and great ability of such men as Corporal A. Whelan, Private T. Cobin, Private J. E. Mooney, Private M. Walsh, Private H. Trask, Private E. O'Brien and Private J. Clark, and the invincible soldier-like spirit of such men as Corporal P. C. Mew, Private M. Power, and Private R. Powers. These men and many others displayed such high soldierly qualities that the Royal Newfoundland Regiment will forever be admired by those who best knew it as a fighting unit. In many ways the engagement was a fitting conclusion to the splendid record that the Regiment had so persistently maintained in every action in which it was called on to take part.

Following is a list of the decorations awarded for conspicuous bravery and devotion to duty in the three engagements reviewed in this chapter:

ARMENTIERES

Captain J. Clift	Military Cross
Second Lieutenant J. Mifflin	Military Cross
Private T. A. Pittman	Distinguished Conduct Medal
Sergeant E. Gulliksen	Distinguished Conduct Medal
C. Q. M. S. W. Haynes	Distinguished Conduct Medal
Lance-Corporal M. Brazil	Military Medal
Sergeant C. Curnew	Military Medal
Private F. Bendell	Military Medal
Lance-Corporal P. Sullivan	Military Medal
Private W. R. Saunders	Military Medal
Private N. Yetman	Military Medal
Private H. Snow	Military Medal
Private S. White	Military Medal
Private G. Thomas	Military Medal
Private J. Gosse	Military Medal
Sergeant D. Burge	Military Medal
Lance-Corporal J. G. W. Hagen	Bar to Military Medal

PASCHENDAELE

Captain J. Frost	Military Cross
Second Lieutenant H. Williamson	Military Cross
Major H. Windeler	Military Cross
Second Lieutenant A. E. Taylor	Bar to Military Cross
Sergeant A. S. Rose	Distinguished Conduct Medal
Sergeant E. Stanford	Distinguished Conduct Medal
Private J. H. O'Quinn	Distinguished Conduct Medal
Private R. Powers	Distinguished Conduct Medal
Sergeant G. L. Greene	Military Medal
Corporal W. Joy	Military Medal
Lance-Corporal J. O'Rourke	Military Medal
Lance-Corporal W. J. Woolfrey	Military Medal
Private J. Murphy	Military Medal
Private J. E. Mooney	Military Medal
Private M. Walsh	Military Medal
Private R. B. Reid	Military Medal
Private W. Gough	Military Medal
Private A. Lee	Military Medal

Private J. Clarke	Military Medal
Private A. Adams	Bar to Military Medal
Private G. Mullett	Bar to Military Medal

LEDGEHEM

Private T. Ricketts	Victoria Cross
Lieutenant A. S. Newman	Military Cross
Lieutenant F. A. Hopson	Military Cross
Lieutenant G. Hicks	Bar to Military Cross
Corporal C. Carter	Distinguished Conduct Medal
Lance-Corporal M. Brazil	Distinguished Conduct Medal
Private W. Anthony	Distinguished Conduct Medal
Private S. Greenslade	Distinguished Conduct Medal
Private T. Corbin	Distinguished Conduct Medal
Corporal A. Whelan	Distinguished Conduct Medal
Lance-Corporal H. Gardner	Military Medal
Private R. Powers	Military Medal
Private D. Curtis	Military Medal
Corporal P. C. Mew	Military Medal
Private A. Smith	Military Medal
Private H. Trask	Military Medal
Private E. O'Brien	Military Medal
Private W. P. King	Military Medal
Private M. Power	Military Medal
Sergeant E. Aitken	Bar to Military Medal

A COMPANY, FIRST NEWFOUNDLAND REGIMENT, AT FORT GEORGE

B COMPANY, FIRST NEWFOUNDLAND REGIMENT, AT FORT GEORGE

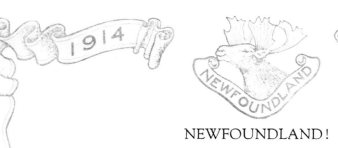

NEWFOUNDLAND!

There lies a land in the west and north
Whither the bravest men went forth,
And daunted not by fog or ice
They came at last to a Paradise.
Full two thousand miles it lay
Washed by a sea of English grey;
And they called it Newfoundland at sight,
It's rather the land of Heart's Delight.

I have seen the Mediterranean's blue
    Lazily lapping the southern shores,
And groves where the orange blossoms grow,
    And the cypress shading cathedral doors.
I have seen the moon in the desert place
Flooding the pyramid's stony face,
And crowned by the banks of the sacred Nile,
Pharoahs, carved in an ancient style;
    All I have loved and known.
But on moonlight nights, in the land I love,
I have slept with the stars and trees above,
By a big log fire that sputters and creeks,
And a river that sobs itself to sleep,
And perhaps with frightened eyes that blink
The timid deer comes down to drink;
    These I have loved and known.

I have seen sweet places in foreign lands,
Gardens tended by cunning hands,
Houses old as the hills in fame,
Bearing the weight of a noble name;
    All I have seen and known.
But Nature gardens the land I choose,
And gives her names such as lovers use;
Fortune Bay—was the fortune Love?
Conception—borrowed from Heaven above;

Breakheart Point—what a world of woe—
A maiden watching her lover go.
Heart's Content—here they came at last,
When the toil and grief of their life was past;
    These I have loved and known.

There lies a land in the west and north
Whither the bravest men went forth;
And daunted not by fog nor ice
They came at last to a Paradise.
A land to be won by the men who durst,
No wonder the British chose it first,
And they called it Newfoundland at sight,
It's rather the land of Heart's Delight.

PART II

The Military Records and Photographs (where obtainable) of the "First Five Hundred."

1914

NEWFOUNDLAND

A HAPPY GROUP OF "BLUE PUTTEES"

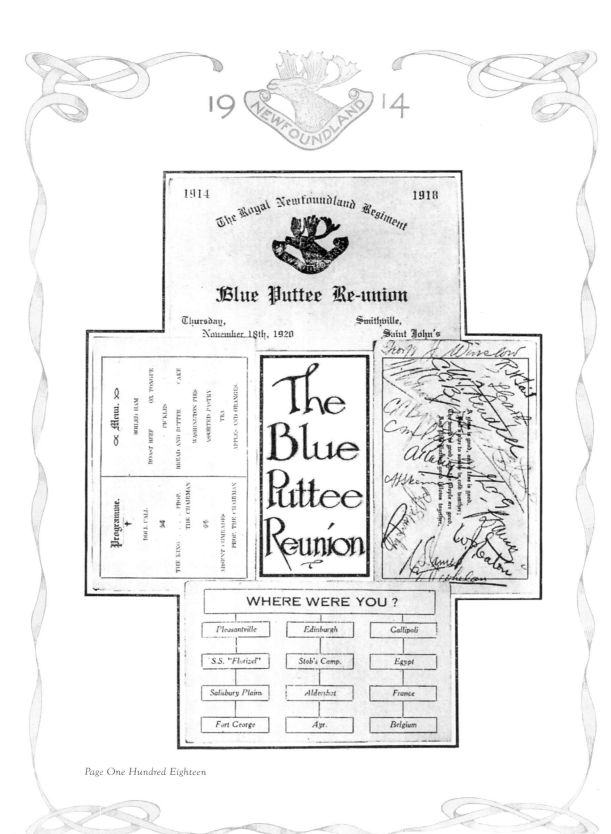

THE BLUE PUTTEE RE-UNION

The first Blue Puttee Reunion was held at Smithville on the evening of November 18, 1920. Ninety-two men of all ranks of the first contingent which left St. John's by the S. S. Florizel on October 4, 1914, sat down at 8:45 p. m. The gathering was a reunion of men who were banded together with a spirit of companionship that is known to very few reunions. It was not a class reunion of some theological institution, nor a gathering of scientists to discuss Darwin's philosophy of the origin of man; it was the first reunion of the Pioneers of the Royal Newfoundland Regiment who had fought through and returned from four years of the bloodiest and most destructive war of history. They had gone, they had fought in a way that brought honor to their Regiment and to Newfoundland, and they had returned. Only they know their feeling; only they can adequately express it.

There were no long and tiresome speeches. The program had but two toasts, "The King" and "Absent Comrades." The latter was honored by all present standing to attention for one minute. It was one minute of supreme solemnity.

Lieutenant-Colonel Carty was chairman, and under his capable guidance the reunion was a great success. During the evening he read messages from Lieutenant-Colonel Paterson and Captain T. Connors, both of whom regretted their enforced absence from the celebration.

After the supper had been thoroughly enjoyed an impromptu concert was given. Songs were rendered by Majors B. Butler, J. W. March and R. H. Tait; Captains G. G. Byrne and J. Snow, Lieutenant Irvine, Sergeant Morrissey, Mike Smythe, Tom Noseworthy and G. Jackman; recitations by Captain H. McNeil and Sergeant-Major F. P. LeGrow.

The item that very much impressed all the men was the roll-call to which the following answered:

Lieutenant-Colonel G. T. Carty	169 J. Whelan
Lieutenant-Colonel W. F. Rendell	182 C. Garland
Major B. Butler	186 Leo O'Dea
Major J. W. March	202 J. Skinner
Major A. Raley	210 R. Clare
Captain C. R. Ayre	211 T. Morrissey
Captain J. Nunns	235 C. Peet
Lieutenant Frank Bennett	263 W. Allan
10 R. Williams	298 H. Thompkinson

1914

19 Ewan Hennebury
20 S. Dewling
26 L. Stone
31 Hector McNeil
33 C. B. Dicks
36 S. Newman
48 W. J. Long
49 J. M. Irvine
50 N. McLellan
52 Eric Chafe
56 Walter Janes
59 S. P. Skeffington
60 C. C. Oke
62 P. S. LeMessurier
68 W. Kearney
71 F. Watts
74 J. H. Snow
75 R. Martin
79 A. Hammond
80 P. Brien
85 Peter Mansfield
102 C. S. James
103 E. Bradbury
111 N. Taylor
113 J. Hickey
114 J. Mahon
118 G. Jackman
121 T. Christopher
126 T. Carmichael
131 J. Cleary
137 W. Eaton
140 H. Maddick
152 R. Voisey
154 A. Goobie
164 J. McGrath
167 C. Belbin

305 H. Wilson
315 J. D. Andrews
317 G. Winslow
318 P. Daniels
336 J. Nicholle
338 N. Galgay
340 G. G. Byrne
347 J. C. Channing
360 T. Hammond
368 W. Roberts
374 J. Caul
378 C. Spurrell
379 A. Smith
401 J. Murphy
404 F. P. LeGrow
430 E. Butcher
432 M. Whelan
452 W. Taylor
461 A. Hennebury
466 A. Stacey
474 J. Dooley
475 H. Wheeler
480 J. J. Robinson
513 Henry Reid
520 W. Newell
523 T. Smyth
527 F. Noseworthy
530 B. Murphy
537 J. Brett
557 J. J. Brown
572 M. Smythe
578 G. Yates
585 A. E. Parsons
608 F. Marshall
612 H. Keats
615 M. Godden

LIEUTENANT H. H. SMALL

Who was Elected as a representative in the House of Assembly by the electoral district of Burgeo and La Poile.

SERGEANT-MAJOR F. P. Le GROW

Who was Elected as a representative in the House of Assembly by the Electoral district of Bay de Verde.

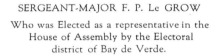

NORMAN HARVEY ALDERDICE

CONN ALEXANDER

CHARLES ROBERT AYRE

ADOLPH ERNEST BERNARD

19 14

Twenty Officers left Newfoundland with the first contingent on October 4, 1914. Colonel Franklin embarked two days earlier, on October 2nd.

NORMAN HARVEY ALDERDICE.

Granted Commission, Lieutenant, Sept. 24, 1914; Relinquished Commission, Oct. 8, 1915, and joined a unit of the Imperial Army.

CONN ALEXANDER

Granted Commission, Captain, Sept. 21, 1914. British Mediterranean Expeditionary Force, Aug. 20, 1915; British Expeditionary Force, March 14, 1916; Relinquished Commission, June 20, 1916.

CHARLES ROBERT AYRE

Granted Commission, Lieutenant, Sept. 24, 1914; Captain, July 28, 1915; Returned to Newfoundland and attached for duty to depot, May 8, 1916; Retired, St. John's, medically unfit, June 7, 1917.

ADOLPH ERNEST BERNARD

Granted Commission, Captain, Sept. 21, 1914; British Mediterranean Expeditionary Force, Aug. 20, 1915; Evacuated Suvla, sick, Dec. 12, 1915; Admitted to hospital, Malta, Dec. 17, 1915; Invalided to England, Jan. 25, 1916; Awarded Military Cross, June 3, 1916; Mentioned in despatches, July 11, 1916; Attached to depot, Ayr, July 12, 1916; Major, Oct. 5, 1916; British Expeditionary Force, Dec. 1, 1916; Decorated with Croix de Guerre, Sept. 1917; Took over command of the First Newfoundland Battalion, June 1, 1918; Returned to U. K. for special Officers' course, June 30, 1918; Returned to B. E. F., Sept. 29, 1918; Rejoined Battalion, Oct. 6, 1918; Assumed command of First Newfoundland Battalion, March 16, 1919; Embarked for Newfoundland, May 22, 1919; Acting Lieutenant-Colonel, Jan. 1, 1919; Retired, July 29, 1919.

BERTRAM BUTLER   REG. No. 146

Enlisted, Sept. 2, 1914; Orderly Room Sergeant, Sept. 3, 1914; Lieutenant, Oct. 4, 1914; British Mediterranean Expeditionary Force, Aug. 20, 1915; Captain, Jan. 10, 1916; British Expeditionary Force, March 14, 1916; Wounded, remained at duty, June 28, 1916; Wounded, Lesfosses Farm, April 23, 1917; Invalided to England; Returned to B. E. F., Nov. 10, 1917; Wounded, Marcoing, Nov. 20, 1917; Transferred to England, Nov. 27, 1917; Awarded Military Cross; Awarded Bar to Military Cross; Awarded Distinguished Service Order, Feb. 4, 1918; Mentioned in Sir Douglas Haig Despatches, April 7, 1918; Returned to Newfoundland on furlough, Sept. 2, 1918; Major, Sept. 15, 1919; Seconded for duty with Civil Re-Establishment Committee, Jan. 14, 1920.

GEORGE THOMAS CARTY

Granted Commission, Captain, Sept. 21, 1914; British Mediterranean Expeditionary Force, Aug. 20, 1915; Evacuated Suvla, sick, Dec. 4, 1915; Admitted to hospital, Malta, Dec. 8, 1915; Invalided to England, April 16, 1916; Embarked for Newfoundland, June 9, 1916; Appointed Transport Officer, July 8, 1916; Major, Oct. 1, 1916; Appointed Officer commanding Depot, St. John's, Oct. 29, 1917; Relinquished Command, July 22, 1918; Lieutenant-Colonel, Jan. 1, 1919; Appointed Staff Officer, Acting D. O. C., Jan. 28, 1919; Relinquished appointment as Acting D. O. C., Sept. 9, 1919; Retired, Sept. 9, 1919.

WILLIAM HODGSON FRANKLIN

Granted Commission, Captain, Sept. 21, 1914; Embarked for U. K., Oct. 2, 1914; Attached to First Battalion Suffolk Regiment, Nov. 18, 1914; Attached to 6th Battalion, Royal Warwick Regiment, March 20, 1915; British Expeditionary Force, March 20, 1915; Major, March 25, 1915; Lieutenant-Colonel, April 15, 1916; In Command of 6th R. W. R.; Wounded, Beaumont Hamel, July 1, 1916; Awarded D. S. O., July 1, 1916; Invalided to England, July 6, 1916; Mentioned in despatches, Jan. 5, 1917; Retired, U. K., with honorary rank of Colonel, Nov. 29, 1919.

HERBERT H. GOODRIDGE

Granted Commission, Lieutenant, Sept. 24, 1914; Relinquished Commission U. K., April 5, 1915.

BERTRAM BUTLER

GEORGE THOMAS CARTY

NEWFOUNDLAND

WILLIAM HODGSON FRANKLIN

HERBERT H. GOODRIDGE

LIEUT. JAMES ALLAN LEDINGHAM

MAJ. JOHN WESLEY MARCH

CAPT. JOE NUNNS

CAPT. AUGUSTUS O'BRIEN

James Allan Ledingham

Granted Commission, Lieutenant, Sept. 24, 1914; Captain, July 28, 1915; British Expeditionary Force, March 13, 1916; Wounded, Beaumont Hamel, July 1, 1916; Invalided to England, July 3, 1916; Attached to Depot, Ayr, Sept. 14, 1916; Returned to B. E. F., Dec. 21, 1916; Appointed Adjutant, Dec. 21, 1916; Rejoined Battalion, May 15, 1917; Killed in Action, Broembeek, Oct. 9, 1917.

John Wesley March

Granted Commission, Captain, Sept. 21, 1914; British Mediterranean Expeditionary Force, Aug. 20, 1915; British Expeditionary Force, March 14, 1916; Awarded Military Cross, Dec. 11, 1916; Evacuated to Hospital, Jan. 20, 1917; Invalided to England, Jan. 21, 1917; Attached to Depot, Ayr, March 14, 1917; Decorated with Croix de Guerre, May 1, 1917; Major, July 1, 1917; Embarked for Newfoundland, May 22, 1919; Retired, July 5, 1919.

Joe Nunns

Granted Commission, Lieutenant, Sept. 24, 1914; British Mediterranean Expeditionary Force, Aug. 20, 1915; Captain, Jan. 10, 1916; British Expeditionary Force, March 14, 1916; Wounded, Beaumont Hamel, July 1, 1916; Invalided to England, July 3, 1916; Attached to Depot, Ayr, Sept. 13, 1916; Returned to B. E. F., Jan. 9, 1917; Evacuated to Hospital, March 13, 1917; Discharged to Duty, May 11, 1917; Awarded Military Cross, Oct. 1, 1917; Returned to U. K. and substituted for rest after 24 months continuous service in the field; Attached to Depot, Winchester, April 5, 1918; Embarked for Newfoundland on special duty, May 13, 1918; Embarked for U. K., Oct. 12, 1918; Attached to Depot, Winchester, Oct. 22, 1918; Returned to Newfoundland, Dec. 12, 1918; Retired, Feb. 1, 1919.

Augustus O'Brien

Granted Commission, Captain, Sept. 21, 1914; British Mediterranean Expeditionary Force, Aug. 20, 1915; Evacuated Suvla, sick, Dec. 21, 1915; Admitted Hospital, Malta, Jan. 18, 1916; Rejoined Battalion, Suez, March 7, 1916; Wounded, Gueudecourt, Oct. 12, 1916; Died of Wounds, Oct. 18, 1916; Mentioned in Despatches, Jan. 5, 1917.

LAMONT PATERSON

Granted Commission. Captain, Sept. 21, 1914; Major, June 3, 1916; Appointed D. D. M S., Nov. 14, 1916; Lieutenant-Colonel, Dec. 7, 1918; Decorated with Order of the British Empire, June 3, 1919; Relinquished Appointment as D. D. M. S., Sept. 9, 1919; Retired, Sept. 9, 1919.

ARTHUR RALEY

Granted Commission, Lieutenant, Sept. 24, 1914; Captain, July 28, 1915; British Mediterranean Expeditionary Force, Aug. 20, 1915; Appointed Adjutant, Sept. 29, 1915; Admitted Hospital, Malta, Dec. 13, 1915; Rejoined Battalion, Suez, Jan. 31, 1916: British Expeditionary Force, March 14, 1916; Awarded Military Cross, Jan. 1, 1917; Wounded, Monchy, April 14, 1917; Invalided to England, April 19, 1917; Attached to Depot, Ayr, May 23, 1917; Returned to B. E. F., Jan. 5, 1918; Rejoined Battalion. Jan. 26, 1918; Appointed Adjutant, June 24, 1918; Temporary Major, Jan 5. 1919; Transferred to England for Officers' course, Jan. 11, 1919; Rejoined 1st Battalion, Winchester, April 23, 1919; Appointed 2nd in command of 1st Battalion, May 20, 1919; Embarked for Newfoundland, May 22, 1919; Decorated with Croix de Guerre with Silver Star, June 19, 1919; Retired, July 29, 1919.

WALTER FREDERICK RENDELL

Granted Commission, Captain, Sept. 21, 1914; British Mediterranean Expeditionary Force, Aug. 20, 1915; Wounded, Suvla Bay, Sept. 20, 1915; Admitted Hospital, Malta, Sept. 26, 1915; Invalided to England, Oct. 8, 1915; Attached to Depot, Ayr, Feb. 8, 1916; Major, April 25, 1916; British Expeditionary Force, Sept. 5, 1916; Wounded, Gueudecourt, Oct. 12, 1916; Invalided to England, Oct. 18, 1916; Attached to Depot, Feb. 20, 1917; Embarked for Newfoundland on special duty, Aug. 21, 1917; Appointed Chief Staff Officer, Department of Militia, Oct. 29, 1917; Lieutenant-Colonel, May. 16, 1918; Awarded C. B. E., Dec. 12, 1919; Still on Strength.

REGINALD S. ROWSELL

Granted Commission, Lieutenant, Sept. 24, 1914; Captain, July 28, 1915; British Mediterranean Expeditionary Force, Aug. 20, 1915; British Expeditionary Force, March 14, 1916; Wounded, Beaumont Hamel, July 1, 1916; Invalided to England, July 3, 1916; Attached to Depot, Ayr, Aug. 23, 1916; Awarded Military Cross, Jan. 1, 1917; Returned to B. E. F., Jan. 9, 1917; Killed in action, Monchy, April 14, 1917.

LAMONT PATERSON

ARTHUR RALEY

WALTER FREDERICK RENDELL

REGINALD S. ROWSELL

MICHAEL FRANCIS SUMMERS

ROBERT HOLLAND TAIT

HENRY ALFRED TIMEWELL

ARTHUR WILLIAM WAKEFIELD

CHARLES WIGHTON

MICHAEL FRANCIS SUMMERS

Appointed Quarter Master, Sept. 21, 1914; British Mediterranean Expeditionary Force, Aug. 20, 1915; Captain, Nov. 23, 1915; British Expeditionary Force, March 14, 1916; Wounded, Beaumont Hamel, July 1, 1916; Died of wounds, July 16, 1916.

ROBERT HOLLAND TAIT

Granted Commission, Lieutenant, Sept. 24, 1914; British Mediterranean Expeditionary Force, Aug. 8, 1915; Admitted Hospital, Cairo, Sept. 8, 1915; Discharged from Hospital, Oct. 4, 1915; Embarked for Gallipoli, Oct. 19, 1915; Captain, Jan. 10, 1916; Admitted Hospital, Cairo, Feb. 28, 1916; Discharged to duty, April 30, 1916; British Expeditionary Force, May 16, 1916; Evacuated to Hospital, May 20, 1916; Discharged to duty, Oct. 19, 1916; Appointed Adjutant, May 23, 1917; Evacuated to Hospital, sick, July 17, 1917; Rejoined Battalion, Aug. 24, 1917; Awarded Military Cross, Oct. 9, 1917; Wounded, Neuve Eglise, April 12, 1918; Invalided to England, April 15, 1918; Embarked for Newfoundland on special duty, May 22, 1918; Appointed Acting Major, June 1, 1919, while commanding Discharge Depot, St. John's; Retired, Oct. 6, 1919.

HENRY ALFRED TIMEWELL

Granted Commission, Captain, Sept. 21, 1914; Appointed Paymaster, Sept. 21, 1914; Embarked for U. K. Nov. 2, 1914; Major, Dec. 1, 1916; Appointed Chief Paymaster and Officer in charge of Records, Oct. 29, 1917; Lieutenant-Colonel, Dec. 7, 1918; Appointed Chief Staff Officer, London, April 26, 1919; Awarded Order of the British Empire, June 3, 1919.

ARTHUR WILLIAM WAKEFIELD

Granted Commission, Lieutenant, Sept. 21, 1914; Struck off Strength, Aldershot, Oct. 2, 1915; transferred to Royal Army Medical Corps.

CHARLES WHIGHTON

Granted Commission, Lieut, Sept. 21, 1914; British Mediterranean Expeditionary Force, Aug. 20, 1915; Captain, Oct. 17, 1915; Killed in action, Suvla Bay, Nov. 25, 1915.

SERGEANT'S GROUP

19 NEWFOUNDLAND 14

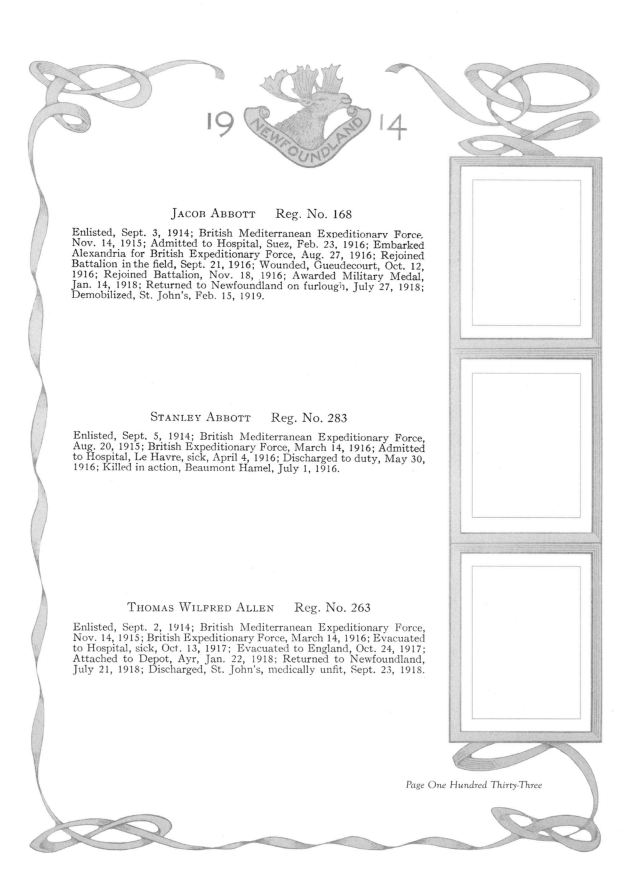

JACOB ABBOTT   Reg. No. 168

Enlisted, Sept. 3, 1914; British Mediterranean Expeditionary Force, Nov. 14, 1915; Admitted to Hospital, Suez, Feb. 23, 1916; Embarked Alexandria for British Expeditionary Force, Aug. 27, 1916; Rejoined Battalion in the field, Sept. 21, 1916; Wounded, Gueudecourt, Oct. 12, 1916; Rejoined Battalion, Nov. 18, 1916; Awarded Military Medal, Jan. 14, 1918; Returned to Newfoundland on furlough, July 27, 1918; Demobilized, St. John's, Feb. 15, 1919.

STANLEY ABBOTT   Reg. No. 283

Enlisted, Sept. 5, 1914; British Mediterranean Expeditionary Force, Aug. 20, 1915; British Expeditionary Force, March 14, 1916; Admitted to Hospital, Le Havre, sick, April 4, 1916; Discharged to duty, May 30, 1916; Killed in action, Beaumont Hamel, July 1, 1916.

THOMAS WILFRED ALLEN   Reg. No. 263

Enlisted, Sept. 2, 1914; British Mediterranean Expeditionary Force, Nov. 14, 1915; British Expeditionary Force, March 14, 1916; Evacuated to Hospital, sick, Oct. 13, 1917; Evacuated to England, Oct. 24, 1917; Attached to Depot, Ayr, Jan. 22, 1918; Returned to Newfoundland, July 21, 1918; Discharged, St. John's, medically unfit, Sept. 23, 1918.

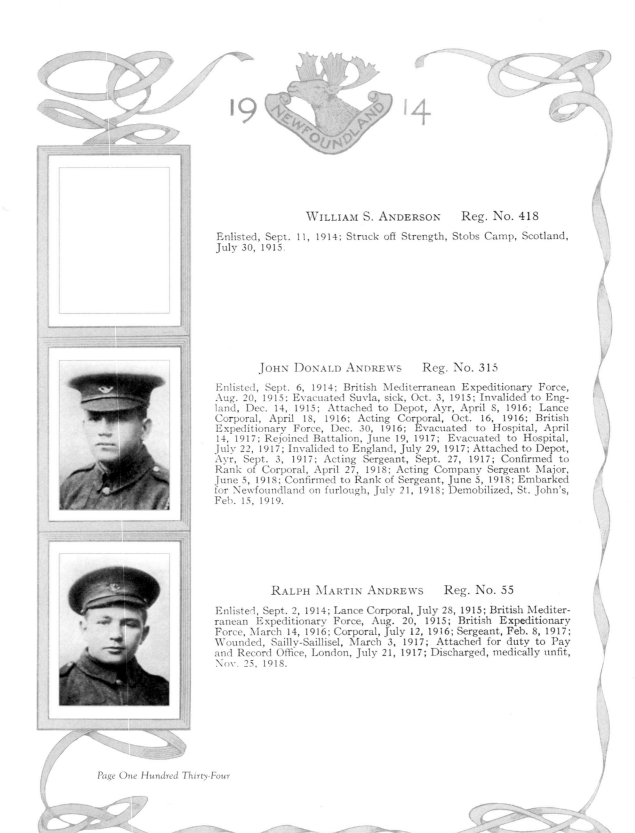

WILLIAM S. ANDERSON   Reg. No. 418

Enlisted, Sept. 11, 1914; Struck off Strength, Stobs Camp, Scotland, July 30, 1915.

JOHN DONALD ANDREWS   Reg. No. 315

Enlisted, Sept. 6, 1914; British Mediterranean Expeditionary Force, Aug. 20, 1915; Evacuated Suvla, sick, Oct. 3, 1915; Invalided to England, Dec. 14, 1915; Attached to Depot, Ayr, April 8, 1916; Lance Corporal, April 18, 1916; Acting Corporal, Oct. 16, 1916; British Expeditionary Force, Dec. 30, 1916; Evacuated to Hospital, April 14, 1917; Rejoined Battalion, June 19, 1917; Evacuated to Hospital, July 22, 1917; Invalided to England, July 29, 1917; Attached to Depot, Ayr, Sept. 3, 1917; Acting Sergeant, Sept. 27, 1917; Confirmed to Rank of Corporal, April 27, 1918; Acting Company Sergeant Major, June 5, 1918; Confirmed to Rank of Sergeant, June 5, 1918; Embarked for Newfoundland on furlough, July 21, 1918; Demobilized, St. John's, Feb. 15, 1919.

RALPH MARTIN ANDREWS   Reg. No. 55

Enlisted, Sept. 2, 1914; Lance Corporal, July 28, 1915; British Mediterranean Expeditionary Force, Aug. 20, 1915; British Expeditionary Force, March 14, 1916; Corporal, July 12, 1916; Sergeant, Feb. 8, 1917; Wounded, Sailly-Saillisel, March 3, 1917; Attached for duty to Pay and Record Office, London, July 21, 1917; Discharged, medically unfit, Nov. 25, 1918.

Archibald Ash   Reg. No. 575

Enlisted, Sept. 22, 1914; Lance Corporal, Sept. 28, 1914; Acting Corporal, Dec. 5, 1915; Sergeant, Feb. 3, 1916; British Expeditionary Force Oct. 3, 1916; Joined Battalion, Oct. 14, 1916; Killed in action, Sailly-Saillisel, Feb. 23, 1917; Mentioned in despatches, April 9, 1917.

Wilfred Douglas Ayre   Reg. No. 164

Enlisted, Sept. 16, 1914; Corporal, Sept. 21, 1914; Sergeant, Oct. 30, 1914; Acting Company Quartermaster Sergeant, July 12, 1915; 2nd Lieutenant, Oct. 16, 1915; British Expeditionary Force, March 13, 1916; Killed in action, Beaumont Hamel, July 1, 1916

Laurie Graham Baine   Reg. No. 592

Enlisted, Sept. 8, 1914; Lance Corporal, March 12, 1915; 2nd Lieutenant, April 6, 1915; British Mediterranean Expeditionary Force, Aug. 20, 1915; Lieutenant, Oct. 15, 1915; Evacuated Suvla, sick Nov. 23, 1915; Invalided to England, Nov. 30, 1915; Attached to Royal Flying Corps, Sept. 25, 1916; Graded Flying Officer, March 30, 1917; British Expeditionary Force with Royal Flying Corps, June 2, 1917; Captain, April 1, 1918; Evacuated to Hospital, Oct. 24, 1918; Transferred to England, Nov. 5, 1918; Rejoined 2nd Battalion, Winchester, March 4, 1919; Embarked for Newfoundland, May 2, 1919; Retired, May 21, 1919.

LAWRENCE BARNES   Reg. No. 528

Enlisted, Sept. 15, 1914; British Mediterranean Expeditionary Force, Aug. 20, 1915; Evacuated Suvla, sick, Oct. 13, 1915; Invalided to England, Oct. 27, 1915; Attached to Depot, Ayr, Jan. 19, 1916; British Expeditionary Force, March 28, 1916; Wounded, Beaumont Hamel, July 1, 1916; Invalided to England, July 5, 1916; Attached to Depot, Ayr, Aug. 25, 1916; British Expeditionary Force, Dec. 12, 1916; Joined Battalion, Dec. 25, 1916; Killed in action, Steenbeke, Aug. 14, 1917.

THOMAS FRANK BARRON   Reg. No. 568

Enlisted, Sept. 17, 1914; British Mediterranean Expeditionary Force, Nov. 14, 1915; British Expeditionary Force, March 14, 1916; Wounded, Beaumont Hamel, July 1, 1916; Invalided to England, July 5, 1916; Attached to Depot, Ayr, Aug. 6, 1916; Rejoined Battalion, Oct. 14, 1916; Evacuated to Hospital, sick, Feb. 11, 1917; Transferred to England, April 22, 1917; Attached to Depot, Ayr, April 29, 1917; Embarked for Newfoundland, July 18, 1917; Discharged, St. John's, medically unfit, July 9, 1918.

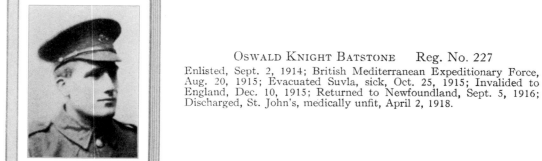

OSWALD KNIGHT BATSTONE   Reg. No. 227

Enlisted, Sept. 2, 1914; British Mediterranean Expeditionary Force, Aug. 20, 1915; Evacuated Suvla, sick, Oct. 25, 1915; Invalided to England, Dec. 10, 1915; Returned to Newfoundland, Sept. 5, 1916; Discharged, St. John's, medically unfit, April 2, 1918.

LEONARD JOSIAH BARRETT   Reg. No. 372

Enlisted, Sept. 5, 1914; British Mediterranean Expeditionary Force, Aug. 20, 1915; British Expeditionary Force, March 14, 1916; Killed in action, Beaumont Hamel, July 1, 1916.

RUBERT WILFRED BARTLETT   Reg. No. 166

Enlisted, Sept. 2, 1914; Lance Corporal, Sept. 21, 1914; Corporal, April 21, 1915; 2nd Lieutenant, April 22, 1915; Lieutenant, Oct. 16, 1915; British Mediterranean Expeditionary Force, Nov. 14, 1915; British Expeditionary Force, March 14, 1916; Wounded, Gueudecourt, Oct. 12, 1916; Evacuated to England, sick, Oct. 15, 1916; Returned to B. E. F., March 12, 1917; Awarded Military Cross, June 18, 1917; Awarded Bar to Military Cross, Sept. 26, 1917; Killed in action, Marcoing, Nov. 30, 1917; Foreign Decoration, Order of the Crown of Italy, Cavalier, Nov. 29, 1918.

WILLIAM WASHER BARTLETT   Reg. No. 270

Enlisted, Sept. 4, 1914; British Mediterranean Expeditionary Force, Aug. 20, 1915; Admitted to Hospital, Lemnos, Sept. 20, 1915; Invalided to England, Feb. 4, 1916; British Expeditionary Force, Oct. 24, 1916; Wounded, Sailly-Saillisel, March 2, 1917; Admitted No. 1, Australian General Hospital, Rouen, March 18, 1917; Died of Wounds, March 19, 1917.

CHESLEY CHARLES BELBIN   Reg. No. 167

Enlisted, Sept. 5, 1914; Lance Corporal, April 17, 1915; British Mediterranean Expeditionary Force, Aug. 20, 1915; Evacuated, Suvla Bay, sick, Nov. 12, 1915; Invalided to England, Jan. 13, 1916; Returned to Newfoundland on furlough, April 4, 1916; Embarked for U. K., July 19, 1916; Proceeded on Cadet Course at Newmarket, Nov. 29, 1916; Commissioned in Rifle Brigade, 12th Battalion, May 21, 1917.

JAMES ALEXANDER BENDELL   Reg. No. 207

Enlisted, Sept. 4, 1914; Lance Corporal, Aug. 18, 1915; British Mediterranean Expeditionary Force, Aug. 20, 1915; Evacuated Suvla, sick, Oct. 31, 1915; Invalided to England, Dec. 27, 1915; Corporal, July 31, 1916; Acting Sergeant, Jan. 1, 1917; Confirmed to Rank of Sergeant, March 23, 1917; British Expeditionary Force, March 25, 1917; Joined Battalion, Aug. 29, 1917; Killed in action, Broembeek, Oct. 9, 1917.

DOMINICI BENNETT   Reg. No. 245

Enlisted, Sept. 2, 1914; Struck off Strength, Newton on Ayr, time expired, Oct. 15, 1915.

Frank Bennett   Reg. No. 284

Enlisted, Sept. 5, 1914; Attached to Pay and Record Staff, St. John's, Sept. 19, 1914; Corporal, Oct. 2, 1914; Embarked for U. K., Nov. 2, 1914; Sergeant, Sept. 4, 1915; 2nd Lieutenant, July 13, 1916; Returned to Newfoundland on furlough, Nov. 11, 1916; Attached to Depot, St. John's, Feb. 16, 1917; Retired, March 15, 1917.

Frank Gordon Best   Reg. No. 42

Enlisted, Sept. 2, 1914; British Mediterranean Expeditionary Force, Aug. 20, 1915; British Expeditionary Force, March 14, 1916; Lance Corporal, June 11, 1916; Wounded, Beaumont Hamel, July 1, 1916; Invalided to England; Returned to B. E. F., Oct. 3, 1916; Wounded, Gueudecourt, Oct. 12, 1916; Invalided to England; Acting Corporal, Jan. 17, 1917; Confirmed to Rank of Corporal, April 24, 1917; Returned to B. E. F., April 25, 1917; Awarded Military Medal, Aug. 8, 1917; Killed in action, Broembeek, Oct. 9, 1917.

Alexander Bishop   Reg. No. 57

Enlisted, Sept. 2, 1914; British Mediterranean Expeditionary Force, Aug. 20, 1915; British Expeditionary Force, March 14, 1916; Wounded, Ypres, Sept. 2, 1916; Lance Corporal, Feb. 19, 1917; Acting Corporal, May 3, 1917; Acting Sergeant, Aug. 1, 1917; Confirmed to Rank of Corporal, April 27, 1918; Returned to Newfoundland on furlough, July 21, 1918; Demobilized, St. John's, May 29, 1919.

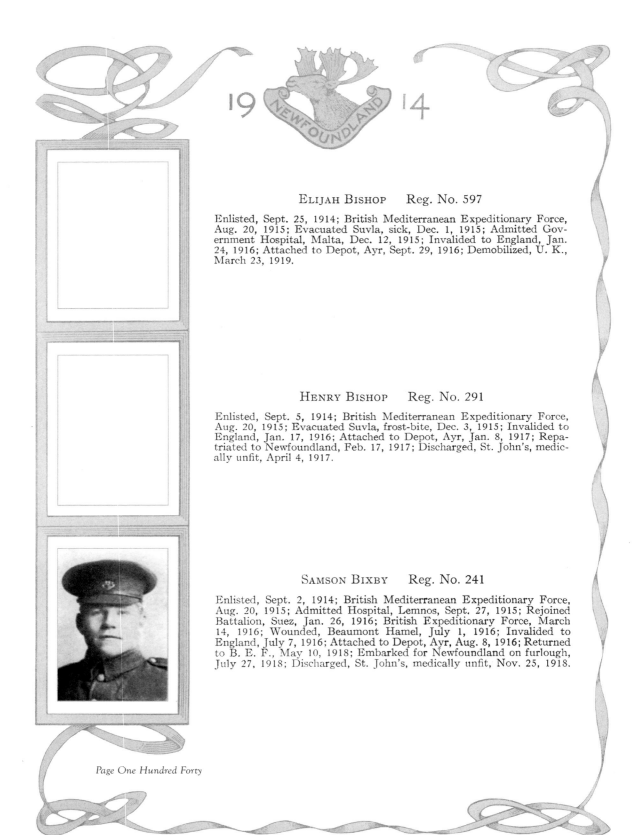

ELIJAH BISHOP   Reg. No. 597

Enlisted, Sept. 25, 1914; British Mediterranean Expeditionary Force, Aug. 20, 1915; Evacuated Suvla, sick, Dec. 1, 1915; Admitted Government Hospital, Malta, Dec. 12, 1915; Invalided to England, Jan. 24, 1916; Attached to Depot, Ayr, Sept. 29, 1916; Demobilized, U. K., March 23, 1919.

HENRY BISHOP   Reg. No. 291

Enlisted, Sept. 5, 1914; British Mediterranean Expeditionary Force, Aug. 20, 1915; Evacuated Suvla, frost-bite, Dec. 3, 1915; Invalided to England, Jan. 17, 1916; Attached to Depot, Ayr, Jan. 8, 1917; Repatriated to Newfoundland, Feb. 17, 1917; Discharged, St. John's, medically unfit, April 4, 1917.

SAMSON BIXBY   Reg. No. 241

Enlisted, Sept. 2, 1914; British Mediterranean Expeditionary Force, Aug. 20, 1915; Admitted Hospital, Lemnos, Sept. 27, 1915; Rejoined Battalion, Suez, Jan. 26, 1916; British Expeditionary Force, March 14, 1916; Wounded, Beaumont Hamel, July 1, 1916; Invalided to England, July 7, 1916; Attached to Depot, Ayr, Aug. 8, 1916; Returned to B. E. F., May 10, 1918; Embarked for Newfoundland on furlough, July 27, 1918; Discharged, St. John's, medically unfit, Nov. 25, 1918.

HERBERT BLACKALL   Reg. No. 448

Enlisted, Sept. 8, 1914; Lance Corporal, Oct. 3, 1914; Corporal, April 23, 1915; Sergeant, July 26, 1915; 2nd Lieutenant, Nov. 27, 1915; Relinquished Commission, Jan. 10, 1916.

MICHAEL JOHN BLYDE   Reg. No. 280

Enlisted, Sept. 5, 1914; British Mediterranean Expeditionary Force, Aug. 20, 1915; Died of Wounds, 88th Field Ambulance, Suvla, Sept. 26, 1915.

HUGH PIERSON BOWDEN   Reg. No. 526

Enlisted Sept. 15, 1914; British Mediterranean Expeditionary Force, Aug. 20, 1915; Evacuated Suvla, sick, Nov. 12, 1915; Invalided to England, Dec. 6, 1915; Attached to Depot, Ayr, Feb. 5, 1916; British Expeditionary Force, March 28, 1916; Joined Battalion, July 4, 1916; Evacuated to Hospital, July 14, 1916; Rejoined Battalion, Sept. 1, 1916; Wounded, Ypres, Sept. 8, 1916; Invalided to England, Sept. 12, 1916; Attached to Depot, Ayr, Oct. 12, 1916; Returned to B. E. F., June 3, 1917; Rejoined Battalion, June 19, 1917; Killed in action, Marcoing, Nov. 20, 1917; Awarded Military Medal, Jan. 14, 1918.

EDWARD CHARLES BRADBURY   Reg. No. 103

Enlisted, Sept. 2, 1914; British Mediterranean Expeditionary Force, Aug. 20, 1915; British Expeditionary Force, March 14, 1916; Lance Corporal, Feb. 9, 1917; Corporal, March 14, 1917; Sergeant, June 14, 1917; Wounded, Steenbeke, Aug. 16, 1917; Repatriated to Newfoundland, Jan. 19, 1918; Discharged, St. John's, medically unfit, March 11, 1918.

WILFRED BRADLEY   Reg. No. 398

Enlisted, Sept. 7, 1914; British Mediterranean Expeditionary Force, Aug. 20, 1915; Admitted to Hospital, Cairo, Sept. 11, 1915; Embarked for Gallipoli, Oct. 18, 1915; Joined Battalion, Suvla, Oct. 24, 1915; British Expeditionary Force, March 14, 1916; Wounded, Gueudecourt, Oct. 12, 1916; Admitted 5th General Hospital, Rouen, Oct. 14, 1916; Died of Wounds, Oct. 17, 1916.

JOHN BREEN   Reg. No. 67

Enlisted, Sept. 2, 1914; British Mediterranean Expeditionary Force, Aug. 20, 1915; British Expeditionary Force, March 14, 1916; Killed n action, Beaumont Hamel, July 1, 1916.

Jonathan Brett   Reg. No. 537

Enlisted, Sept. 16, 1914; British Mediterranean Expeditionary Force, Aug. 20, 1915; Lance Corporal, Nov. 20, 1915; Evacuated Suvla, sick, Dec. 3, 1915; Admitted to Hospital, Malta, Dec. 14, 1915; Invalided to England, Jan. 17, 1916; Reported for duty at Pay and Record Office, London, Sept. 20, 1916; Embarked for Newfoundland, Nov. 1, 1916; Discharged, St. John's, medically unfit, Dec. 16, 1916.

Patrick Brien   Reg. No. 80

Enlisted, Sept. 2, 1914; British Mediterranean Expeditionary Force, Aug. 20, 1915; Corporal, Feb. 27, 1916; British Expeditionary Force, March 14, 1916; Wounded, Beaumont Hamel, July 1, 1916; Acting Sergeant, Aug. 22, 1916; Returned to Newfoundland on duty, June 15, 1917; Demobilized, St. John's, Feb. 17, 1919.

Edward John Brown   Reg. No. 545

Enlisted, Sept. 16, 1914; British Mediterranean Expeditionary Force, Aug. 20, 1915; British Expeditionary Force, March 14, 1916; Killed in action, Beaumont Hamel, July 1, 1916.

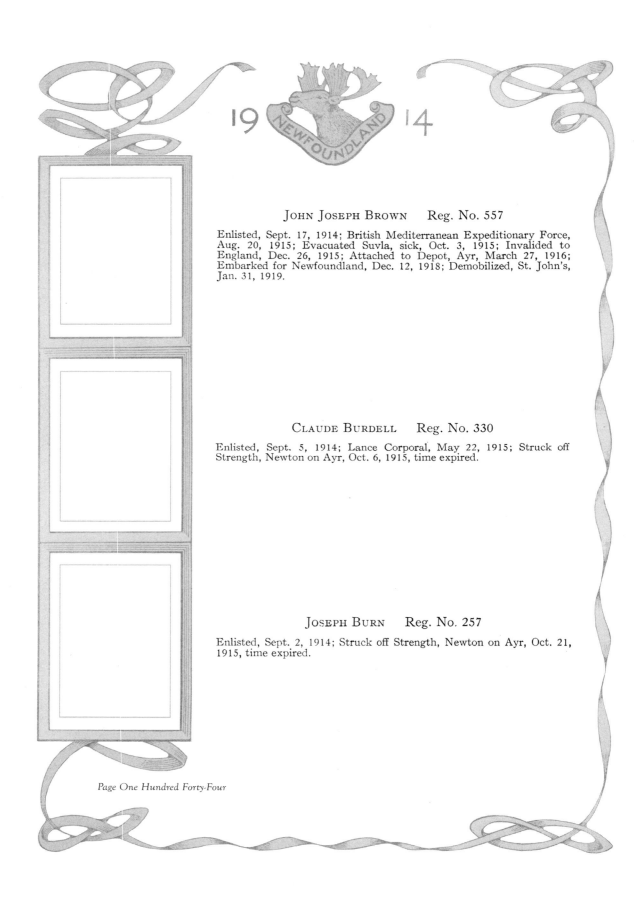

19 NEWFOUNDLAND 14

JOHN JOSEPH BROWN   Reg. No. 557

Enlisted, Sept. 17, 1914; British Mediterranean Expeditionary Force, Aug. 20, 1915; Evacuated Suvla, sick, Oct. 3, 1915; Invalided to England, Dec. 26, 1915; Attached to Depot, Ayr, March 27, 1916; Embarked for Newfoundland, Dec. 12, 1918; Demobilized, St. John's, Jan. 31, 1919.

CLAUDE BURDELL   Reg. No. 330

Enlisted, Sept. 5, 1914; Lance Corporal, May 22, 1915; Struck off Strength, Newton on Ayr, Oct. 6, 1915, time expired.

JOSEPH BURN   Reg. No. 257

Enlisted, Sept. 2, 1914; Struck off Strength, Newton on Ayr, Oct. 21, 1915, time expired.

William G. H. Burns   Reg. No. 160

Enlisted, Sept. 2, 1914; Lance Corporal, Sept. 21, 1914; Corporal, June 7, 1915; Acting Sergeant, Nov. 4, 1915; Returned to Newfoundland on duty, May 8, 1916; Embarked for U. K., Aug. 28, 1916; British Expeditionary Force, Oct. 30, 1916; Company Sergeant Major, Feb. 9, 1917; Wounded, LesFosses Farm, April 23, 1917; Evacuated to England, April 26, 1917; Returned to B. E. F., May 10, 1918; 2nd Lieutenant, June 28, 1918; Acting R. S. M., July 23, 1918; Wounded, Ledgeham, Oct. 20, 1918; Evacuated to England, Oct. 29, 1918; Returned to Newfoundland, June 24, 1919; Retired, July 17, 1919.

Hubert Frederick Burridge   Reg. No. 191

Enlisted, Sept. 9, 1914; British Mediterranean Expeditionary Force Aug. 20, 1915; Evacuated Suvla, sick, Nov. 29, 1915; British Expeditionary Force, May 20, 1916: Joined Battalion in the Field, June 9, 1916; Wounded, Beaumont Hamel, July 1, 1916; Invalided to England, July 3, 1916; Returned to B. E. F., Dec. 12, 1916; Joined Battalion, Feb. 17, 1917; Wounded, Steenbeke, Aug. 16, 1917; Invalided to England, Aug. 19, 1917; Lance Corporal, Nov. 27, 1917; Returned to B. E. F., Feb. 8, 1918; Corporal, April 26, 1918; Returned to Newfoundland on furlough, July 27, 1918; Demobilized, St. John's Feb. 15, 1919.

Gladstone R. Burt   Reg. No. 54

Enlisted, Sept. 2, 1914; British Mediterranean Expeditionary Force Aug. 20, 1915; Attached to Pay and Record Office, London, March 1916; Acting Corporal, June 10, 1916; Acting Staff Sergeant, Dec. 23, 1916; Acting Staff Quartermaster Sergeant, Nov. 24, 1917; 2nd Lieutenant, Nov. 18, 1918; Retired, Oct. 27, 1919.

Harold Burt   Reg. No. 323

Enlisted, Sept. 14, 1914; Struck off Strength, Newton on Ayr, Oct. 15, 1915; time expired and medically unfit.

Ernest Butcher   Reg. No. 430

Enlisted, Sept. 8, 1914; Lance Corporal, Sept. 21, 1914; Corporal, Nov. 13, 1914; Sergeant, April 27, 1915; British Mediterranean Expeditionary Force, Aug. 20, 1915; Wounded, Suvla, Oct. 26, 1915; Invalided to England, Nov. 16, 1915; Attached to Depot, Ayr, Feb. 7, 1916; Embarked for Newfoundland, March 10, 1916; Returned to U. K. and attached to Depot, Ayr, June 11, 1917; British Expeditionary Force, July 22, 1917; Joined Battalion, Aug. 28, 1917; Wounded, Marcoing, Nov. 30, 1917; Invalided to England, Dec. 17, 1917; Awarded Meritorious Service Medal, Jan. 14, 1918; Attached to 2nd Battalion, Winchester, June 21, 1918; Embarked for Newfoundland, July 21, 1918; Discharged, St. John's, medically unfit, Aug. 31, 1918.

Alfred Francis Butler   Reg. No. 460

Enlisted, Sept. 2, 1914; British Mediterranean Expeditionary Force, Aug. 20, 1915; Evacuated Suvla, sick, Oct. 31, 1915; Invalided to England, Jan. 20, 1916; Attached to Depot, Ayr, April 24, 1916; British Expeditionary Force, Aug. 24, 1916; Wounded, Gueudecourt, Oct. 12, 1916; Invalided to England, Oct. 18, 1916; Attached to Depot, Ayr, Feb. 8, 1917; Returned to B. E. F., Sept. 14, 1917; Rejoined Battalion, Oct. 12, 1917; Embarked for Newfoundland on furlough, July 27, 1918; Discharged, St. John's, medically unfit, Dec. 14, 1918.

Charles Oakley Butler   Reg. No. 205

Enlisted, Sept. 4, 1914; British Mediterranean Expeditionary Force, Aug. 20, 1915; Admitted Hospital, Cairo, Dec. 21, 1915; British Expeditionary Force, April 26, 1916; Joined Battalion, June 1, 1916; Wounded, June 28, 1916; Invalided to England, July 4, 1916; Attached to Depot, 2nd Battalion, Winchester, Sept. 13, 1916; Lance Corporal, Nov. 16, 1916; Acting Corporal, May 11, 1917; Acting Sergeant, Dec. 19, 1917; Confirmed to rank of Corporal, April 27, 1918; Returned to Newfoundland on furlough, July 21, 1918; Demobilized, St. John's, Feb. 15, 1919.

George Butler   Reg. No. 457

Enlisted, Sept. 8, 1914; British Mediterranean Expeditionary Force, Aug. 20, 1915; Lance Corporal, Feb. 27, 1916; British Expeditionary Force, March 14, 1916; Wounded, Beaumont Hamel, July 1, 1916; Rejoined Battalion, Aug. 14, 1916; Wounded, Gueudecourt, Oct. 12, 1916; Invalided to England, Nov. 2, 1916; Attached to Depot, Ayr, March 16, 1917; Repatriated to Newfoundland, April 10, 1917; Discharged, St. John's, medically unfit, May 11, 1917.

Henry Albert Butler   Reg. No. 325

Enlisted, Sept. 5, 1914; British Mediterranean Expeditionary Force, Aug. 20, 1915; Evacuated Suvla, sick, Dec. 3, 1915; Invalided to England, Feb. 2, 1916; Attached to Depot, Ayr, June 22, 1916; Lance Corporal, Sept. 16, 1916; Corporal, Nov. 16, 1916; Granted Commission with 3rd Reserve Garrison Battalion, March 11, 1917.

19 14

GERALD GUY BYRNE   Reg. No. 340

Enlisted, Sept. 8, 1914; Lance Corporal, Oct. 3, 1914; Corporal, April 7, 1915; Sergeant, June 14, 1915; British Mediterranean Expeditionary Force, Aug. 20, 1915; Evacuated Suvla, frost-bite, Dec. 3, 1915; Admitted to Hospital, Malta, Dec. 13, 1915; Discharged to duty, March 23, 1916; British Expeditionary Force, April 13, 1916; Wounded, Beaumont Hamel, July 1, 1916; 2nd Lieutenant, July 1, 1916; Invalided to England, July 7, 1916; Attached to Depot, Ayr, Aug. 21, 1916; Returned to B. E. F., Jan. 9, 1917; Awarded Military Cross, March 3, 1917; Evacuated to Hospital, Rouen, March 13, 1917; Invalided to England, March 13, 1917; Attached to Depot, Ayr, April 21, 1917; Lieutenant, July 1, 1917; Embarked for Newfoundland on special duty, Aug. 31, 1917; Appointed Military Secretary, Department of Militia, St. John's, Oct. 29, 1917; Temporary Captain, May 7, 1918; Confirmed to Rank of Captain, Sept. 1, 1918; Seconded for duty with Civil Re-Establishment Committee, Dec. 22, 1919.

MARTIN JOSEPH CAHILL   Reg. No. 258

Enlisted, Sept. 2, 1914; British Mediterranean Expeditionary Force, Aug. 20, 1915; British Expeditionary Force, March 14, 1916; Killed in action, Beaumont Hamel, July 1, 1916.

JOHN CALDWELL   Reg. No. 151

Enlisted, Sept. 3, 1914; British Mediterranean Expeditionary Force, Nov. 14, 1915; British Expeditionary Force, Dec. 30, 1916; Wounded, Beaumont Hamel, July 1, 1916; Evacuated to England, July 9, 1916; Transferred to England, "Permanent Base," July 27, 1917; Discharged, U. K., medically unfit, Oct. 26, 1917.

Roger John Callahan   Reg. No. 344

Enlisted, Sept. 8, 1914; British Mediterranean Expeditionary Force, Aug. 20, 1915; Evacuated Suvla, sick, Dec. 5, 1915; Invalided to England, Dec. 26, 1915; Attached to Depot, Ayr, March 3, 1916; British Expeditionary Force, March 28, 1916; Joined Battalion, April 15, 1916; Killed in action, Beaumont Hamel, July 1, 1916.

Arthur R. Canham   Reg. No. 221

Enlisted, Sept. 2, 1914; Sergeant, Sept. 21, 1914; Acting Company Sergeant Major, Dec. 11, 1915; Acting Staff Sergeant, April 5, 1916; Demobilized, U. K., March 5, 1919; Awarded Meritorious Service Medal, June 3, 1919.

Maurice Carberry   Reg. No. 382

Enlisted, Sept. 5, 1914; British Mediterranean Expeditionary Force, Aug. 20, 1915; Evacuated Suvla, sick, Dec. 3, 1915; Invalided to England, Dec. 25, 1915; Attached to Depot, Ayr, Feb. 24, 1916; Embarked for Newfoundland on furlough, July 21, 1918; Demobilized, St John's Feb 15, 1919

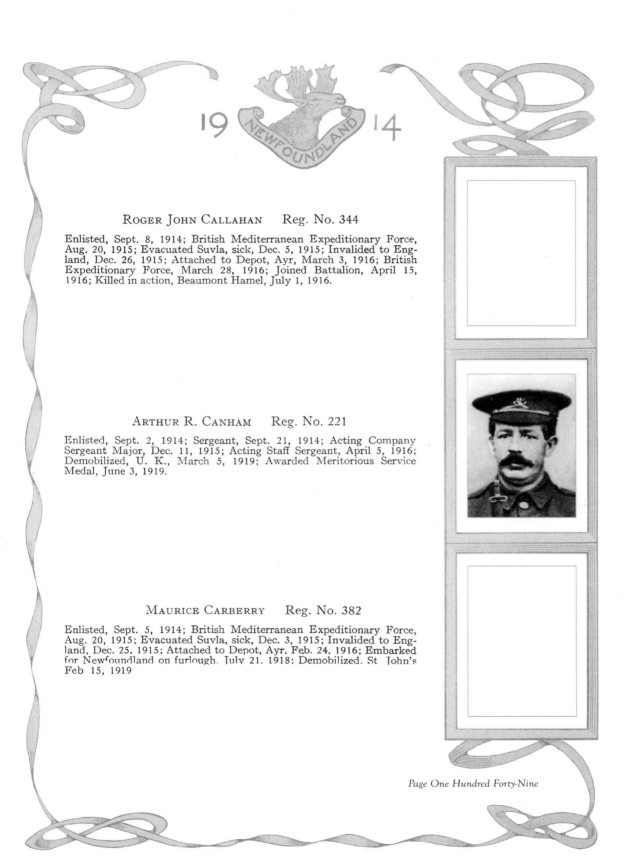

QUARTERMASTERS PERSONAL STAFF

Left to Right, Capt. Hector McNeil, Capt. M. F. Summers, Pte. Harris B. Oke, Lance-Corporal T. W. Wyatt.

1914 NEWFOUNDLAND

WILLIAM PATRICK CAREW   Reg. No. 469

Enlisted, Sept. 16, 1914; British Mediterranean Expeditionary Force, Aug. 20, 1915; Lance Corporal, Feb. 27, 1916; British Expeditionary Force, March 14, 1916; Wounded, Somme raid, June 28, 1916; Rejoined Battalion, July 21, 1916; Sergeant, Sept. 28, 1916; Wounded, Gueude-court, Oct. 12, 1916; Invalided to England, Oct. 16, 1916; Attached to Depot, Ayr, Dec. 4, 1916; Returned to B. E. F., Sept. 7, 1917; Wounded, Broembeek, Oct. 9, 1917; Rejoined Battalion, Oct. 25, 1917; Evacuated to Hospital, Jan. 21, 1918; Rejoined Battalion, March 18, 1918; Wounded, Passchendaele, April 12, 1918; Invalided to England, April 16, 1918; Attached to Depot, Winchester, June 24, 1918; Embarked for Newfoundland on furlough, July 21, 1918; Demobilized, St. John's Feb. 15, 1919.

THOMAS COLTON CARMICHAEL   Reg. No. 126

Enlisted, Sept. 2, 1914; British Mediterranean Expeditionary Force Aug. 20, 1915; Evacuated to England, sick, Dec. 5, 1915; British Expeditionary Force, March 28, 1916; Lance Corporal, Aug. 8, 1916; Corporal, Sept. 14, 1916; Sergeant, April 18, 1917; Company Quarter-master, Sergeant Dec. 26, 1917; Company Sergeant Major, April 25, 1918; Returned to Newfoundland on furlough, July 27 1918; Attached for duty to Depot, St. John's, Nov. 28, 1918; Demobilized, St. John's Aug. 25, 1919.

THOMAS CARROLL   Reg. No. 274

Enlisted, Sept. 2, 1914; British Mediterranean Expeditionary Force, Aug. 20, 1915; Corporal, Feb. 27, 1916; British Expeditionary Force, March 14, 1916; Sergeant, June 11, 1916; Killed in action, Beaumont Hamel, July 1, 1916.

James Carter   Reg. No. 269

Enlisted, Sept. 2, 1914; British Mediterranean Expeditionary Force Aug. 20, 1915; Evacuated Suvla, sick, Nov. 16, 1915; Joined Battalion Suez, Jan. 31, 1916; British Expeditionary Force, March 14, 1916; Wounded, Beaumont Hamel, July 1, 1916; Invalided to England, July 3, 1916; Repatriated to Newfoundland, March 9, 1917; Discharged, St. John's, medically unfit, April 11, 1917.

James Henry Carter   Reg. No. 222

Enlisted, Sept. 2, 1914; British Mediterranean Expeditionary Force Aug. 20, 1915; Lance Corporal, Nov. 14, 1915; Served with 1st Composite Battalion, Western Egyptian Frontier, Dec. 1915 to Feb. 1916; British Expeditionary Force, March 2, 1916; Evacuated to Hospital, April 12, 1916; Invalided to England, April 23, 1916; Attached to 2nd Battalion, Aug. 1, 1916; Returned to B. E. F., Sept. 7, 1917; Killed in action, Marcoing, Nov. 20, 1917.

Llewellyn James Carter   Reg. No. 198

Enlisted, Sept. 14, 1914; British Mediterranean Expeditionary Force, Aug. 20, 1915; Evacuated Suvla, sick, Nov. 26, 1915; Invalided to England, Jan. 2, 1916; British Expeditionary Force, March 28, 1916; Wounded, Beaumont Hamel, July 1, 1916; Died of wounds, July 2, 1916.

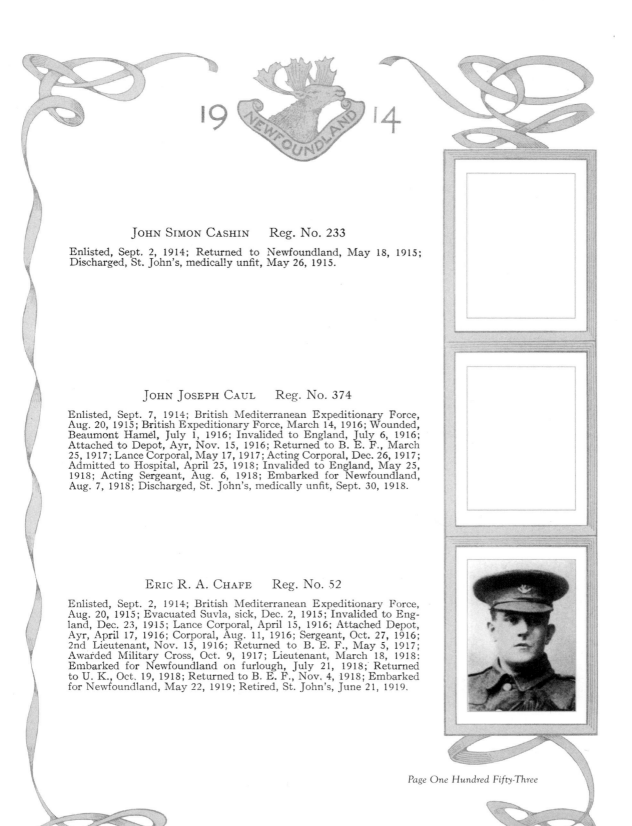

John Simon Cashin   Reg. No. 233

Enlisted, Sept. 2, 1914; Returned to Newfoundland, May 18, 1915; Discharged, St. John's, medically unfit, May 26, 1915.

John Joseph Caul   Reg. No. 374

Enlisted, Sept. 7, 1914; British Mediterranean Expeditionary Force, Aug. 20, 1915; British Expeditionary Force, March 14, 1916; Wounded, Beaumont Hamél, July 1, 1916; Invalided to England, July 6, 1916; Attached to Depot, Ayr, Nov. 15, 1916; Returned to B. E. F., March 25, 1917; Lance Corporal, May 17, 1917; Acting Corporal, Dec. 26, 1917; Admitted to Hospital, April 25, 1918; Invalided to England, May 25, 1918; Acting Sergeant, Aug. 6, 1918; Embarked for Newfoundland, Aug. 7, 1918; Discharged, St. John's, medically unfit, Sept. 30, 1918.

Eric R. A. Chafe   Reg. No. 52

Enlisted, Sept. 2, 1914; British Mediterranean Expeditionary Force, Aug. 20, 1915; Evacuated Suvla, sick, Dec. 2, 1915; Invalided to England, Dec. 23, 1915; Lance Corporal, April 15, 1916; Attached Depot, Ayr, April 17, 1916; Corporal, Aug. 11, 1916; Sergeant, Oct. 27, 1916; 2nd Lieutenant, Nov. 15, 1916; Returned to B. E. F., May 5, 1917; Awarded Military Cross, Oct. 9, 1917; Lieutenant, March 18, 1918: Embarked for Newfoundland on furlough, July 21, 1918; Returned to U. K., Oct. 19, 1918; Returned to B. E. F., Nov. 4, 1918; Embarked for Newfoundland, May 22, 1919; Retired, St. John's, June 21, 1919.

GEORGE WILBUR CHANCEY   Reg. No. 78

Enlisted, Sept. 5, 1914; Corporal, Sept. 21, 1914; Sergeant, Oct. 3, 1914; British Mediterranean Expeditionary Force, Aug. 20, 1915; British Expeditionary Force, March 14, 1916; Wounded, Sailly-Saillisel, March 3, 1917; Company Quartermaster Sergeant, May 20, 1917; Invalided to England; Returned to B. E. F., May 10, 1918; Returned to Newfoundland on duty, July 18, 1918; Demobilized, St. John's, Nov. 3, 1919.

JOHN CUTHBERT CHANNING   Reg. No. 347

Enlisted, Sept. 7, 1914; Repatriated to Newfoundland, Dec. 14, 1914; Discharged, St. John's, medically unfit, Jan. 7, 1915.

JOHN FIELDING CHAPLIN   Reg. No. 584

Enlisted, Sept. 22, 1914; Died at Fort George, Jan. 1, 1915.

19 14

Thomas Christopher Reg. No. 121

Enlisted, Sept. 4, 1914; Lance Corporal, July 28, 1915; British Mediterranean Expeditionary Force, Aug. 20, 1915; Evacuated to England, March 26, 1916; Returned to Newfoundland on furlough, Aug. 3, 1916; Corporal, April 24, 1917; Embarked for U. K., Dec. 31, 1917; Sergeant, Jan. 2, 1918; Attached for duty to Pay and Record Office, London, May 29, 1918; Repatriated to Newfoundland on compassionate grounds, Nov. 20, 1918; Demobilized, St. John's, Oct. 18. 1919.

Ernest St. Claire Churchill Reg. No. 281

Enlisted, Sept. 8, 1914; Lance Corporal, Sept. 21, 1914; Corporal, Oct. 3, 1914; Sergeant, April 21, 1915; 2nd Lieutenant, Aug. 16, 1915; British Mediterranean Expeditionary Force, Aug. 20, 1915; Evacuated Suvla, sick, Nov. 6, 1915; Invalided to England, April 4, 1916; Attached to Depot, Ayr, July 4, 1916; Returned to Newfoundland, Aug. 23, 1916; Arrived U. K., April 30, 1917; British Expeditionary Force, May 4, 1917; Evacuated to Hospital, June 21, 1917; Invalided to England, July 8, 1917; Attached to Depot, Ayr, Nov. 29, 1917; Returned to B. E. F., Jan 5, 1918; Wounded, Belgium, March 28, 1918; Invalided to England, March 31, 1918; Returned to Newfoundland, May 22, 1919; Retired, July 5, 1919.

William Maxse Churchill Reg. No. 4

Enlisted, Sept. 2, 1914; Lance Corporal, April 21, 1915; Corporal, July 27, 1915; British Mediterranean Expeditionary Force, Aug. 20, 1915; Sergeant, Aug. 26, 1915; Evacuated Suvla, sick, Nov. 26, 1915; Invalided to England, Jan. 3, 1916; Attached to Depot, Ayr, Feb. 24, 1916; Company Quartermaster Sergeant, April 10, 1916; Company Sergeant Major, April 14, 1916; 2nd Lieutenant, April 15, 1916; Embarked for Newfoundland, Aug. 23, 1916; Retired, March 15, 1917; Reattested and placed on active list, April 1, 1918; Embarked for U. K., June 22, 1918; British Expeditionary Force, Aug. 13, 1918; Evacuated to Hospital, sick, Oct. 13, 1918; Rejoined Battalion, Jan. 4, 1919; Transferred to U. K., Jan. 11, 1919; Embarked for Newfoundland, Jan. 30, 1919; Retired, Feb. 15, 1919.

Lawrence Edward Clare   Reg. No. 343

Enlisted, Sept. 8, 1914; British Mediterranean Expeditionary Force, Aug. 20, 1915; Served with 1st Composite Battalion on Western Egyptian Frontier, Nov. 1915 to Feb. 1916; British Expeditionary Force, March 2, 1916; Lance Corporal, Aug. 11, 1916; Corporal, Sept. 28, 1916; Killed in action, Gueudecourt, Oct. 12, 1916.

Robert Clare   Reg. No. 210

Enlisted, Sept. 3, 1914; British Mediterranean Expeditionary Force Aug. 20, 1915; Evacuated Suvla, sick, Oct. 14, 1915; Rejoined Battalion, Suez, Jan. 26, 1916; British Expeditionary Force, March 18 1916; Wounded, Beaumont Hamel, July 1, 1916; Invalided to England July 4, 1916; Lance Corporal, Feb. 12, 1917; Returned to B. E. F. April 25, 1917; Rejoined Battalion, June 7, 1917; Corporal, July 18 1917; Wounded, Steenbeke, Aug. 23, 1917; Invalided to England Nov. 14, 1917; Still on Strength.

William Joseph Clare   Reg. No. 536

Enlisted, Sept. 16, 1914; British Mediterranean Expeditionary Force, Aug. 20, 1915; Sergeant, Sept. 21, 1915; British Expeditionary Force, March 14, 1916; Company Sergeant Major, April 29, 1916; 2nd Lieutenant, July 1, 1916; Evacuated to Hospital, Oct. 22, 1916; Invalided to England, Oct. 23, 1916; Attached to Depot, Ayr, Jan. 17, 1917; Returned to B. E. F., March 12, 1917; Wounded, Monchy, April 14, 1917; Invalided to England, April 20, 1917; Attached to Depot, Ayr, Nov. 10, 1917; Lieutenant, Jan. 1, 1918; Embarked for Newfoundland on special duty, March 13, 1918; Retired, St. John's, medically unfit, Oct. 7, 1918.

1914 NEWFOUNDLAND

GEORGE S. CLARIDGE   Reg. No. 110

Enlisted, Sept. 2, 1914; British Mediterranean Expeditionary Force, Aug. 20, 1915; Evacuated to England, Jan. 11, 1916; Attached to Depot 2nd Battalion, May 1, 1916; Lance Corporal, Sept. 16, 1916; Acting Corporal, Nov. 16, 1916; Acting Company Quartermaster Sergeant, Jan. 13, 1917; Confirmed to Rank of Sergeant, April 27, 1918; Honorary 2nd Lieutenant, March 17, 1919; Retired, March 17, 1919.

SELBY CLARK   Reg. No. 239

Enlisted, Sept. 2, 1914; British Mediterranean Expeditionary Force, Aug. 20, 1915; Admitted to Hospital, Lemnos, Sept. 20, 1915; Invalided to England, Nov. 21, 1915; Reported to Depot, Ayr, Feb. 1, 1916; British Expeditionary Force, March 28, 1916; Wounded, Beaumont Hamel, July 1, 1916; Invalided to England, July 3, 1916; Returned to Newfoundland on furlough, Oct. 10, 1916; Discharged, St. John's, medically unfit, March 8, 1918.

GEORGE CLARKE   Reg. No. 271

Enlisted, Sept. 5, 1914; British Mediterranean Expeditionary Force, Aug. 20, 1915; Evacuated Suvla, sick, Oct. 25, 1915; Died at 16th Stationary Hospital, Mudros, Nov. 24, 1915.

John Cleary   Reg. No. 288

Enlisted, Sept. 8, 1914; British Mediterranean Expeditionary Force, Aug. 20, 1915; Evacuated Suvla, sick, Nov. 25, 1915; Rejoined Battalion, Jan. 31, 1916; British Expeditionary Force, March 14, 1916; Killed in action, Beaumont Hamel, July 1, 1916.

John Sullivan Cleary   Reg. No. 131

Enlisted, Sept. 2, 1914; British Mediterranean Expeditionary Force, Aug. 20, 1915; British Expeditionary Force, March 14, 1916; Wounded, Beaumont Hamel, July 1, 1916; Evacuated to England, July 8, 1916; Lance Corporal, Nov. 16, 1916; Corporal, Jan. 17, 1917; Returned to B. E. F., April 25, 1917; Wounded, Steenbeke, Aug. 16, 1917; Evacuated to England, Sept. 11, 1917; Acting Sergeant, Oct. 16, 1917; Repatriated to Newfoundland, Oct. 18, 1917; Discharged, St. John's, medically unfit, Nov. 22, 1917.

William Cleary   Reg. No. 384

Enlisted, Sept. 7, 1914; British Mediterranean Expeditionary Force, Aug. 20, 1915; Lance Corporal, Feb. 27, 1916; British Expeditionary Force, March 14, 1916; Wounded, Beaumont Hamel, July 1, 1916, Invalided to England, July 5, 1916; Attached to Depot, Ayr, Sept. 16, 1916; Embarked for Newfoundland on furlough, Sept. 27, 1916; Discharged, St. John's, medically unfit, March, 8, 1918.

19 NEWFOUNDLAND 14

CECIL BAYLY CLIFT   Reg. No. 505

Enlisted, Sept. 7, 1914; Lance Corporal, April 26, 1915; 2nd Lieutenant, June 29, 1915; British Mediterranean Expeditionary Force, Aug. 20, 1915; Lieutenant, Jan. 1, 1916; British Expeditionary Force, March 14, 1916; Evacuated to Hospital, April 20, 1916; Rejoined Battalion, July 14, 1916; Killed in action, Gueudecourt, Oct. 12, 1916.

JOHN CLIFT   Reg. No. 503

Enlisted, Sept. 7, 1914; Lance Corporal, April 26, 1915; Struck off Strength, Commissioned with Cameron Highlanders, April 8, 1915; Transferred from Cameron Highlanders to Newfoundland Regiment, Captain Clift, Oct. 26, 1917; British Expeditionary Force, Nov. 10, 1917; Awarded Military Cross, Sept. 16, 1918; Embarked for Newfoundland, Jan. 30, 1919; Retired, Feb. 25, 1919.

FREDERICK AUGUSTUS CLOUTER   Reg. No. 422

Enlisted, Sept. 2, 1914; British Mediterranean Expeditionary Force, Aug. 20, 1915; Evacuated Suvla, sick, Nov. 30, 1915; Invalided to England, Jan. 17, 1916; Attached to Depot, Ayr, April 28, 1916; Embarked for Newfoundland, Sept. 8, 1916; Discharged, St. John's medically unfit, Dec. 22, 1916.

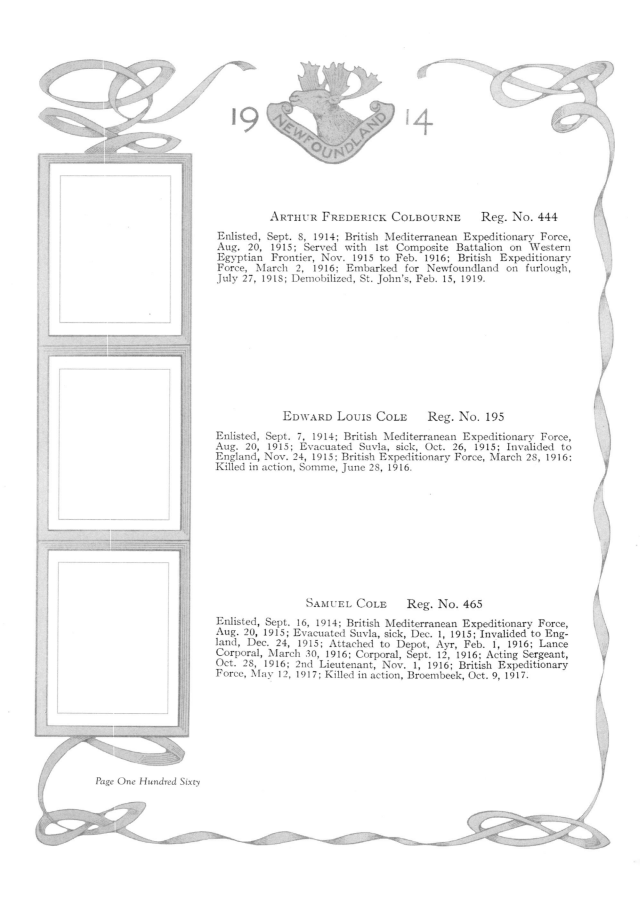

ARTHUR FREDERICK COLBOURNE   Reg. No. 444

Enlisted, Sept. 8, 1914; British Mediterranean Expeditionary Force, Aug. 20, 1915; Served with 1st Composite Battalion on Western Egyptian Frontier, Nov. 1915 to Feb. 1916; British Expeditionary Force, March 2, 1916; Embarked for Newfoundland on furlough, July 27, 1918; Demobilized, St. John's, Feb. 15, 1919.

EDWARD LOUIS COLE   Reg. No. 195

Enlisted, Sept. 7, 1914; British Mediterranean Expeditionary Force, Aug. 20, 1915; Evacuated Suvla, sick, Oct. 26, 1915; Invalided to England, Nov. 24, 1915; British Expeditionary Force, March 28, 1916: Killed in action, Somme, June 28, 1916.

SAMUEL COLE   Reg. No. 465

Enlisted, Sept. 16, 1914; British Mediterranean Expeditionary Force, Aug. 20, 1915; Evacuated Suvla, sick, Dec. 1, 1915; Invalided to England, Dec. 24, 1915; Attached to Depot, Ayr, Feb. 1, 1916; Lance Corporal, March 30, 1916; Corporal, Sept. 12, 1916; Acting Sergeant, Oct. 28, 1916; 2nd Lieutenant, Nov. 1, 1916; British Expeditionary Force, May 12, 1917; Killed in action, Broembeek, Oct. 9, 1917.

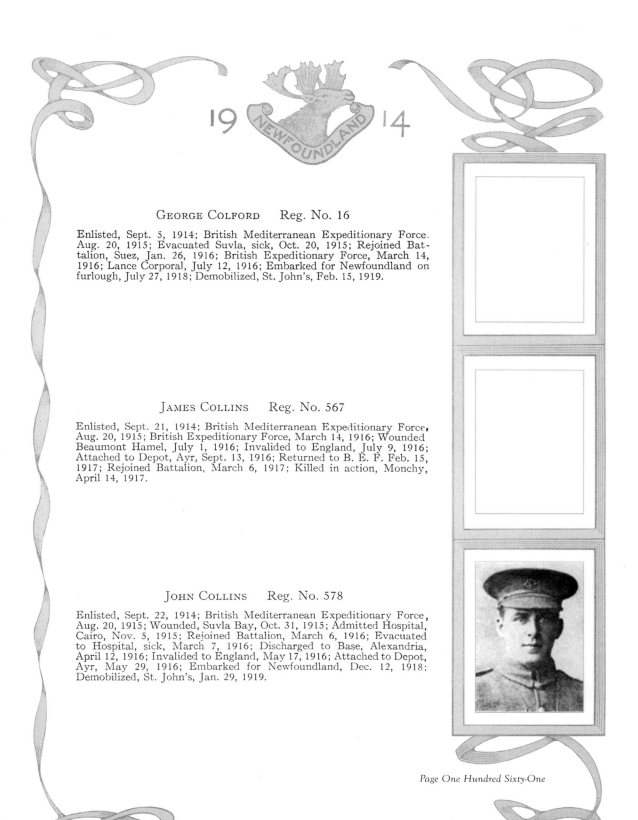

GEORGE COLFORD   Reg. No. 16

Enlisted, Sept. 5, 1914; British Mediterranean Expeditionary Force.
Aug. 20, 1915; Evacuated Suvla, sick, Oct. 20, 1915; Rejoined Battalion, Suez, Jan. 26, 1916; British Expeditionary Force, March 14,
1916; Lance Corporal, July 12, 1916; Embarked for Newfoundland on
furlough, July 27, 1918; Demobilized, St. John's, Feb. 15, 1919.

JAMES COLLINS   Reg. No. 567

Enlisted, Sept. 21, 1914; British Mediterranean Expeditionary Force,
Aug. 20, 1915; British Expeditionary Force, March 14, 1916; Wounded
Beaumont Hamel, July 1, 1916; Invalided to England, July 9, 1916;
Attached to Depot, Ayr, Sept. 13, 1916; Returned to B. E. F. Feb. 15,
1917; Rejoined Battalion, March 6, 1917; Killed in action, Monchy,
April 14, 1917.

JOHN COLLINS   Reg. No. 578

Enlisted, Sept. 22, 1914; British Mediterranean Expeditionary Force,
Aug. 20, 1915; Wounded, Suvla Bay, Oct. 31, 1915; Admitted Hospital,
Cairo, Nov. 5, 1915; Rejoined Battalion, March 6, 1916; Evacuated
to Hospital, sick, March 7, 1916; Discharged to Base, Alexandria,
April 12, 1916; Invalided to England, May 17, 1916; Attached to Depot,
Ayr, May 29, 1916; Embarked for Newfoundland, Dec. 12, 1918;
Demobilized, St. John's, Jan. 29, 1919.

WILLIAM JOSEPH COLLINS   Reg. No. 82

Enlisted, Sept. 2, 1914; British Mediterranean Expeditionary Force, Aug. 20, 1915; Evacuated Suvla, sick, Oct. 10, 1915; Died at 19th General Hospital, Alexandria, Oct. 28, 1915.

JAMES PATRICK CONNORS   Reg. No. 209

Enlisted, Sept. 5, 1914; British Mediterranean Expeditionary Force, Aug. 20, 1915; Evacuated Suvla, sick, Dec. 3, 1915; Invalided to England, Jan. 2, 1916; British Expeditionary Force, March 28, 1916; Killed in action, Beaumont Hamel, July 1, 1916

THOMAS JOSEPH CONNORS   Reg. No. 170

Enlisted, Sept. 3, 1914; Lance Corporal, Oct. 3, 1914; Transferred to Royal Division, Leith, and Struck off Strength, May 21, 1915.

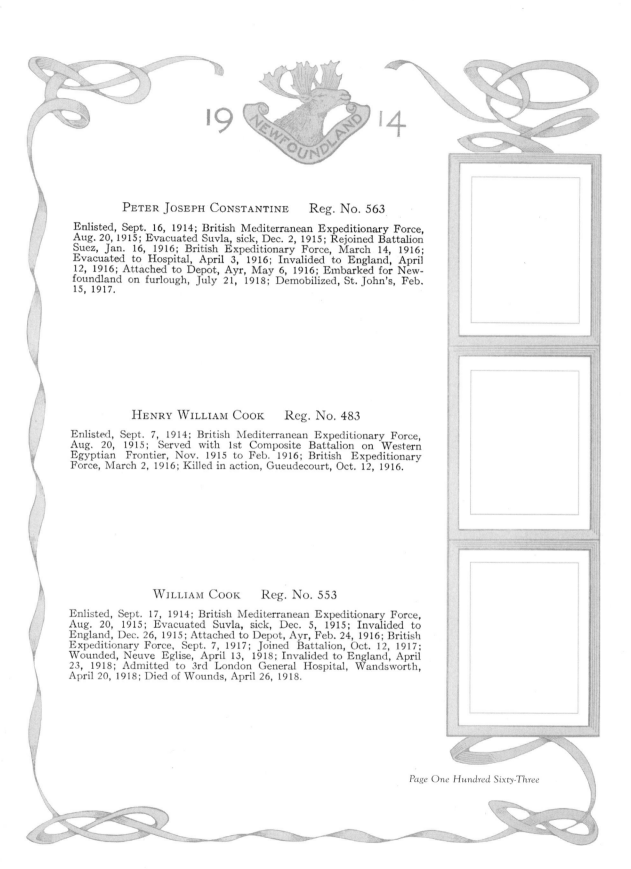

Peter Joseph Constantine   Reg. No. 563

Enlisted, Sept. 16, 1914; British Mediterranean Expeditionary Force, Aug. 20, 1915; Evacuated Suvla, sick, Dec. 2, 1915; Rejoined Battalion Suez, Jan. 16, 1916; British Expeditionary Force, March 14, 1916; Evacuated to Hospital, April 3, 1916; Invalided to England, April 12, 1916; Attached to Depot, Ayr, May 6, 1916; Embarked for Newfoundland on furlough, July 21, 1918; Demobilized, St. John's, Feb. 15, 1917.

Henry William Cook   Reg. No. 483

Enlisted, Sept. 7, 1914; British Mediterranean Expeditionary Force, Aug. 20, 1915; Served with 1st Composite Battalion on Western Egyptian Frontier, Nov. 1915 to Feb. 1916; British Expeditionary Force, March 2, 1916; Killed in action, Gueudecourt, Oct. 12, 1916.

William Cook   Reg. No. 553

Enlisted, Sept. 17, 1914; British Mediterranean Expeditionary Force, Aug. 20, 1915; Evacuated Suvla, sick, Dec. 5, 1915; Invalided to England, Dec. 26, 1915; Attached to Depot, Ayr, Feb. 24, 1916; British Expeditionary Force, Sept. 7, 1917; Joined Battalion, Oct. 12, 1917; Wounded, Neuve Eglise, April 13, 1918; Invalided to England, April 23, 1918; Admitted to 3rd London General Hospital, Wandsworth, April 20, 1918; Died of Wounds, April 26, 1918.

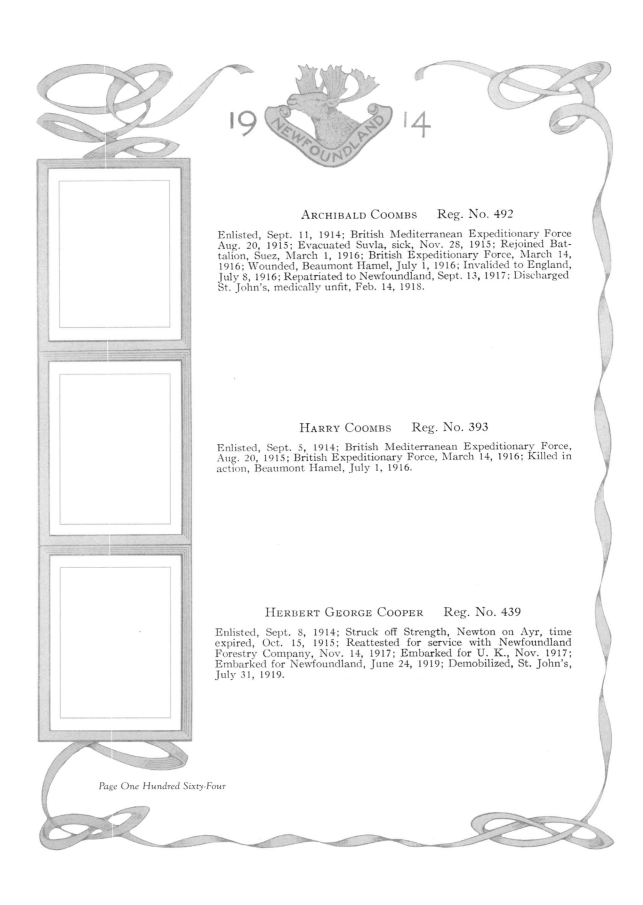

ARCHIBALD COOMBS　　Reg. No. 492

Enlisted, Sept. 11, 1914; British Mediterranean Expeditionary Force Aug. 20, 1915; Evacuated Suvla, sick, Nov. 28, 1915; Rejoined Battalion, Suez, March 1, 1916; British Expeditionary Force, March 14, 1916; Wounded, Beaumont Hamel, July 1, 1916; Invalided to England, July 8, 1916; Repatriated to Newfoundland, Sept. 13, 1917; Discharged St. John's, medically unfit, Feb. 14, 1918.

HARRY COOMBS　　Reg. No. 393

Enlisted, Sept. 5, 1914; British Mediterranean Expeditionary Force, Aug. 20, 1915; British Expeditionary Force, March 14, 1916; Killed in action, Beaumont Hamel, July 1, 1916.

HERBERT GEORGE COOPER　　Reg. No. 439

Enlisted, Sept. 8, 1914; Struck off Strength, Newton on Ayr, time expired, Oct. 15, 1915; Reattested for service with Newfoundland Forestry Company, Nov. 14, 1917; Embarked for U. K., Nov. 1917; Embarked for Newfoundland, June 24, 1919; Demobilized, St. John's, July 31, 1919.

James Cooper   Reg. No. 98

Enlisted, Sept. 2, 1914; British Mediterranean Expeditionary Force, Aug. 20, 1915; Invalided to England, Oct. 21, 1915; British Expeditionary Force, March 28, 1915; Wounded, Beaumont Hamel, July 1 1916; Invalided to England; Returned to B. E. F., March 25, 1917; Lance, Corporal, Nov. 1, 1917; Acting Corporal, Dec. 26, 1917; Embarked for Newfoundland on duty, May 22, 1918; Discharged, St. John's, medically ufiut, Dec. 7, 1918.

Eugene Cornect   Reg. No. 429

Enlisted, Sept. 2, 1914; British Mediterranean Expeditionary Force, Aug. 20, 1915; Evacuated Suvla, sick, Oct. 31, 1915; Rejoined Battalion, Suez, Jan. 26, 1916; British Expeditionary Force, March 14, 1916; Wounded, Beaumont Hamel, July 1, 1916; Invalided to England, July 3, 1916; Repatriated to Newfoundland, Feb. 17, 1917; Discharged, St. John's, medically unfit, March 28, 1917.

Edwin Cornick   Reg. No. 377

Enlisted, Sept. 5, 1914; British Mediterranean Expeditionary Force, Aug. 20, 1915; Evacuated Suvla, sick, Oct. 22, 1915; Invalided to England, Dec. 26, 1915; Attached to Depot, Ayr, April 26, 1916, British Expeditionary Force, June 25, 1916; Wounded, Gueudecourt, Oct. 12, 1916; Invalided to England, Oct. 16, 1916; Attached to Depot, Ayr, Nov. 30, 1916; Lance Corporal, Jan. 17, 1917; Returned to B. E. F. Jan. 31, 1917; Admitted to Hospital, Rouen, Feb. 3, 1917; Rejoined Battalion, May 7, 1917; Wounded, Marcoing, Nov. 20, 1917; Invalided to England, Nov. 24, 1917; Attached to Depot, Ayr, Jan. 7, 1918; Returned to B. E. F., Feb. 4, 1918; Corporal, March 16, 1918; Sergeant, April 25, 1918; Embarked for Newfoundland on special duty, May 22, 1918; Returned to U. K., Oct. 12, 1918; Joined Battalion, Jan. 5, 1919; Embarked for Newfoundland, April 23, 1919; Demobilized, St. John's, June 10, 1919.

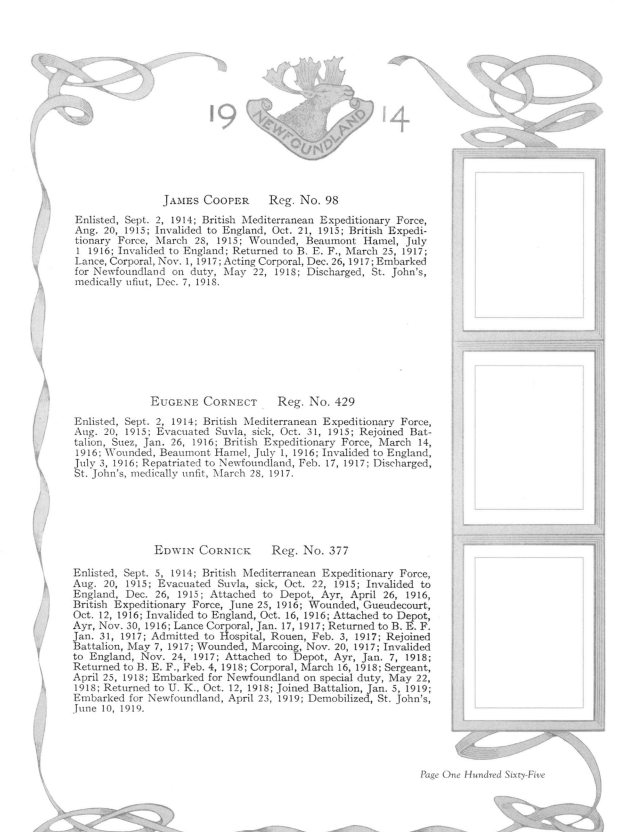

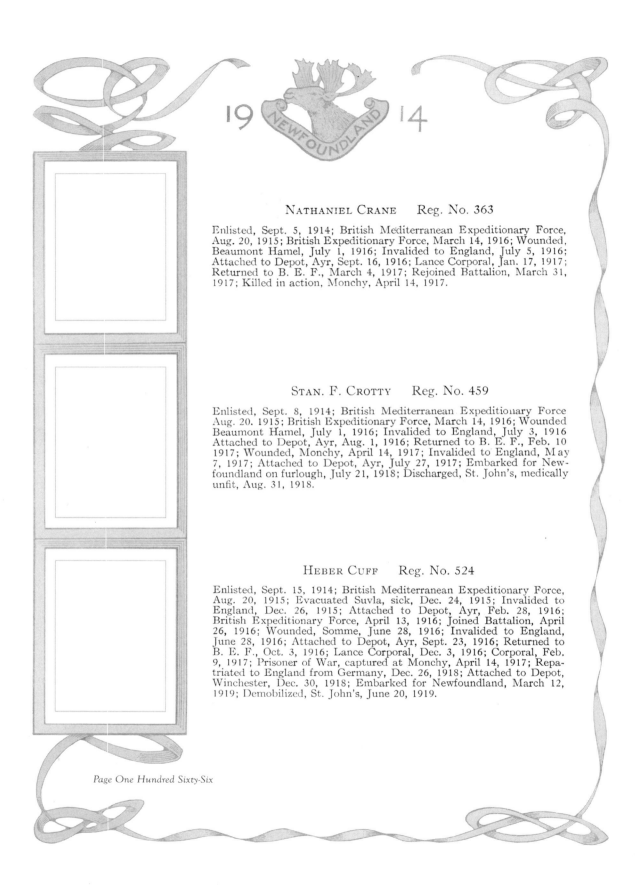

19 NEWFOUNDLAND 14

NATHANIEL CRANE   Reg. No. 363

Enlisted, Sept. 5, 1914; British Mediterranean Expeditionary Force, Aug. 20, 1915; British Expeditionary Force, March 14, 1916; Wounded, Beaumont Hamel, July 1, 1916; Invalided to England, July 5, 1916; Attached to Depot, Ayr, Sept. 16, 1916; Lance Corporal, Jan. 17, 1917; Returned to B. E. F., March 4, 1917; Rejoined Battalion, March 31, 1917; Killed in action, Monchy, April 14, 1917.

STAN. F. CROTTY   Reg. No. 459

Enlisted, Sept. 8, 1914; British Mediterranean Expeditionary Force Aug. 20. 1915; British Expeditionary Force, March 14, 1916; Wounded Beaumont Hamel, July 1, 1916; Invalided to England, July 3, 1916 Attached to Depot, Ayr, Aug. 1, 1916; Returned to B. E. F., Feb. 10 1917; Wounded, Monchy, April 14, 1917; Invalided to England, May 7, 1917; Attached to Depot, Ayr, July 27, 1917; Embarked for Newfoundland on furlough, July 21, 1918; Discharged, St. John's, medically unfit, Aug. 31, 1918.

HEBER CUFF   Reg. No. 524

Enlisted, Sept. 15, 1914; British Mediterranean Expeditionary Force, Aug. 20, 1915; Evacuated Suvla, sick, Dec. 24, 1915; Invalided to England, Dec. 26, 1915; Attached to Depot, Ayr, Feb. 28, 1916; British Expeditionary Force, April 13, 1916; Joined Battalion, April 26, 1916; Wounded, Somme, June 28, 1916; Invalided to England, June 28, 1916; Attached to Depot, Ayr, Sept. 23, 1916; Returned to B. E. F., Oct. 3, 1916; Lance Corporal, Dec. 3, 1916; Corporal, Feb. 9, 1917; Prisoner of War, captured at Monchy, April 14, 1917; Repatriated to England from Germany, Dec. 26, 1918; Attached to Depot, Winchester, Dec. 30, 1918; Embarked for Newfoundland, March 12, 1919; Demobilized, St. John's, June 20, 1919.

19 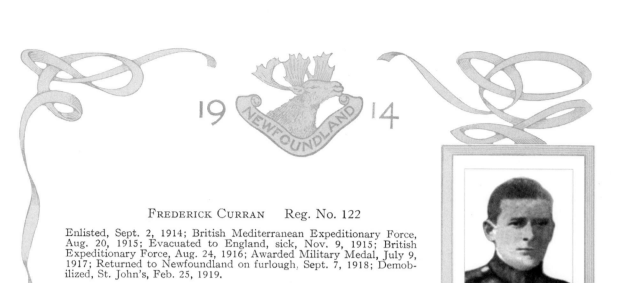 **14**

FREDERICK CURRAN   Reg. No. 122

Enlisted, Sept. 2, 1914; British Mediterranean Expeditionary Force, Aug. 20, 1915; Evacuated to England, sick, Nov. 9, 1915; British Expeditionary Force, Aug. 24, 1916; Awarded Military Medal, July 9, 1917; Returned to Newfoundland on furlough, Sept. 7, 1918; Demobilized, St. John's, Feb. 25, 1919.

PETER DANIELS   Reg. No. 318

Enlisted, Sept. 7, 1914; British Mediterranean Expeditionary Force, Aug. 20, 1915; Lance Corporal, Dec. 10, 1915; Admitted to Hospital, Malta, Jan. 8, 1916; Discharged to duty, March 4, 1916; British Expeditionary Force, March 18, 1916; Evacuated to Hospital, June 15, 1916; Invalided to England, June 25, 1916; Attached to Depot, Ayr, July 18, 1916; Acting Corporal, Aug. 11, 1916; Sergeant, Oct. 27, 1916; Acting Company Quartermaster Sergeant, Aug. 24, 1917; Company Sergeant Major, Oct. 4, 1918; Wounded, Ledgeham, Oct. 14, 1918; Invalided to England, Dec. 4, 1918; Repatriated to Newfoundland, Feb. 15, 1919; Demobilized, St. John's, Aug. 30, 1919.

HENRY CHARLES DAWE   Reg. No. 589

Enlisted, Sept. 24, 1914; British Mediterranean Expeditionary Force, Aug. 20, 1915; British Expeditionary Force, March 14, 1916; Killed in action, Beaumont Hamel, July 1, 1916.

19 NEWFOUNDLAND 14

CAPTAIN R. H. TAIT'S PLATOON

Page One Hundred Sixty-Eight

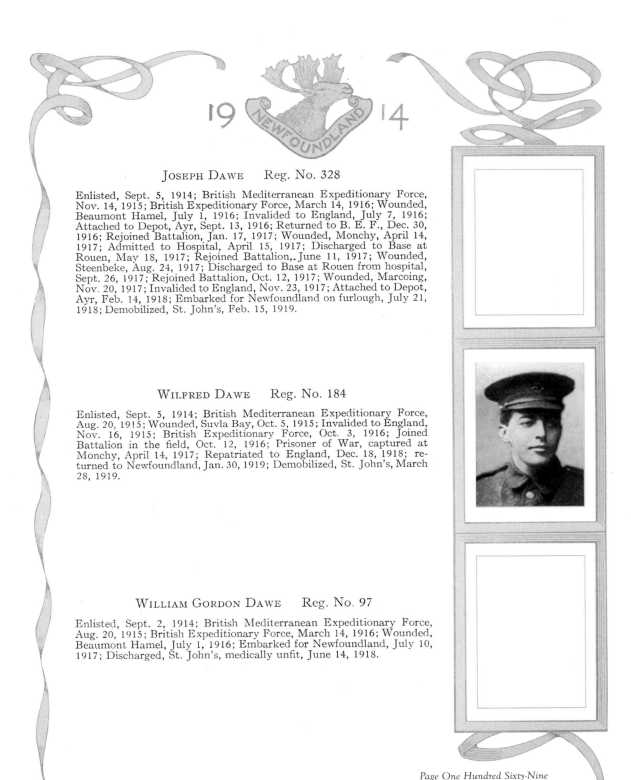

Joseph Dawe   Reg. No. 328

Enlisted, Sept. 5, 1914; British Mediterranean Expeditionary Force, Nov. 14, 1915; British Expeditionary Force, March 14, 1916; Wounded, Beaumont Hamel, July 1, 1916; Invalided to England, July 7, 1916; Attached to Depot, Ayr, Sept. 13, 1916; Returned to B. E. F., Dec. 30, 1916; Rejoined Battalion, Jan. 17, 1917; Wounded, Monchy, April 14, 1917; Admitted to Hospital, April 15, 1917; Discharged to Base at Rouen, May 18, 1917; Rejoined Battalion,.June 11, 1917; Wounded, Steenbeke, Aug. 24, 1917; Discharged to Base at Rouen from hospital, Sept. 26, 1917; Rejoined Battalion, Oct. 12, 1917; Wounded, Marcoing, Nov. 20, 1917; Invalided to England, Nov. 23, 1917; Attached to Depot, Ayr, Feb. 14, 1918; Embarked for Newfoundland on furlough, July 21, 1918; Demobilized, St. John's, Feb. 15, 1919.

Wilfred Dawe   Reg. No. 184

Enlisted, Sept. 5, 1914; British Mediterranean Expeditionary Force, Aug. 20, 1915; Wounded, Suvla Bay, Oct. 5, 1915; Invalided to England, Nov. 16, 1915; British Expeditionary Force, Oct. 3, 1916; Joined Battalion in the field, Oct. 12, 1916; Prisoner of War, captured at Monchy, April 14, 1917; Repatriated to England, Dec. 18, 1918; returned to Newfoundland, Jan. 30, 1919; Demobilized, St. John's, March 28, 1919.

William Gordon Dawe   Reg. No. 97

Enlisted, Sept. 2, 1914; British Mediterranean Expeditionary Force, Aug. 20, 1915; British Expeditionary Force, March 14, 1916; Wounded, Beaumont Hamel, July 1, 1916; Embarked for Newfoundland, July 10, 1917; Discharged, St. John's, medically unfit, June 14, 1918.

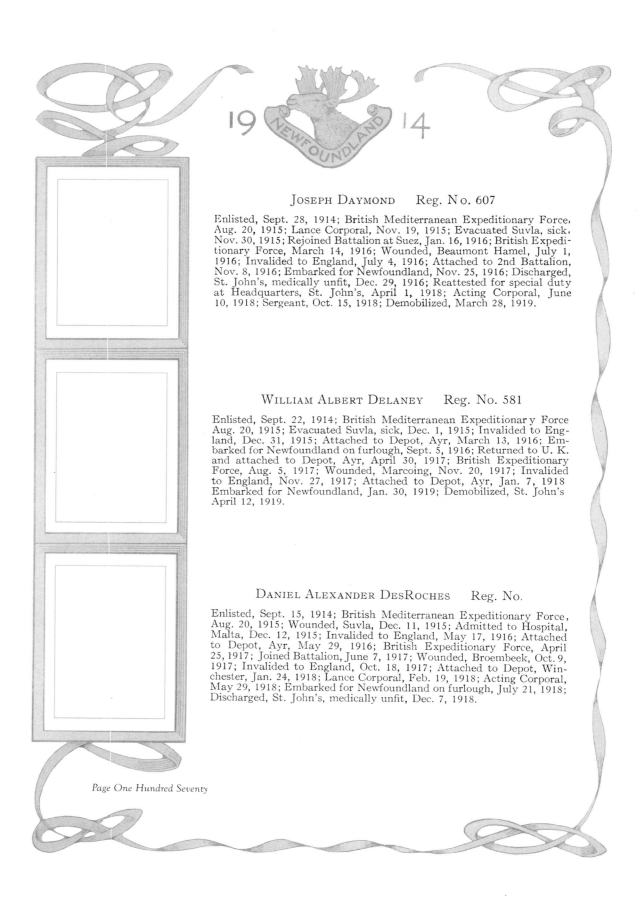

JOSEPH DAYMOND   Reg. No. 607

Enlisted, Sept. 28, 1914; British Mediterranean Expeditionary Force, Aug. 20, 1915; Lance Corporal, Nov. 19, 1915; Evacuated Suvla, sick, Nov. 30, 1915; Rejoined Battalion at Suez, Jan. 16, 1916; British Expeditionary Force, March 14, 1916; Wounded, Beaumont Hamel, July 1, 1916; Invalided to England, July 4, 1916; Attached to 2nd Battalion, Nov. 8, 1916; Embarked for Newfoundland, Nov. 25, 1916; Discharged, St. John's, medically unfit, Dec. 29, 1916; Reattested for special duty at Headquarters, St. John's, April 1, 1918; Acting Corporal, June 10, 1918; Sergeant, Oct. 15, 1918; Demobilized, March 28, 1919.

WILLIAM ALBERT DELANEY   Reg. No. 581

Enlisted, Sept. 22, 1914; British Mediterranean Expeditionary Force Aug. 20, 1915; Evacuated Suvla, sick, Dec. 1, 1915; Invalided to England, Dec. 31, 1915; Attached to Depot, Ayr, March 13, 1916; Embarked for Newfoundland on furlough, Sept. 5, 1916; Returned to U. K. and attached to Depot, Ayr, April 30, 1917; British Expeditionary Force, Aug. 5, 1917; Wounded, Marcoing, Nov. 20, 1917; Invalided to England, Nov. 27, 1917; Attached to Depot, Ayr, Jan. 7, 1918 Embarked for Newfoundland, Jan. 30, 1919; Demobilized, St. John's April 12, 1919.

DANIEL ALEXANDER DesRoches   Reg. No.

Enlisted, Sept. 15, 1914; British Mediterranean Expeditionary Force, Aug. 20, 1915; Wounded, Suvla, Dec. 11, 1915; Admitted to Hospital, Malta, Dec. 12, 1915; Invalided to England, May 17, 1916; Attached to Depot, Ayr, May 29, 1916; British Expeditionary Force, April 25, 1917; Joined Battalion, June 7, 1917; Wounded, Broembeek, Oct. 9, 1917; Invalided to England, Oct. 18, 1917; Attached to Depot, Winchester, Jan. 24, 1918; Lance Corporal, Feb. 19, 1918; Acting Corporal, May 29, 1918; Embarked for Newfoundland on furlough, July 21, 1918; Discharged, St. John's, medically unfit, Dec. 7, 1918.

1914

HERBERT DEWLING   Reg. No. 45

Enlisted, Sept. 2, 1914; Lance Corporal, July 28, 1915; British Mediterranean Expeditionary Force, Aug. 20, 1915; Evacuated Suvla, sick, Sept. 23, 1915; Admitted to Hospital, Alexandria, Sept. 26, 1915; Discharged to duty, Oct. 25, 1915; Attached for duty to 3rd Echelon, Alexandria, Oct. 28, 1915; British Expeditionary Force, March 18, 1916; Acting Sergeant, April 14, 1916; Admitted to hospital, Rouen, Dec. 9, 1916; Invalided to England, Dec. 20, 1916; Returned to B. E. F., Sept. 26, 1917; Orderly Room Sergeant, Oct. 3, 1917; Invalided to England, July 26, 1918; Discharged to duty, Aug. 27, 1918; Returned to B. E. F., Sept. 7, 1918; and rejoined 3rd Echelon; Taken on Strength of 1st Battalion, April 3, 1919; Attached for duty to Pay and Record Office, London, April 23, 1919; Acting Staff Sergeant, April 23, 1919; Demobilized, U. K., June 24, 1919.

STEWART DEWLING   Reg. No. 20

Enlisted, Sept. 2, 1914; British Mediterranean Expeditionary Force, Aug. 20, 1915; British Expeditionary Force, March 2, 1916; Awarded Military Medal, July 1, 1916; Corporal, Feb. 9, 1917; Sergeant, May 8, 1917; Wounded, Steenbeke, Aug. 14, 1917; Invalided to England, Aug. 18, 1917; Embarked for Newfoundland on duty, May 6, 1918; Acting Company Sergeant Major, March 24, 1919.

CHRISTOPHER BERTRAM DICKS   Reg. No. 33

Enlisted, Sept. 1, 1914; Acting Quartermaster, Sept. 5, 1914; Acting Sergeant, Sept. 26, 1914; Company Sergeant Major, Oct. 29, 1914; British Mediterranean Expeditionary Force, Aug. 20, 1915; British Expeditionary Force, March 14, 1916; Acting Regimental Sergeant Major, May 29, 1916; 2nd Lieutenant, June 11, 1916; Wounded, Beaumont Hamel, July 1, 1916; Invalided to England; Returned to B. E. F., April 23, 1917; Repatriated to Newfoundland, Feb. 6, 1918; Assistant Director recruiting, St. John's, April 9, 1918; Captain, Sept. 1, 1918; Demobilization Officer, Nov. 25, 1918; Retired, March 31, 1919.

WILLIAM PATRICK DOHANEY   Reg. No. 496

Enlisted, Sept. 14, 1914; British Mediterranean Expeditionary Force, Aug. 20, 1915; Evacuated Suvla, sick, Nov. 25, 1915; Rejoined Battalion, Suez, Jan. 26, 1916; British Expeditionary Force, March 14, 1916; Killed in action, Beaumont Hamel, July 1, 1916.

JOHN JOSEPH DOOLEY   Reg. No. 474

Enlisted, Sept. 10, 1914; British Mediterranean Expeditionary Force, Aug. 20, 1915; Evacuated Suvla, sick, Nov. 29, 1915; Invalided to England, Dec. 24, 1915; Attached to Depot, Ayr, March 3, 1916; British Expeditionary Force, March 28, 1916; Evacuated to Hospital, June 11, 1916; Rejoined Battalion, July 29, 1916; Lance Corporal, Aug. 11, 1916; Wounded, Gueudecourt, Oct. 12, 1916; Invalided to England, Oct. 22, 1916; Attached to Depot, Ayr, March 1, 1917; Corporal, April 9, 1917; Embarked for Newfoundland, April 10, 1917; Discharged, St John's, medically unfit, May 11, 1917; Reattested for special duty at Heart's Content, June 21, 1917; Sergeant, June 21, 1917; Demobilized, St. John's, May 1, 1919.

JOHN DUNN   REG. No. 173

Enlisted, Sept, 4, 1914; British Mediterranean Expeditionary Force, Aug. 20, 1915; Served with 1st Composite Battalion on Western Egyptian Frontier, Nov. 1915 to Feb. 1916; British Expeditionary Force, March 2, 1916; Lance Corporal, Nov. 5, 1916; Corporal, May 11, 1917; Acting Sergeant, July 24, 1917; Returned to Newfoundland on furlough, July 27, 1918; Demobilized, St. John's, Feb. 15, 1919.

1914

John Dunphy   Reg. No. 44

Enlisted, Sept. 2, 1914; British Mediterranean Expeditionary Force, Aug. 20, 1915; Killed in Action, Suvla Bay, Dec. 12, 1915

William Dunphy   Reg. No. 15

Enlisted, Sept. 2, 1914; British Mediterranean Expeditionary Force, Aug. 20, 1915; British Expeditionary Force, March 14, 1916; Killed in action, Beaumont Hamel, July 1, 1916.

William John Eaton   Reg. No. 137

Enlisted, Sept. 4, 1914; British Mediterranean Expeditionary Force, Aug. 20, 1915; Appointed Orderly Room Clerk in the Field, Feb. 1, 1916; British Expeditionary Force, March 14, 1916; Corporal, July 12, 1916; Sergeant, Oct. 22, 1916; Staff Sergeant, April 25, 1918; Acting Regimental Quartermaster Sergeant, Sept. 4, 1918; Returned to Newfoundland on furlough, July 27, 1918; Attached to Depot, St. John's, for duty, Nov. 28, 1918; Still on Strength.

HUBERT EDGAR EBSARY   Reg. No. 339

Enlisted, Sept. 7, 1914; Lance Corporal, April 24, 1915; British Mediterranean Expeditionary Force, Aug. 20, 1915; Wounded, Suvla Bay, Dec. 1, 1915; Died of wounds at 88th Field Ambulance, Dec. 1, 1915.

SAMUEL JOSEPH EBSARY   Reg. No. 501

Enlisted, Sept. 2, 1914; Sergeant, Sept. 21, 1914; Company Sergeant Major, Oct. 29, 1914; British Mediterranean Expeditionary Force, Aug. 20, 1915; Acting Regimental Sergeant Major, Aug. 23, 1915; Evacuated Suvla, sick, Dec. 2, 1915; Rejoined Battalion, Suez, March 1, 1916; British Expeditionary Force, March 14, 1916; 2nd Lieutenant, July 1, 1916; Wounded, Gueudecourt, Oct. 12, 1916; Admitted 8th General Hospital, Rouen, Oct. 14, 1916; Died of wounds, Oct. 15, 1916.

CHARLES LeGALLAIS EDGAR   Reg. No. 199

Enlisted, Sept. 4, 1914; Lance Corporal, April 8, 1915; Corporal, July 27, 1915; British Mediterranean Expeditionary Force, Aug. 20, 1915; Acting Company Quartermaster Sergeant, Nov. 11, 1915; Sergeant Nov. 14, 1915; Wounded, Suvla Bay, Dec. 5, 1915; Discharged to duty, Jan. 19, 1916; Confirmed to Rank of Company Quartermaster Sergeant, Jan. 31, 1916; British Expeditionary Force, March 14, 1916; 2nd Lieutenant, June 5, 1916; Returned to Newfoundland on duty, July 11, 1916; Embarked for U. K., Aug. 28, 1916; Returned to B. E. F., Oct. 27, 1916; Killed in action, Sailly-Saillisel, Feb. 26, 1917.

EDWARD FRANCIS EDGECOMBE   Reg. No. 40

Enlisted, Sept. 2, 1914; British Mediterranean Expeditionary Force, Aug. 20, 1915; Evacuated Suvla, sick, Nov. 1, 1915; Invalided to England, Nov. 30, 1915; Attached to Depot, Ayr, April 3, 1916; British Expeditionary Force, Dec. 12, 1916; Evacuated to Hospital, March 17, 1917; Invalided to England, March 29, 1917; Attached to Depot, Ayr, April 13, 1917; Returned to B. E. F., June 3, 1917; Killed in action at Centre Sector, Steenbeke, Aug. 21, 1917.

JOHN CHARLES EDWARDS   Reg. No. 450

Enlisted, Sept. 8, 1914; British Mediterranean Expeditionary Force, Aug. 20, 1915; Evacuated Suvla, sick, Nov. 26, 1915; Rejoined Battalion, Suez, March 1, 1916; British Expeditionary Force, March 14, 1916; Wounded, Beaumont Hamel, July 1, 1916; Invalided to England, July 4, 1916; Admitted to Royal Victoria Hospital, Netley, July 5, 1916; Died of wounds, July 21, 1916.

JOHN ELLIOTT   Reg. No. 22

Enlisted, Sept. 2, 1914; British Mediterranean Expeditionary Force, Nov. 14, 1915; British Expeditionary Force, March 14, 1916; Killed in action, Beaumont Hamel, July 1, 1916.

John Joseph Ellis   Reg. No. 443

Enlisted, Sept. 8, 1914; British Mediterranean Expeditionary Force, Aug. 20, 1915; Evacuated Suvla, sick, Nov. 15, 1915; Rejoined Battalion, Suez, March 1, 1916; British Expeditionary Force, March 14, 1916; Lance Corporal, May 18, 1916; Killed in action, Beaumont Hamel, July 1, 1916.

Joseph Erley   Reg. No. 116

Enlisted, Sept. 2, 1914; British Mediterranean Expeditionary Force, Aug. 20, 1915; British Expeditionary Force, May 9, 1915; Lance Corporal, Oct. 1, 1916; Evacuated to England, sick, March 15, 1917; Returned to B. E. F., Aug. 5, 1917; Wounded, Broembeek, Oct. 9, 1917; Evacuated to England, Oct. 13, 1917; Acting Corporal, May 29, 1918; Returned to Newfoundland on furlough, July 21, 1918; Demobilized, St. John's, Feb. 15, 1919.

Joseph Wellington Evans   Reg. No. 181

Enlisted, Sept. 5, 1914; British Mediterranean Expeditionary Force, Aug. 20, 1915; British Expeditionary Force, March 14, 1916; Killed in action, Beaumont Hamel, July 1, 1916.

STEWART SMALL FERGUSON   Reg. No. 95

Enlisted, Sept. 2, 1914; Lance Corporal, Sept. 21, 1914; Corporal, April 23, 1915; Signal Sergeant, July 10, 1915; British Mediterranean Expeditionary Force, Aug. 20, 1915; British Expeditionary Force, March 14, 1916; Killed in action, Beaumont Hamel, July 1, 1916.

SAMUEL FIANDER   Reg. No. 467

Enlisted, Sept. 9, 1914; British Mediterranean Expeditionary Force, Aug. 20, 1915; Evacuated Suvla, sick, Oct. 20, 1915; Invalided to England, Nov. 24, 1915; Attached to Depot, Ayr, Aug. 12, 1916; British Expeditionary Force, Dec. 12, 1916; Wounded, Monchy, April 14, 1917; Invalided to England, April 21, 1917; Attached to Depot, Ayr, May 19, 1917; Returned to B. E. F., Aug. 5, 1917; Wounded, Broembeek, Oct. 9, 1917; Joined Base Depot, Rouen, Nov. 12, 1917; Joined Battalion, Dec. 4, 1917; Lance Corporal, Dec. 26, 1917; Embarked for Newfoundland on furlough, July 27, 1918; Demobilized, St. John's, Feb. 15, 1919.

CHARLES WILLIAM FIELD   Reg. No. 115

Enlisted, Sept. 2, 1914; British Mediterranean Expeditionary Force, Aug. 20, 1915; Wounded, Suvla Bay, Nov. 8, 1915; Evacuated to England, sick, Nov. 30, 1915; British Expeditionary Force, April 6, 1918; Embarked for Newfoundland on furlough, Sept. 7, 1918; Demobilized, St. John's, Feb. 15, 1919.

LARRY FIELD   Reg. No. 153

Enlisted, Sept. 3, 1914; British Mediterranean Expeditionary Force, Aug. 20, 1915; British Expeditionary Force, March 28, 1916; Lance Corporal, July 12, 1916; Wounded, Belgium, Aug. 18, 1916; Evacuated to England, Aug. 30, 1916; Repatriated to Newfoundland, April 10, 1917; Discharged, St. John's, medically unfit, May 11, 1917; Reattested for duty at Depot, St. John's, June 21, 1917; Acting Corporal, May 22, 1918; Demobilized, St. John's, Sept. 30, 1919.

ISAAC FIFIELD   Reg. No. 420

Enlisted, Sept. 4, 1914; British Mediterranean Expeditionary Force, Aug. 20, 1915; British Expeditionary Force, March 14, 1916; Lance Corporal, June 11, 1916; Corporal, July 12, 1916; Wounded, Somme raid, Nov. 30, 1916; Invalided to England, Dec. 25, 1916; Attached to Depot, Ayr, April 2, 1917; Embarked for Newfoundland on duty, July 18, 1917; Discharged, St. John's, medically unfit, April 2, 1918.

MAXIMILLIAM WILLIAM FILLIER   Reg. No. 507

Enlisted, Sept. 15, 1914; British Mediterranean Expeditionary Force, Nov. 14, 1915; British Expeditionary Force, March 14, 1916; Wounded, Beaumont Hamel, July 1, 1916; Invalided to England, July 4, 1916; Attached to Depot, Ayr, Aug. 18, 1916; Embarked for Newfoundland, July 10, 1917; Attached for duty to Headquarters, St. John's, Oct. 6, 1917; Demobilized, July 25, 1919.

John Fitzgerald   Reg. No. 295

Enlisted, Sept. 8, 1914; British Mediterranean Expeditionary Force, Aug. 20, 1915; Killed in action, Suvla, Dec. 1, 1915; Mentioned in despatches, London Gazette, July 11, 1916.

Richard Francis Fleming   Reg. No. 357

Enlisted, Sept. 5, 1914; British Mediterranean Expeditionary Force, Aug. 20, 1915; Evacuated, Suvla, sick, Oct. 19, 1915; Rejoined Battalion, Suez, Jan. 16, 1916; British Expeditionary Force, March 14, 1916; Wounded, Beaumont Hamel, July 1, 1916; Invalided to England, July 4, 1916; Attached to Depot, Ayr, Aug. 1, 1916; Returned to B. E. F., Oct. 3, 1916; Evacuated to Hospital, Nov. 25, 1916; Joined Battalion, March 2, 1917; Lance Corporal, Oct. 16, 1918; Evacuated to Hospital, Oct. 23, 1918; Rejoined Battalion, Dec. 31, 1918; Embarked for Newfoundland, Jan. 30, 1919; Demobilized, St. John's, March 10, 1919.

Bernard Forsey   Reg. No. 12

Enlisted, Sept. 2, 1914; British Mediterranean Expeditionary Force, Aug. 20, 1915; British Expeditionary Force, March 3, 1916; Wounded, Beaumont Hamel, July 1, 1916; Invalided to England, July 5, 1916; Attached to Depot, Aug. 17, 1916; Lance Corporal, Aug. 22, 1916; Corporal, Oct. 27, 1916; Acting Sergeant, Jan. 17, 1917; Second Lieutenant, Sept. 25, 1917; Returned to B. E. F., Jan. 5, 1918; Embarked for Newfoundland on furlough, July 24, 1918; Returned to U. K., Oct. 19, 1918; Returned to B. E. F., Nov. 4, 1918; Lieutenant, March 25, 1919; Transferred to U. K., April 27, 1919; Embarked for Newfoundland, May 22, 1919; Retired, St. John's, July 5, 1919.

James Francis Fowler   Reg. No. 311

Enlisted, Sept. 2, 1914; British Mediterranean Expeditionary Force, Aug. 20, 1915; British Expeditionary Force, March 14, 1916; Wounded Aug. 11, 1916; Rejoined Battalion, Oct. 22, 1916; Lance Corporal, Dec. 26, 1917; Embarked for Newfoundland on furlough, July 27, 1918; Demobilized, St. John's, Feb. 15, 1919.

William Fowler   Reg. No. 81

Enlisted, Sept. 2, 1914; British Mediterranean Expeditionary Force, Aug. 20, 1915; British Expeditionary Force, March 14, 1916; Killed in action, Beaumont Hamel, July 1, 1916.

John Ed. Joseph Fox   Reg. No. 142

Enlisted, Sept. 4, 1914; Lance Corporal, Sept. 21, 1914; Corporal, Nov. 13, 1914; Sergeant, Feb. 24, 1915; 2nd Lieutenant, March 29, 1915; British Mediterranean Expeditionary Force, Aug. 20, 1915; Lieutenant, Oct. 15, 1915; Evacuated, Suvla, sick, Nov. 3, 1915; Rejoined Battalion, Suez, Jan. 26, 1916; British Expeditionary Force, March 14, 1916; Evacuated to England, sick, April 27, 1916; Captain, Nov. 16, 1916; Appointed Demobilization Officer, London, Nov. 11, 1918; Returned to Newfoundland, May 22, 1919; Relinquished appointment, June 2, 1919; Retired, June 23, 1919.

CHARLES SYDNEY FROST   Reg. No. 58

Enlisted, Sept. 7, 1914; Lance Corporal, July 14, 1915; British Mediterranean Expeditionary Force, Aug. 20, 1915; 2nd Lieutenant, April 15, 1916; British Expeditionary Force, June 5, 1916; Wounded, Gueudecourt, Oct. 12, 1916; Invalided to England; Lieutenant, May 15, 1917; Returned to B. E. F., Nov. 10, 1917; Captain, March 18, 1918; Awarded Military Cross, Sept. 28, 1918; Retired and placed on reserve of Officers, St. John's, June 2, 1919.

JOHN JOSEPH FRENCH   Reg. No. 63

Enlisted, Sept. 2, 1914; British Mediterranean Expeditionary Force, Aug. 20, 1915; British Expeditionary Force, March 14, 1916; Missing, believed killed, Beaumont Hamel, July 1, 1916.

NICHOLAS AUGUSTUS GALGAY   Reg. No. 338

Enlisted, Sept. 7, 1914; British Mediterranean Expeditionary Force, Aug. 20, 1915; Evacuated Suvla, sick, Oct. 20, 1915; Invalided to England, Dec, 6, 1915; Attached to Depot, Ayr, Feb. 4, 1916; British Expeditionary Force, March 20, 1916; Wounded, Beaumont Hamel, July 1, 1916; Invalided to England, July 3, 1916; Attached to Depot, Ayr, Aug. 11, 1916; Lance Corporal, Sept. 4, 1916; Acting Corporal, Nov. 16, 1916; Returned to B. E. F., Nov. 30, 1916; Admitted to Hospital, Rouen, Dec. 5, 1916; Joined Battalion, Feb. 5, 1917; Wounded, Monchy, April 14, 1917; Invalided to England, April 20, 1917; Attached to Depot, Ayr, July 10, 1917; Acting Sergeant, Sept. 27, 1917; Confirmed to rank of Corporal, April 27, 1918; Confirmed to rank of Sergeant, July 31, 1918; Acting Company Sergeant Major, July 31, 1918; Acting Regimental Sergeant Major, May 19, 1919; Confirmed to rank of R. S. M., June 20, 1919; Embarked for Newfoundland, June 24, 1919; Demobilized, St. John's, Aug. 15, 1919.

19 14

John Gardner   Reg. No. 144

Enlisted, Sept. 3, 1914; Corporal, Sept. 21, 1914; Sergeant, Oct. 3, 1914; British Mediterranean Expeditionary Force, Aug. 20, 1915; British Expeditionary Force, March 14, 1916; Wounded, Beaumont Hamel, July 1, 1916; Evacuated to England, July 11, 1916; Returned to Newfoundland, Sept. 27, 1916; Rejoined 2nd Battalion, Ayr, Dec. 31, 1917; Returned to B. E. F., Feb. 18, 1918; Transferred to England "Permanent Base," March 1, 1918; Returned to Newfoundland on duty, May 13, 1918; Acting Company Sergeant Major, July 22, 1918; Demobilized, St.John;'s, Jan. 23, 1919.

Frederick Garf   Reg. No. 125

Enlisted, Sept. 2, 1914; British Mediterranean Expeditionary Force, Aug. 20, 1915; British Expeditionary Force, March 14, 1916; Killed in action, Beaumont Hamel, July 1, 1916.

Charles Frederick Garland   Reg. No. 182

Enlisted, Sept. 3, 1914; Lance Corporal, Sept. 21, 1914; Corporal, June 7, 1915; British Mediterranean Expeditionary Force, Aug. 20, 1915; Sergeant, Oct. 28, 1915; British Expeditionary Force, March 14, 1916; Wounded, Beaumont Hamel, July 1, 1916; Evacuated to England, July 6, 1916; 2nd Lieutenant, Nov. 1, 1916; Attached to 2nd Battalion, Depot, for duty, Nov. 10, 1916; Lieutenant, May 1, 1918; Returned to Newfoundland, May 22, 1919; Retired, July 5, 1919.

George Stanley Garland   Reg. No. 200

Enlisted, Sept. 3, 1914; British Mediterranean Expeditionary Force, Aug. 20, 1915; Wounded, Suvla, Sept. 29, 1915; Admitted to Hospital Alexandria, Oct. 4, 1915; Invalided to England, Dec. 26, 1915; Repatriated to Newfoundland, June 9, 1916; Discharged, St. John's, medically unfit, June 24, 1916.

William Thomas Gellately   Reg. No. 100

Enlisted, Sept. 2, 1914; British Mediterranean Expeditionary Force, Aug. 20, 1915; Wounded, Suvla, Oct. 5, 1915; Invalided to England, Dec. 3, 1915; British Expeditionary Force, March 28, 1916; Wounded, Beaumont Hamel, July 1, 1916; Invalided to England, July 3, 1916; Returned to B. E. F. Nov. 6, 1917; Invalided to England, Dec. 29, 1917; Embarked for Newfoundland on furlough, July 21, 1918; Discharged, St. John's, Feb. 15, 1919.

Arthur Wilfred Gillam   Reg. No. 454

Enlisted, Sept. 8, 1914; British Mediterranean Expeditionary Force, Aug. 20, 1915; Lance Corporal, Feb. 27, 1916; British Expeditionary Force, March 14, 1916; Killed in action, Beaumont Hamel, July 1, 1916.

Edward Francis Gladney   Reg. No. 335

Enlisted, Sept. 8, 1914; Lance Corporal, April 17, 1915; Corporal, July 27, 1915; British Mediterranean Expeditionary Force, Aug. 20, 1915; British Expeditionary Force, March 14, 1916; Evacuated to Hospital, April 22, 1916; Rejoined Battalion, May 2, 1916; Sergeant, June 11, 1916; Killed in action, Beaumont Hamel, July 1, 1916.

William Joseph Gladney   Reg. No. 417

Enlisted, Sept. 3, 1914; British Mediterranean Expeditionary Force, Aug. 20, 1915; Evacuated, Suvla, sick, Dec. 1, 1915; Invalided to England, Dec. 21, 1915; Attached to Depot, Ayr, May 9, 1916; Awarded Distinguished Conduct Medal, June 3, 1916; Mentioned in despatches, July 11, 1916; Embarked for Newfoundland on furlough, July 20, 1916; Lance Corporal, March 10, 1917; Returned to U. K. and attached to Depot, Ayr, April 30, 1917; British Expeditionary Force, Aug. 5, 1917; Wounded, Elverdinge, Sept. 27, 1917; Invalided to England, Sept. 30, 1917; Attached to Depot, Ayr, Dec. 23, 1917; Acting Corporal, May 29, 1918; Acting Sergeant, Nov. 7, 1918; Confirmed to rank of Corporal, March 12, 1919; Confirmed to rank of Sergeant, April 24, 1919; Embarked for Newfoundland, May 22, 1919; Demobilized, St. John's, June 29, 1919.

Malcolm Godden   Reg. No. 615

Enlisted, Sept. 2, 1914; Corporal, Sept. 24, 1914; Sergeant, Oct. 10, 1914; Company Sergeant Major, July 30, 1915; British Mediterranean Expeditionary Force, Aug. 20, 1915; British Expeditionary Force, March 14, 1916; Evacuated to Hospital, Aug. 23, 1916; Invalided to England, Sept. 4, 1916; Attached to Depot, Ayr, Nov. 6, 1916; 2nd Lieutenant, Nov. 1, 1916; Lieutenant, May 1, 1918; Embarked for Newfoundland on furlough, July 21, 1918; Returned to U. K., Oct. 19, 1918; Evacuated to Hospital, Nov. 28, 1918; Attached to 2nd Battalion. Winchester, April 28, 1919; Embarked for Newfoundland, Sept. 5, 1919; Retired, Oct. 14, 1919.

19 14

Archibald Gooby   Reg. No. 154

Enlisted, Sept. 2, 1914; British Mediterranean Expeditionary Force, Aug. 20, 1915; Lance Corporal, Feb. 27, 1916; British Expeditionary Force, March 14, 1916; Corporal, May 8, 1916; Sergeant, Feb. 9, 1917; Awarded Military Medal, June 18, 1917; Wounded, Belgium, March 13, 1918; Evacuated to England, March 19, 1918; Returned to Newfoundland on duty, May 22, 1918; Acting Company Sergeant Major, March 24, 1919; Demobilized, St. John's, Sept. 1, 1919.

Robert Joseph Good   Reg. No. 219

Enlisted, Sept. 2, 1914; British Mediterranean Expeditionary Force, Aug. 20, 1915; Evacuated, Suvla, sick, Oct. 15, 1915; Rejoined Battalion, Suez, March 7, 1916; British Expeditionary Force, March 14, 1916; Admitted to Hospital in England while on leave from B. E. F., Dec. 28, 1916; Joined 2nd Battalion, Ayr, Jan. 10, 1917; Repatriated to Newfoundland, Jan. 26, 1917; Transferred to Forestry Company, May 18, 1917; Discharged, St. John's, medically unfit, April 11, 1918.

Josiah Robert Goodyear   Reg. No. 573

Enlisted, Sept. 18, 1914; British Mediterranean Expeditionary Force, Aug. 20, 1915; Lance Corporal, Nov. 14, 1915; Served with 1st Composite Battalion on Western Egyptian Frontier, Nov. 1915 to Feb. 1916; British Expeditionary Force, March 2, 1916; Transport Sergeant, June 3, 1916; Wounded, Nov. 21, 1916; Invalided to England, Dec. 4, 1916; Attached to Depot, Ayr, April 21, 1917; Embarked for Newfoundland, May 4, 1917; Discharged, St. John's, medically unfit, June 6, 1917; Granted Commission, Captain, with Newfoundland Forestry Corps, July 18, 1917; Embarked for U. K., Dec. 11, 1917; Returned to Newfoundland, June 1, 1919; Retired, June 19, 1919.

CAPTAIN M. F. SUMMERS, QUARTERMASTER, AND HIS STAFF.

19 NEWFOUNDLAND 14

STANLEY CHARLES GOODYEAR   Reg. No. 334

Enlisted, Sept. 8, 1914; Lance Corporal, Oct. 3, 1914; Corporal, Feb. 13, 1915; Transport Sergeant, June 14, 1915; British Mediterranean Expeditionary Force, Aug. 20, 1915; Served with 1st Composite Battalion on Western Egyptian Frontier, Nov. 1915 to Feb., 1916; British Expeditionary Force, March 2, 1916; 2nd Lieutenant, May 10, 1916; Lieutenant, Aug. 1, 1917; Killed in action, Broembeek, Oct. 10, 1917; Awarded Military Cross, Dec. 28, 1917.

GILBERT THOMAS GORDON   Reg. No. 64

Enlisted, Sept. 2, 1914; Lance Corporal, Sept. 21, 1914; Corporal, Nov. 13, 1914; Transferred to the Gordon Highlanders as Commissioned Officer and Struck off the Strength, Nov. 30, 1914.

FRANK GEORGE GOUGH   Reg. No. 132

Enlisted, Sept. 3, 1914; British Mediterranean Expeditionary Force, Aug. 20, 1915; British Expeditionary Force, March 14, 1916; Wounded, Beaumont Hamel, July 1, 1916; Evacuated to England, July 3, 1916; Returned to B. E. F., March 25, 1917; Wounded, Broembeek, Oct. 9, 1917; Rejoined Unit in the Field, Nov. 10, 1917; Wounded, Marcoing, Nov. 20, 1917; Evacuated to England, Dec. 13, 1917; Transferred to Forestry Corps, June 25, 1918; Returned to Newfoundland on furlough, July 21, 1918; Demobilized, St. John's, Feb. 15, 1919.

19 14

WILLIAM HOYES GRANT   Reg. No. 410

Enlisted, Sept. 11, 1914; Lance Corporal, May 21, 1915; 2nd Lieutenant Oct. 16, 1915; British Expeditionary Force, March 23, 1916; Killed in action, in the line near Beaumont Hamel, July 16, 1916.

AUGUSTUS PETER GREEN   Reg. No. 251

Enlisted, Sept. 2, 1914; British Mediterranean Expeditionary Force, Aug. 20, 1915; Evacuated Suvla, sick, Oct. 16, 1915; Rejoined Battalion, Suez, March 7, 1916; British Expeditionary Force, March 14, 1916; Wounded, Beaumont Hamel, July 1, 1916; Invalided to England, July 4, 1916; Attached to Depot, Ayr, Aug. 6, 1916; Returned to Newfoundland on furlough, Sept. 27, 1916; Discharged, St. John's, medically unfit, March 21, 1917.

JOHN HENRY STANLEY GREEN   Reg. No. 108

Enlisted, Sept. 2, 1914; British Mediterranean Expeditionary Force Aug. 20, 1915; Evacuated to England, sick, Oct. 29, 1915; 2nd Lieutenant, July 12, 1916; Attached to 57th Squadron Royal Flying Corp as Flying Officer, March 12, 1917; British Expeditionary Force, March 21, 1917; Killed in action, July 7, 1917.

19 NEWFOUNDLAND 14

GORDON GREEN   Reg. No. 156

Enlisted, Sept. 2, 1914; British Mediterranean Expeditionary Force, Aug. 20, 1915; Evacuated Suvla Bay, sick, Dec. 1, 1915; Invalided to England, Feb. 11, 1916; Returned to Newfoundland on furlough, April 17, 1916; Discharged, St. John's, medically unfit, Aug. 28, 1916.

WALTER MARTIN GREENE   Reg. No. 266

Enlisted, Sept. 2, 1914; Lance Corporal, Sept. 21, 1914; Corporal, Nov. 13, 1914; Provost Sergeant, April 23, 1915; British Mediterranean Expeditionary Force, Aug. 20, 1915; Awarded Distinguished Conduct Medal, Jan. 24, 1916; British Expeditionary Force, March 14, 1916; 2nd Lieutenant, June 5, 1916; Wounded, Somme Raid, June 28, 1916; Invalided to England, July 5, 1916; Returned to B. E. F., May 4, 1917; Lieutenant, Nov. 1, 1917; Killed in action, Marcoing, Nov. 20, 1917.

WILLIAM JOSEPH GREENE   Reg. No. 320

Enlisted, Sept. 8, 1914; British Mediterranean Expeditionary Force, Aug. 20, 1915; Wounded, Suvla Bay, Nov. 5, 1915; Attached to Depot, Ayr, March 9, 1916; British Expeditionary Force, March 28, 1916; Joined Battalion, April 15, 1916; Wounded, Gueudecourt, Oct. 12, 1916; Invalided to England, Oct. 24, 1916; Repatriated to Newfoundland, Feb. 23, 1918; Discharged, St. John's, medically unfit, June 8, 1918.

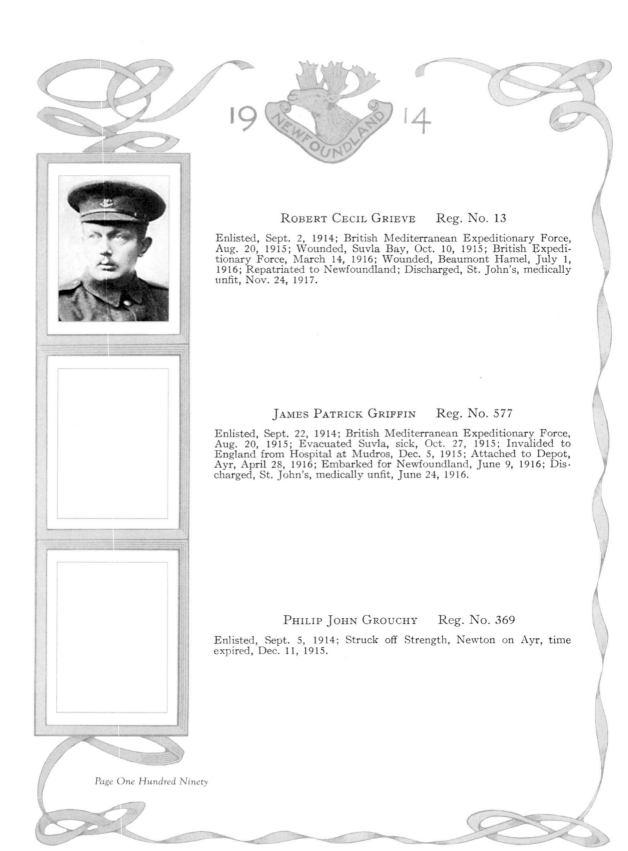

ROBERT CECIL GRIEVE   Reg. No. 13

Enlisted, Sept. 2, 1914; British Mediterranean Expeditionary Force, Aug. 20, 1915; Wounded, Suvla Bay, Oct. 10, 1915; British Expeditionary Force, March 14, 1916; Wounded, Beaumont Hamel, July 1, 1916; Repatriated to Newfoundland; Discharged, St. John's, medically unfit, Nov. 24, 1917.

JAMES PATRICK GRIFFIN   Reg. No. 577

Enlisted, Sept. 22, 1914; British Mediterranean Expeditionary Force, Aug. 20, 1915; Evacuated Suvla, sick, Oct. 27, 1915; Invalided to England from Hospital at Mudros, Dec. 5, 1915; Attached to Depot, Ayr, April 28, 1916; Embarked for Newfoundland, June 9, 1916; Discharged, St. John's, medically unfit, June 24, 1916.

PHILIP JOHN GROUCHY   Reg. No. 369

Enlisted, Sept. 5, 1914; Struck off Strength, Newton on Ayr, time expired, Dec. 11, 1915.

19 **NEWFOUNDLAND** 14

T. J. HACKETT   Reg. No. 408

Enlisted, Sept. 8, 1914; Struck off Strength, Salisbury Plain, Oct. 31 1914.

ROBERT HALEY   Reg. No. 489

Enlisted, Sept. 11, 1914; British Mediterranean Expeditionary Force, Aug. 20, 1915; Served with 1st Composite Battalion on Western Egyptain Frontier, Nov. 1915 to Feb., 1916; British Expeditionary Force, March 2, 1916; Evacuated to Hospital, sick, July 9, 1916; Discharged to duty, July 13, 1916; Wounded, Elverdinghe, Sept. 23, 1917; Invalided to England, Oct. 25, 1917; Embarked for Newfoundland, Feb. 23, 1918; Discharged, St. John's, medically unfit, April 10, 1918.

WILLIAM HALL   Reg. No. 352

Enlisted, Sept. 5, 1914; British Mediterranean Expeditionary Force, Aug. 20, 1915; British Expeditionary Force, March 14, 1916; Embarked for Newfoundland on furlough, Oct. 10, 1916; Returned to U. K., and attached to Depot, Ayr, April 30, 1917; Acting Sergeant July 18, 1917; Confirmed to Rank of Sergeant, July 1, 1918; Returned to B. E. F., July 2, 1918; Joined Battalion, July 9, 1918; Killed in action, Ledgeham, Oct. 14, 1918.

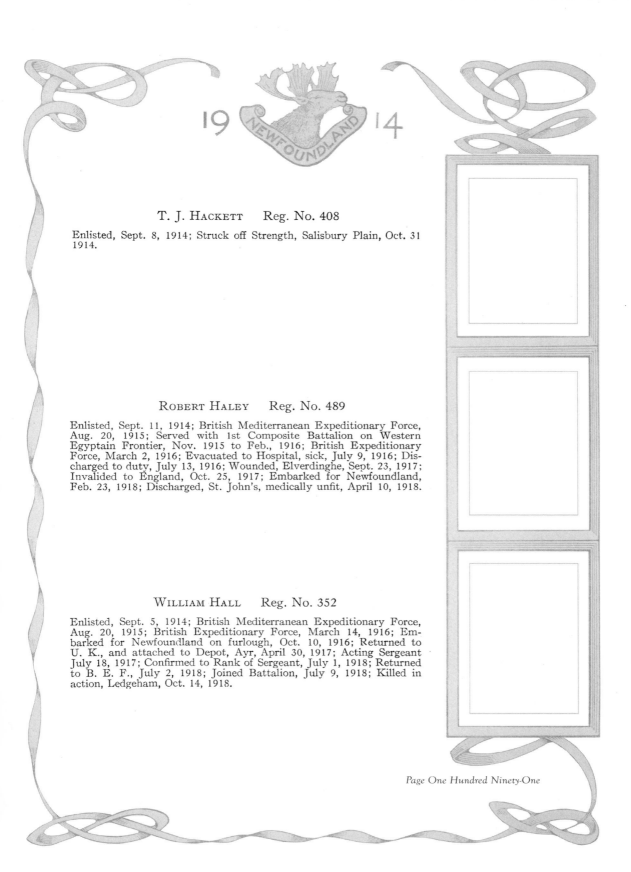

ARTHUR HAMMOND   Reg. No. 79

Enlisted, Sept. 2, 1914; Lance Corporal, Sept. 21, 1914; Corporal, July 2, 1915; British Mediterranean Expeditionary Force, Aug. 20, 1915; Ambulance Sergeant, Nov. 14, 1915; British Expeditionary Force, March 14, 1916; Awarded Military Medal, Oct. 18, 1917; Returned to Newfoundland on furlough, July 27, 1918; Returned to U. K., Sept. 22, 1918; Acting Company Sergeant Major, Nov. 12, 1918; Attached to Pay and Record Office, London, Nov. 21, 1918; Returned to Newfoundland, May 22, 1919; Demobilized, St. John's, Oct. 14, 1919.

CHARLES HAMMOND   Reg. No. 594

Enlisted, Sept. 26, 1914; British Mediterranean Expeditionary Force, Aug. 20, 1915; Evacuated Suvla, sick, Dec. 5, 1915; Invalided to England, Dec. 26, 1915; Attached to Depot, Ayr, Feb. 24, 1916; British Expeditionary Force with band, March 1, 1917; Returned to U. K., and joined Depot, Ayr, April 18, 1917; Returned to B. E. F., with band, July 1, 1918; Embarked for Newfoundland on furlough, July 7, 1918; Demobilized, St. John's, Feb. 15, 1919.

THOMAS HAMMOND   Reg. No. 360

Enlisted, Sept. 5, 1914; British Mediterranean Expeditionary Force, Aug. 20, 1915; British Expeditionary Force, March 14, 1916; Evacuated to Hospital, July 27, 1916; Invalided to England, Aug. 2, 1916; Attached to Depot, Ayr, Aug. 22, 1916; Embarked for Newfoundland, Oct. 27, 1916; Attached for duty to Headquarters, St. John's, Jan. 5, 1917; Lance Corporal, Jan. 15, 1917; Acting Corporal, March 9, 1917; Sergeant, Aug. 17, 1917; Acting Staff Sergeant, March 24, 1919; Awarded Meritorious Service Medal, June 3, 1919; Still on Strength.

19 NEWFOUNDLAND 14

JAMES PATRICK HANEY   Reg. No. 476

Enlisted, Sept. 10, 1914; British Mediterranean Expeditionary Force, Aug. 20, 1915; British Expeditionary Force, March 14, 1916; Killed in action, Beaumont Hamel, July 1, 1916.

JACOB HANN   Reg. No. 90

Enlisted, Sept. 4, 1914; British Mediterranean Expeditionary Force, Aug. 20, 1915; British Expeditionary Force, March 14, 1916; Evacuated to England, sick, Sept. 14, 1917; Returned to B. E. F., Feb. 4, 1918; Returned to Newfoundland on Blue Puttee leave, July 24, 1918; Demobilized, St. John's, Feb. 15, 1919.

HERBERT HARDING   Reg. No. 353

Enlisted, Sept. 7, 1914; British Mediterranean Expeditionary Force, Aug. 20, 1915; Served with 1st Composite Battalion, Western Egyptian Frontier, Nov. 1915 to Feb. 1916; British Expeditionary Force, March 2, 1916; Admitted to Hospital, Aug. 8, 1916; Rejoined Battalion, Aug. 26, 1916; Wounded, Belgium, Sept. 5, 1916; Discharged to Base, Rouen, Oct. 20, 1916; Rejoined Battalion, Nov. 7, 1916; Lance Corporal April 16, 1917; Killed in action Monchy, April 23, 1917.

19 NEWFOUNDLAND 14

WILLIAM FRANK HARDY   Reg. No. 179

Enlisted, Sept. 4, 1914; British Mediterranean Expeditionary Force, Aug. 20, 1915; Killed in action, Suvla Bay, Sept. 23, 1915.

WALTER JOSEPH HARNETT   Reg. No. 458

Enlisted, Sept. 8, 1914; British Mediterranean Expeditionary Force, Aug. 20, 1915; Served with 1st Composite Battalion on Western Egyptian Frontier, Nov. 1915 to Feb. 1916; British Expeditionary Force, March 2, 1916; Evacuated to Hospital, Sept. 2, 1916; Rejoined Battalion, Sept. 21, 1916; Embarked for Newfoundland on furlough, July 27, 1918; Demobilized, St. John's, Feb. 15, 1919.

LAWRENCE GEORGE HARSANT   Reg. No. 431

Enlisted, Sept. 7, 1914; British Mediterranean Expeditionary Force, Aug. 20, 1915; Lance Corporal, Sept. 6, 1915; Corporal, Nov. 2, 1915; British Expeditionary Force, March 14, 1916; Wounded, Beaumont Hamel, July 1, 1916; Invalided to England, July 5, 1916; Attached to Depot, Ayr, Sept. 20, 1916; Acting Sergeant, Nov. 16, 1916; Acting Company Quartermaster Sergeant, April 6, 1918; Confirmed to Rank of Sergeant, April 27, 1918; Embarked for Newfoundland on furlough July 27, 1918; Demobilized, St. John's, Feb. 15, 1919.

ARTHUR PIERCEY HARTLEY Reg. No. 174

Enlisted, Sept. 4, 1914; Lance Corporal, June 22, 1915; British Mediterranean Expeditionary Force, Aug. 20, 1915; British Expeditionary Force, March 14, 1916; Corporal, Oct. 12, 1916; Reported missing, Monchy, April 14, 1917; Later reported prisoner of war, Germany; Repatriated to England, Dec. 2, 1918; Demobilized, U. K., March 1, 1919.

LEONARD VINCENT HARTLEY Reg. No. 294

Enlisted, Sept. 11, 1914; Lance Corporal, July 20, 1915; British Mediterranean Expeditionary Force, Aug. 20, 1915; British Expeditionary Force, March 14, 1916; Evacuated to Hospital, June 28, 1916; Rejoined Battalion, July 12, 1916; Corporal, Oct. 12, 1916; Wounded, Gueudecourt, Oct. 12, 1916; Evacuated to England, Oct. 17, 1916; Attached to Pay and Record Office, London, March 13, 1917; Discharged, U. K., medically unfit, March 29, 1918.

GERALD HARVEY Reg. No. 333

Enlisted, Sept. 10, 1914; 2nd Lieutenant, April 6, 1915; British Mediterranean Expeditionary Force, Aug. 20, 1915; Wounded, Suvla, Oct. 3, 1915; Invalided to England, Oct. 6, 1915; Lieutenant, Oct. 15, 1915; Attached to Depot, Ayr, April 11, 1916; Returned to Newfoundland on furlough, April 17, 1916; Returned to U. K., July 27, 1916; Attached to Royal Flying Corps, Sept. 26, 1916; Rejoined 2nd Battalion, March 7, 1917; British Expeditionary Force, May 4, 1917; Wounded, Belgium, Oct. 7, 1917; Invalided to England, Oct. 23, 1917; Returned to Newfoundland, Jan. 30, 1919; Retired, Feb. 25, 1919.

Wilfred Eric Harvey   Reg. No. 324

Enlisted, Sept. 4, 1914; British Mediterranean Expeditionary Force, Aug. 20, 1915; Evacuated Suvla, sick, Dec. 7, 1915; Invalided to England, Dec. 14, 1915; Attached to Depot, Ayr, April 14, 1916; British Expeditionary Force, Aug. 5, 1917; Embarked for Newfoundland on furlough, July 27, 1918; Demobilized, St. John's, Feb. 15, 1919.

George Bernard Hatfield   Reg. No. 65

Enlisted, Sept. 2, 1914; British Mediterranean Expeditionary Force, Aug. 20, 1915; British Expeditionary Force, April 8, 1916; Killed in action, Beaumont Hamel, July 1, 1916.

Herbert Stephen Heater   Reg. No. 180

Enlisted, Sept. 5, 1914; British Mediterranean Expeditionary Force, Aug. 20, 1915; Evacuated Suvla, sick, Oct. 6, 1915; Invalided to England, Oct. 16, 1915; Lance Corporal, April 20, 1916; Acting Corporal, Aug. 11, 1916; Acting Sergeant, Oct. 28, 1916; Confirmed to Rank of Sergeant, March 23, 1917; British Expeditionary Force, March 25, 1917; Evacuated to Hospital, May 18, 1917; Invalided to England, June 9, 1917; Returned to Newfoundland on furlough, July 27, 1918; Demobilized, Feb. 8, 1919.

Robert Henderson   Reg. No. 471

Enlisted, Sept. 9, 1914; British Mediterranean Expeditionary Force, Aug. 20, 1915; Evacuated Suvla, sick, Dec. 3, 1915; Invalided to England, Dec. 28, 1915; Attached to Depot, Ayr, Feb. 25, 1916; Repatriated to Newfoundland, Dec. 12, 1918; Demobilized, St. John's, Jan. 31, 1919.

Alexander Hennebury   Reg. No. 461

Enlisted, Sept. 11, 1914; British Mediterranean Expeditionary Force, Aug. 20, 1915; Wounded, Suvla, Sept. 29, 1915; Rejoined Battalion, Suez, March 1, 1916; British Expeditionary Force, March 14, 1916; Awarded Military Medal, Jan. 14, 1918; Embarked for Newfoundland on furlough, July 27, 1918; Demobilized, St. John's, Feb. 15, 1919.

Ewan Hennebury   Reg. No. 19

Enlisted, Sept. 3, 1914; Lance Corporal, Sept. 21, 1914; Corporal, July 30, 1915; British Mediterranean Expeditionary Force, Aug. 20, 1915; Evacuated Suvla, sick, Nov. 7, 1915; Rejoined Battalion, Feb. 21, 1916; British Expeditionary Force, March 14, 1916; Wounded, Gueudecourt, Oct. 12, 1916; Invalided to England, Oct. 17, 1916; Repatriated to Newfoundland, May 4, 1917; Discharged, medically unfit, June 6, 1917; Reattested for home defence duty, June 21, 1917; Acting Sergeant, Dec. 13, 1917; Discharged, medically unfit, Nov. 18, 1918.

HUBERT CLINTON HERDER   Reg. No. 3

Enlisted, Sept. 2, 1914; Lance Corporal, Sept. 21, 1914; Corporal, Nov. 15, 1914; 2nd Lieutenant, April 6, 1915; British Mediterranean Expeditionary Force, Aug. 20, 1915; Lieutenant, Oct. 15, 1915; Served with 1st Composite Battalion on Western Egyptian Frontier, Nov. 1915, to Feb. 1916; British Expeditionary Force, March 10, 1916; Killed in action, Beaumont Hamel, July 1, 1916.

RALPH BARNES HERDER   Reg. No. 34

Enlisted, Sept. 2, 1914; Lance Corporal, July 26, 1915; British Mediterranean Expeditionary Force, Aug. 20, 1915; Corporal, Dec. 11, 1915; British Expeditionary Force, March 14, 1916; 2nd Lieutenant, July 1, 1916; Wounded, Beaumont Hamel, July 1, 1916; Invalided to England; Returned to B. E. F., Oct. 27, 1916; Wounded, Monchy, April 14, 1917; Repatriated to Newfoundland; Lieutenant, Jan. 1, 1918; Retired, June 30, 1918.

JAMES FRANCIS HIBBS   Reg. No. 299

Enlisted, Sept. 8, 1914; British Mediterranean Expeditionary Force; Aug. 20, 1915; British Expeditionary Force, March 14, 1916; Evacuated to Hospital, sick, March 19, 1918; Discharged to duty, March 27, 1918, Embarked for Newfoundland on furlough, July 27, 1918; Demobilized, St. John's, Feb. 15, 1919.

James Joseph Hickey   Reg. No. 113

Enlisted, Sept. 2, 1914; British Mediterranean Expeditionary Force, Aug. 20, 1915; British Expeditionary Force, March 14, 1916; Wounded, Elverdinghe, Sept. 26, 1917; Returned to Newfoundland on furlough, July 21, 1918; Demobilized, St. John's, Feb. 15, 1919.

John Joseph Hickey   Reg. No. 586

Enlisted, Sept. 22, 1914; British Mediterranean Expeditionary Force, Aug. 20, 1915; British Expeditionary Force, March 14, 1916; Wounded, Beaumont Hamel, July 1, 1916; Joined Base Depot, Rouen, July 13, 1916; Rejoined Battalion, Aug. 7, 1916; Wounded, Gueudecourt, Oct. 12, 1916; Invalided to England, Oct. 18, 1916; Attached to Depot, Ayr, Nov. 15, 1916; Returned to B. E. F., Aug. 5, 1917; Joined Battalion, Aug. 28, 1917; Wounded, Marcoing, Nov. 20, 1917; Invalided to England, Nov. 24, 1917; Attached to Depot, Winchester, Jan. 5, 1918; Embarked for Newfoundland on furlough, July 21, 1918; Demobilized, St. John's, Feb. 15, 1919.

John Hickey   Reg. No. 252

Enlisted, Sept. 2, 1914; British Mediterranean Expeditionary Force, Aug. 20, 1915; British Expeditionary Force, March 14, 1916; Wounded, Beaumont Hamel, July 1, 1916; Invalided to England, July 7, 1916; Attached to Depot, Ayr, Oct. 10, 1916; Returned to Newfoundland, Jan. 26, 1917; Discharged, St. John's, medically unfit, April 25, 1917.

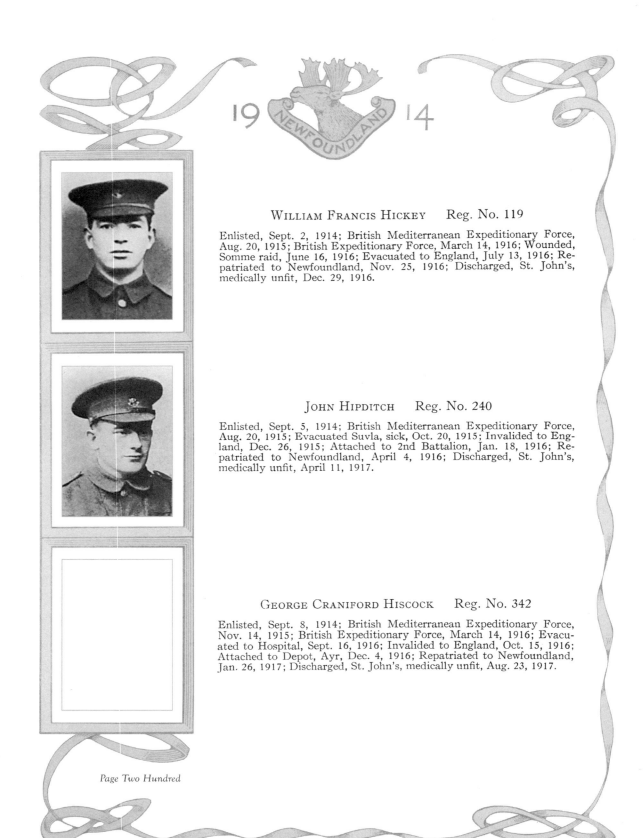

WILLIAM FRANCIS HICKEY   Reg. No. 119

Enlisted, Sept. 2, 1914; British Mediterranean Expeditionary Force, Aug. 20, 1915; British Expeditionary Force, March 14, 1916; Wounded, Somme raid, June 16, 1916; Evacuated to England, July 13, 1916; Repatriated to Newfoundland, Nov. 25, 1916; Discharged, St. John's, medically unfit, Dec. 29, 1916.

JOHN HIPDITCH   Reg. No. 240

Enlisted, Sept. 5, 1914; British Mediterranean Expeditionary Force, Aug. 20, 1915; Evacuated Suvla, sick, Oct. 20, 1915; Invalided to England, Dec. 26, 1915; Attached to 2nd Battalion, Jan. 18, 1916; Repatriated to Newfoundland, April 4, 1916; Discharged, St. John's, medically unfit, April 11, 1917.

GEORGE CRANIFORD HISCOCK   Reg. No. 342

Enlisted, Sept. 8, 1914; British Mediterranean Expeditionary Force, Nov. 14, 1915; British Expeditionary Force, March 14, 1916; Evacuated to Hospital, Sept. 16, 1916; Invalided to England, Oct. 15, 1916; Attached to Depot, Ayr, Dec. 4, 1916; Repatriated to Newfoundland, Jan. 26, 1917; Discharged, St. John's, medically unfit, Aug. 23, 1917.

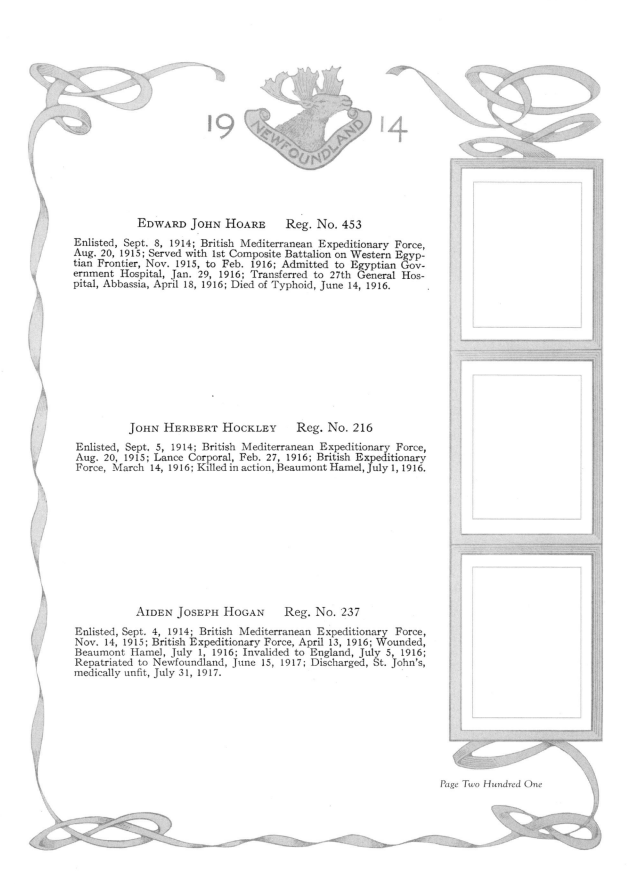

EDWARD JOHN HOARE   Reg. No. 453

Enlisted, Sept. 8, 1914; British Mediterranean Expeditionary Force, Aug. 20, 1915; Served with 1st Composite Battalion on Western Egyptian Frontier, Nov. 1915, to Feb. 1916; Admitted to Egyptian Government Hospital, Jan. 29, 1916; Transferred to 27th General Hospital, Abbassia, April 18, 1916; Died of Typhoid, June 14, 1916.

JOHN HERBERT HOCKLEY   Reg. No. 216

Enlisted, Sept. 5, 1914; British Mediterranean Expeditionary Force, Aug. 20, 1915; Lance Corporal, Feb. 27, 1916; British Expeditionary Force, March 14, 1916; Killed in action, Beaumont Hamel, July 1, 1916.

AIDEN JOSEPH HOGAN   Reg. No. 237

Enlisted, Sept. 4, 1914; British Mediterranean Expeditionary Force, Nov. 14, 1915; British Expeditionary Force, April 13, 1916; Wounded, Beaumont Hamel, July 1, 1916; Invalided to England, July 5, 1916; Repatriated to Newfoundland, June 15, 1917; Discharged, St. John's, medically unfit, July 31, 1917.

LUKE HOLDEN   Reg. No. 329

Enlisted, Sept. 5, 1914; British Mediterranean Expeditionary Force, Aug. 20, 1915; British Expeditionary Force, March 14, 1916; Killed in action, Beaumont Hamel, July 1, 1916.

PATRICK HOLDEN   Reg. No. 555

Enlisted, Sept. 16, 1914; British Mediterranean Expeditionary Force, Aug. 20. 1915; Wounded, Suvla, Dec. 14, 1915; Admitted to Valletta Hospital, Malta, Dec. 22, 1915; Died of wounds, Jan. 29, 1916.

ALBERT NORMAN HOOPER   Reg. No. 248

Enlisted, Sept. 2, 1914; British Mediterranean Expeditionary Force, Nov. 14, 1915; British Expeditionary Force, March 14, 1916; Wounded, Beaumont Hamel, July 1, 1916; Invalided to England, July 4, 1916; Attached to Depot, Ayr, Aug. 21, 1916; Returned to B. E. F., March 1, 1918; Joined Battalion, April 5, 1918; Wounded, Neuve Eglise, April 13, 1918; Invalided to England, May 7, 1918; Repatriated to Newfoundland, May 22, 1919; Demobilized, St. John's, July 12, 1919.

Thomas Anthony Horan   Reg. No. 212

Enlisted, Sept. 3, 1914; British Mediterranean Expeditionary Force, Aug. 20, 1915; British Expeditionary Force, March 14, 1916; Wounded, Beaumont Hamel, July 1, 1916; Invalided to England, July 4, 1916; Repatriated to Newfoundland, Nov. 25, 1916; Discharged, St. John's, medically unfit, Dec. 29, 1916.

Lawrence Amour Hoskins   Reg. No. 449

Enlisted, Sept. 8, 1914; British Mediterranean Expeditionary Force Aug. 20, 1915; Evacuated Suvla, sick, Dec. 5, 1915; Rejoined Battalion at Suez, March 1, 1916; British Expeditionary Force, March 14, 1916; Admitted to Hospital, Rouen, Feb. 27, 1917; Rejoined Battalion, May 7, 1917; Wounded, Marcoing, Nov. 20, 1917; Invalided to England, Nov. 23, 1917; Attached to Depot, Ayr, Jan. 3, 1918; Embarked for Newfoundland on furlough, July 21, 1918; Demobilized, St. John's Feb. 15, 1919.

James Patrick Houlahan   Reg. No. 500

Enlisted, Sept. 14, 1914; Lance Corporal, Aug. 18, 1915; British Mediterranean Expeditionary Force, Aug. 20, 1915; British Expeditionary Force, March 14, 1916; Wounded, Beaumont Hamel, July 1, 1916; Invalided to England, July 7, 1916; Attached to Pay and Record Office, London, Dec. 20, 1916; Admitted to 3rd London General Hospital, Wandsworth, June 19, 1917; Discharged to duty, Nov. 30, 1917; Attached to Depot, Ayr, Dec. 6, 1917; Discharged, U. K., medically unfit, Sept. 17, 1918.

19 **NEWFOUNDLAND** 14

JAMES JOHN HOWARD   Reg. No. 560

Enlisted, Sept. 16, 1914; British Mediterranean Expeditionary Force, Aug. 20, 1915; British Expeditionary Force, March 14, 1916; Killed in action, Beaumont Hamel, July 1, 1916.

MOSES HOWELL   Reg. No. 462

Enlisted, Sept. 8, 1914; Struck off Strength, Newton on Ayr, medically unfit, Nov. 26, 1915.

THOMAS HUMPHREY   Reg. No. 375

Enlisted, Sept. 8, 1914; British Mediterranean Expeditionary Force, Aug. 20, 1915; Evacuated Suvla, sick, Nov. 25, 1915; British Expeditionary Force, March 18, 1916; Admitted to Hospital, Rouen, March 30, 1916; Invalided to England, April 12, 1916; Attached to Depot, Ayr, Aug. 1, 1916; Returned to B. E. F., Aug. 5, 1917; Admitted to Hospital, March 1, 1918; Invalided to England, March 15, 1918; Attached to Depot, Ayr, May 2, 1918; Embarked for Newfoundland on furlough, July 21, 1918; Demobilized, St. John's, Feb. 15, 1919.

19 14

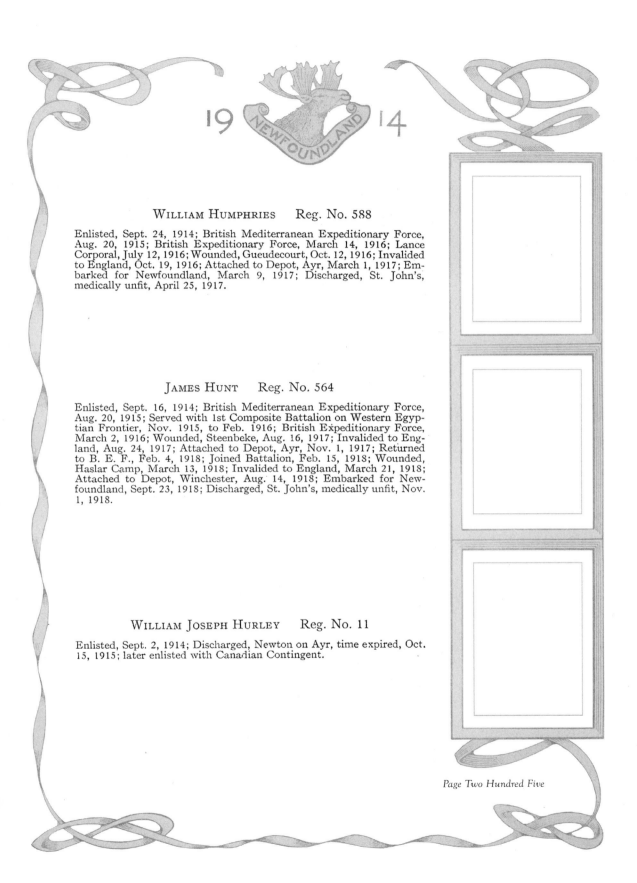

WILLIAM HUMPHRIES   Reg. No. 588

Enlisted, Sept. 24, 1914; British Mediterranean Expeditionary Force, Aug. 20, 1915; British Expeditionary Force, March 14, 1916; Lance Corporal, July 12, 1916; Wounded, Gueudecourt, Oct. 12, 1916; Invalided to England, Oct. 19, 1916; Attached to Depot, Ayr, March 1, 1917; Embarked for Newfoundland, March 9, 1917; Discharged, St. John's, medically unfit, April 25, 1917.

JAMES HUNT   Reg. No. 564

Enlisted, Sept. 16, 1914; British Mediterranean Expeditionary Force, Aug. 20, 1915; Served with 1st Composite Battalion on Western Egyptian Frontier, Nov. 1915, to Feb. 1916; British Expeditionary Force, March 2, 1916; Wounded, Steenbeke, Aug. 16, 1917; Invalided to England, Aug. 24, 1917; Attached to Depot, Ayr, Nov. 1, 1917; Returned to B. E. F., Feb. 4, 1918; Joined Battalion, Feb. 15, 1918; Wounded, Haslar Camp, March 13, 1918; Invalided to England, March 21, 1918; Attached to Depot, Winchester, Aug. 14, 1918; Embarked for Newfoundland, Sept. 23, 1918; Discharged, St. John's, medically unfit, Nov. 1, 1918.

WILLIAM JOSEPH HURLEY   Reg. No. 11

Enlisted, Sept. 2, 1914; Discharged, Newton on Ayr, time expired, Oct. 15, 1915; later enlisted with Canadian Contingent.

COCHRANE STREET CHURCH GROUP

Jack Spooner, Harold Janes, George Taylor, Stanley Garland, Harry Wilson

William Thomas Hussey   Reg. No. 356

Enlisted, Sept. 7, 1914; British Mediterranean Expeditionary Force, March 20, 1915; Appointed Master Cook, Oct. 24, 1915; British Expeditionary Force, March 14, 1916; Sergeant, June 11, 1916; Killed in action, Monchy, April 14, 1917.

Harold Hutchings   Reg. No. 602

Enlisted, Sept. 28, 1914; British Mediterranean Expeditionary Force, Aug. 20, 1915; Served with 1st Composite Battalion on Western Egyptian Frontier, Nov. 1915 to Feb. 1916; British Expeditionary Force, March 2, 1916; Killed in action, Beaumont Hamel, July 1, 1916.

William F. C. Hutchings   Reg. No. 538

Enlisted, Sept. 16, 1914; Lance Corporal, Sept. 21, 1914; Corporal, July 2, 1915; British Mediterranean Expeditionary Force, Aug. 20, 1915; Evacuated Suvla, sick, Nov. 26, 1915; Admitted to Hospital, Malta, Dec. 3, 1915; Invalided to England, Jan. 24, 1916; Attached to Depot, Ayr, March 4, 1916; Attached to Pay and Record Office, London, June 16, 1916; Acting Staff Sergeant, Nov. 24, 1917; Embarked for Newfoundland on furlough, July 21, 1918; Returned to U. K. and re-attached to Pay and Record Office, Nov. 18, 1918; Embarked for Newfoundland, Jan. 3, 1919; Demobilized, St. John's, Feb. 27, 1919.

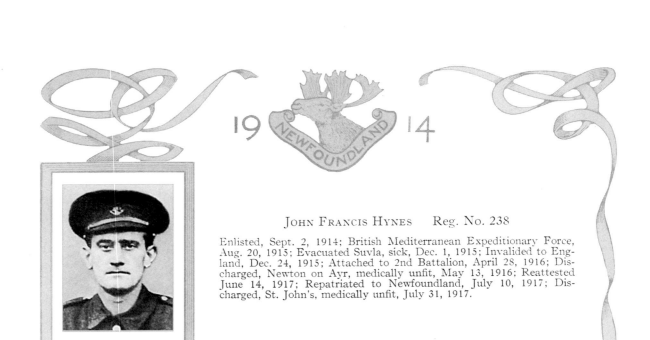

JOHN FRANCIS HYNES   Reg. No. 238

Enlisted, Sept. 2, 1914; British Mediterranean Expeditionary Force, Aug. 20, 1915; Evacuated Suvla, sick, Dec. 1, 1915; Invalided to England, Dec. 24, 1915; Attached to 2nd Battalion, April 28, 1916; Discharged, Newton on Ayr, medically unfit, May 13, 1916; Reattested June 14, 1917; Repatriated to Newfoundland, July 10, 1917; Discharged, St. John's, medically unfit, July 31, 1917.

JAMES MAIN IRVINE   Reg. No. 49

Enlisted, Sept. 2, 1914; Lance Corporal, Sept. 21, 1914; Corporal, Oct. 3, 1914; Sergeant, Nov. 16, 1914; Company Sergeant Major, Oct. 21, 1915; 2nd Lieutenant, Oct. 30, 1915; British Expeditionary Force, June 5, 1916; Admitted to Hospital in England, Jan. 13, 1917; Returned to B. E. F., April 23, 1917; Lieutenant, Aug. 1, 1917; Admitted to Hospital, Dec. 16, 1917; Transferred to England , Dec. 29, 1917; Attached to Depot, Winchester, March 29, 1918; Embarked for Newfoundland on furlough, July 21, 1918; Returned to U. K., Oct. 19, 1918; Returned to B. E. F., Nov. 19, 1918; Admitted to Hospital, Nov. 26, 1918; Discharged to duty, March 8, 1919; Transferred to U. K., April 22, 1919; Embarked for Newfoundland, May 22, 1919; Retired, July 29, 1919.

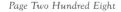

ARTHUR JOSEPH JACKMAN   Reg. No. 533

Enlisted, Sept. 15, 1914; British Mediterranean Expeditionary Force, Aug. 20, 1915; Evacuated Suvla, sick, Nov. 29, 1915; Invalided to England Dec. 24, 1915; Attached to Depot, Ayr, Feb. 14, 1916; British Expeditionary Force, March 28, 1916; Joined Battalion, April 15, 1916; Killed in action, Monchy, April 14, 1917.

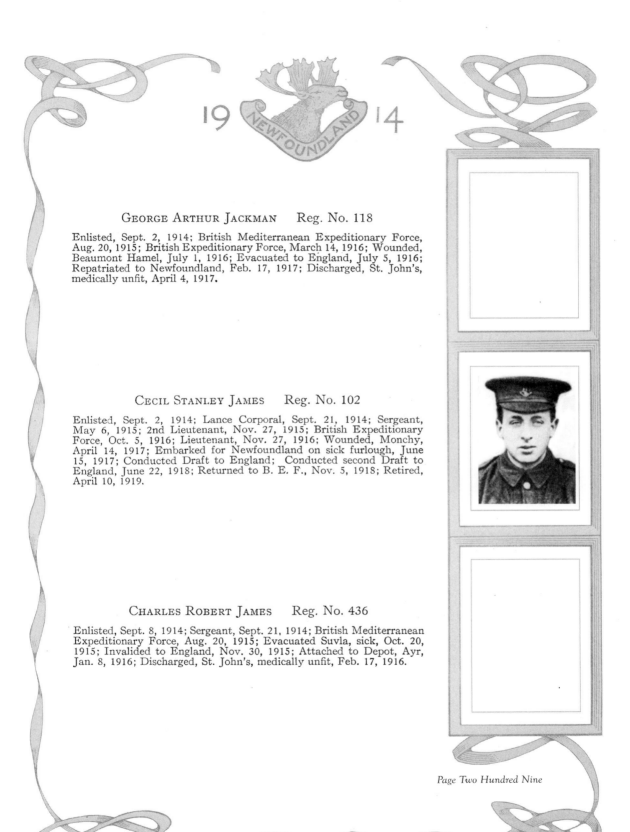

George Arthur Jackman   Reg. No. 118

Enlisted, Sept. 2, 1914; British Mediterranean Expeditionary Force, Aug. 20, 1915; British Expeditionary Force, March 14, 1916; Wounded, Beaumont Hamel, July 1, 1916; Evacuated to England, July 5, 1916; Repatriated to Newfoundland, Feb. 17, 1917; Discharged, St. John's, medically unfit, April 4, 1917.

Cecil Stanley James   Reg. No. 102

Enlisted, Sept. 2, 1914; Lance Corporal, Sept. 21, 1914; Sergeant, May 6, 1915; 2nd Lieutenant, Nov. 27, 1915; British Expeditionary Force, Oct. 5, 1916; Lieutenant, Nov. 27, 1916; Wounded, Monchy, April 14, 1917; Embarked for Newfoundland on sick furlough, June 15, 1917; Conducted Draft to England; Conducted second Draft to England, June 22, 1918; Returned to B. E. F., Nov. 5, 1918; Retired, April 10, 1919.

Charles Robert James   Reg. No. 436

Enlisted, Sept. 8, 1914; Sergeant, Sept. 21, 1914; British Mediterranean Expeditionary Force, Aug. 20, 1915; Evacuated Suvla, sick, Oct. 20, 1915; Invalided to England, Nov. 30, 1915; Attached to Depot, Ayr, Jan. 8, 1916; Discharged, St. John's, medically unfit, Feb. 17, 1916.

Thomas Lincoln James   Reg. No. 370

Enlisted, Sept. 5, 1914: Struck off Strength, Newton on Ayr, time expired and medically unfit, Oct. 15, 1915.

Harold Clark Janes   Reg. No. 109

Enlisted, Sept. 2, 1914; Lance Corporal, Nov. 13, 1914; Corporal, June 14, 1915: British Mediterranean Expeditionary Force, Aug. 20, 1915; Orderly Room Sergeant, Sept. 13, 1915; Employed at General Head Office Staff, 3rd Echelon, Alexandria, Sept. 13, 1915; British Expeditionary Force, March 18, 1916; Employed at Headquarters Staff, 3rd Echelon, Rouen, March 29, 1916; Returned to Newfoundland on sick furlough, July 10, 1917: Attached for duty to Militia Department, Jan. 24, 1918; Acting Staff Sergeant Major, June 25, 1918; Awarded Meritorious Service Medal, June 3, 1919; Honorary 2nd Lieutenant, Sept. 1, 1919; Still on Strength.

Harold Wesley Janes   Reg. No. 197

Enlisted, Sept. 4, 1914; British Mediterranean Expeditionary Force, Aug. 20, 1915; Evacuated Suvla, sick, Nov. 28, 1915; Invalided to England, Feb. 5, 1916; Attached to Depot, 2nd Battalion, March 30, 1916; Returned to Newfoundland on furlough, July 21, 1918; Demobilized, St. John's, Feb. 15, 1919.

1914 NEWFOUNDLAND

THOMAS PATRICK JANES   Reg. No. 136

Enlisted, Sept. 3, 1914; British Mediterranean Expeditionary Force, Aug. 20, 1915; British Expeditionary Force, March 18, 1916; Wounded, Beaumont Hamel, July 1, 1916; Evacuated to England, July 4, 1916; Returned to B. E. F., Aug. 5, 1917; Transferred to England, "Permanent Base," Aug. 12, 1917; Repatriated to Newfoundland, July 21, 1918; Discharged, St. John's, medically unfit, Sept. 2, 1918.

WALTER HAROLD JANES   Reg. No. 56

Enlisted, Sept. 2, 1914; British Mediterranean Expeditionary Force, Aug. 20, 1915; Lance Corporal, Nov. 20, 1915; British Expeditionary Force, March 2, 1916; Corporal, Sept. 28, 1916; Acting Sergeant, Nov. 7, 1916; Confirmed to Rank of Sergeant, Feb. 9, 1917; Wounded, Steenbeke, Aug. 16, 1917; Attached to Pay and Record Office, London, for duty, Jan. 9, 1918; Demobilized, St. John's, March 20, 1919.

JOHN ALLAN JEANS   Reg. No. 424

Enlisted, Sept. 3, 1914; British Mediterranean Expeditionary Force, Aug. 20, 1915; Evacuated to Hospital, sick, Nov. 30, 1915; Discharged to duty, Dec. 31, 1915; Rejoined Battalion, Suez, Jan. 16, 1916; British Expeditionary Force, March 14, 1916; Killed in action, Beaumont Hamel, July 1, 1916.

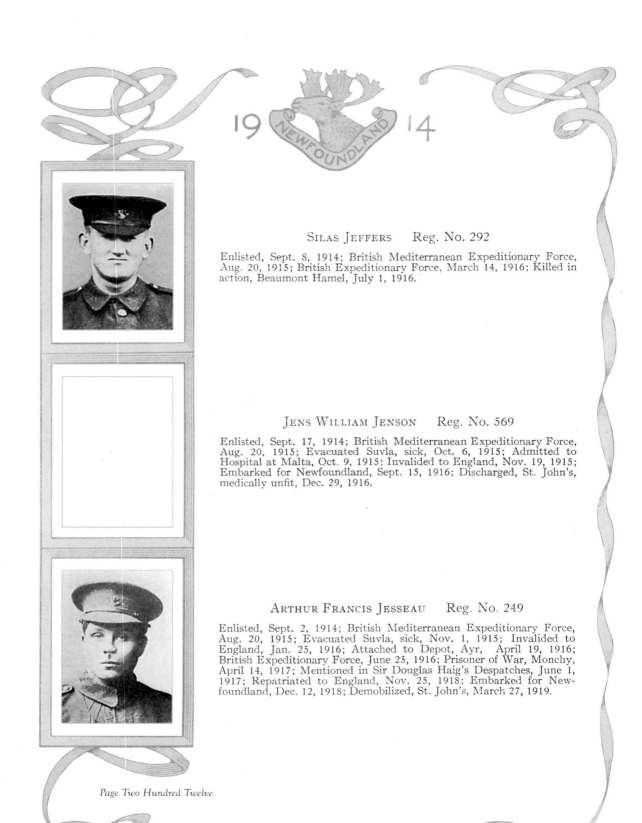

1914

Silas Jeffers   Reg. No. 292

Enlisted, Sept. 8, 1914; British Mediterranean Expeditionary Force, Aug. 20, 1915; British Expeditionary Force, March 14, 1916; Killed in action, Beaumont Hamel, July 1, 1916.

Jens William Jenson   Reg. No. 569

Enlisted, Sept. 17, 1914; British Mediterranean Expeditionary Force, Aug. 20, 1915; Evacuated Suvla, sick, Oct. 6, 1915; Admitted to Hospital at Malta, Oct. 9, 1915; Invalided to England, Nov. 19, 1915; Embarked for Newfoundland, Sept. 15, 1916; Discharged, St. John's, medically unfit, Dec. 29, 1916.

Arthur Francis Jesseau   Reg. No. 249

Enlisted, Sept. 2, 1914; British Mediterranean Expeditionary Force, Aug. 20, 1915; Evacuated Suvla, sick, Nov. 1, 1915; Invalided to England, Jan. 25, 1916; Attached to Depot, Ayr, April 19, 1916; British Expeditionary Force, June 25, 1916; Prisoner of War, Monchy, April 14, 1917; Mentioned in Sir Douglas Haig's Despatches, June 1, 1917; Repatriated to England, Nov. 25, 1918; Embarked for Newfoundland, Dec. 12, 1918; Demobilized, St. John's, March 27, 1919.

1914

JOHN JOSEPH JOHNSON   Reg. No. 135

Enlisted, Sept. 3, 1914; British Mediterranean Expeditionary Force, Aug. 20, 1915; Admitted to Hospital at Cairo, Sept. 11, 1915; Discharged to Base, Alexandria, Sept. 22, 1915; Embarked for Gallipoli, Oct. 25, 1915; British Expeditionary Force, March 14, 1916; Wounded, remained at duty, April 29, 1916; Killed in action, Beaumont Hamel, July 1, 1916.

EDWARD JOY   Reg. No. 502

Enlisted, Sept. 14, 1914; British Mediterranean Expeditionary Force, Aug. 20, 1915; British Expeditionary Force, March 14, 1916; Evacuated to Hospital, Feb. 2, 1917; Discharged to duty, March 5, 1917; Lance Corporal, Aug. 20, 1917; Corporal, Nov. 1, 1917; Awarded Military Medal, Nov. 20, 1917; Acting Sergeant, Dec. 26, 1917; Confirmed to Rank of Sergeant, March 16, 1918; Embarked for Newfoundland on special duty, May 22, 1918; Returned to U. K., Oct. 12, 1918; Died of Pneumonia at Military Hospital, Devonport, Oct. 14, 1918; Awarded Bar to Military Medal, May 21, 1919.

CLIFFORD H. O. JUPP   Reg. No. 157

Enlisted, Sept. 5, 1914; Lance Corporal, June 12, 1915; British Mediterranean Expeditionary Force, Aug. 20, 1915; Corporal, Sept. 26, 1915; Sergeant, Nov. 14, 1915; British Expeditionary Force, March 14, 1916; Acting Company Quartermaster Sergeant, May 29, 1916; 2nd Lieutenant, June 11, 1916; Killed in action, Beaumont Hamel, July 1, 1916.

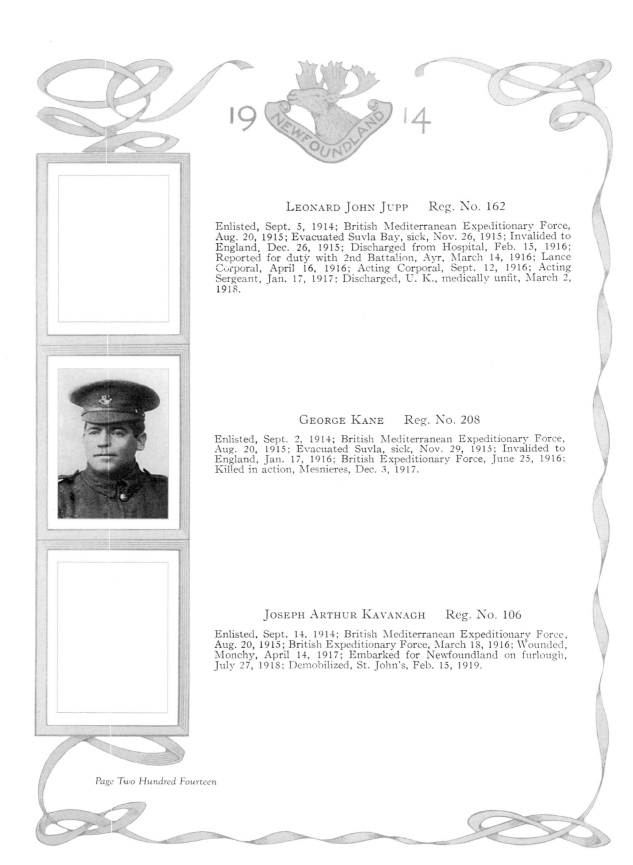

LEONARD JOHN JUPP Reg. No. 162

Enlisted, Sept. 5, 1914; British Mediterranean Expeditionary Force, Aug. 20, 1915; Evacuated Suvla Bay, sick, Nov. 26, 1915; Invalided to England, Dec. 26, 1915; Discharged from Hospital, Feb. 15, 1916; Reported for duty with 2nd Battalion, Ayr, March 14, 1916; Lance Corporal, April 16, 1916; Acting Corporal, Sept. 12, 1916; Acting Sergeant, Jan. 17, 1917; Discharged, U. K., medically unfit, March 2, 1918.

GEORGE KANE Reg. No. 208

Enlisted, Sept. 2, 1914; British Mediterranean Expeditionary Force, Aug. 20, 1915; Evacuated Suvla, sick, Nov. 29, 1915; Invalided to England, Jan. 17, 1916; British Expeditionary Force, June 25, 1916; Killed in action, Mesnieres, Dec. 3, 1917.

JOSEPH ARTHUR KAVANAGH Reg. No. 106

Enlisted, Sept. 14, 1914; British Mediterranean Expeditionary Force, Aug. 20, 1915; British Expeditionary Force, March 18, 1916; Wounded, Monchy, April 14, 1917; Embarked for Newfoundland on furlough, July 27, 1918; Demobilized, St. John's, Feb. 15, 1919.

WALTER KEARLEY   Reg. No. 552

Enlisted, Sept. 16, 1914; British Mediterranean Expeditionary Force, Aug. 20, 1915; Evacuated Suvla, sick, Oct. 11, 1915; Admitted to Hospital, Malta, Nov. 26, 1915; Invalided to England, Nov. 29, 1915; Attached to Depot, Ayr, April 12, 1916; British Expeditionary Force, June 25, 1916; Wounded, Sailly-Saillisel, March 3, 1917; Invalided to England, March 6, 1917; Attached to Depot, Ayr, April 18, 1917; Returned to B. E. F., Aug. 5, 1917; Joined Battalion, Aug. 28, 1917; Wounded, Broembeek, Oct. 9, 1917; Invalided to England, Oct. 21, 1917; Attached to Depot, Winchester, May 15, 1919; Embarked for Newfoundland, May 22, 1919; Demobilized, St. John's, June 29, 1919.

WILLIAM WALLACE KEARNEY   Reg. No. 68

Enlisted, Sept. 2, 1914; British Mediterranean Expeditionary Force, Aug. 20, 1915; Wounded, Suvla Bay, Oct. 31, 1915; Repatriated to Newfoundland, Jan. 17, 1916; Discharged, St. John's, medically unfit, March 31, 1916.

HUBERT JOHN KEATS   Reg. No. 613

Enlisted, Oct. 1, 1914; British Mediterranean Expeditionary Force, Aug. 20, 1915; Evacuated Suvla, sick, Oct. 21, 1915; Rejoined Battalion, Suez, Jan. 31, 1916; British Expeditionary Force, March 14, 1916; Evacuated to Hospital, May 7, 1916; Discharged to duty, May 27, 1916; Wounded, Monchy, April 14, 1917; Invalided to England, April 20, 1917; Repatriated to Newfoundland, May 13, 1918; Discharged, St. John's, medically unfit, Aug. 1, 1918.

WILLIAM KEATS   Reg. No. 203

Enlisted, Sept. 2, 1914; British Mediterranean Expeditionary Force, Aug. 20, 1915; British Expeditionary Force, March 14, 1916; Wounded, Beaumont Hamel, July 1, 1916; Evacuated to England, July 4, 1916; Returned to B. E. F., Jan. 31, 1917; Killed in action, Monchy, April 14, 1917.

FREDERICK KEEL   Reg. No. 490

Enlisted, Sept. 11, 1914; British Mediterranean Expeditionary Force, Nov. 14, 1915; British Expeditionary Force, March 14, 1916; Wounded Somme Raid, June 20, 1916; Invalided to England, July 1, 1916; Attached to Depot, Ayr, April 19, 1917; Demobilized, U. K., May 19, 1919.

ERNEST KELLY   Reg. No. 27

Enlisted, Sept. 2, 1914; British Mediterranean Expeditionary Force, Aug. 20, 1915; British Expeditionary Force, March 14, 1916; Wounded, Beaumont Hamel, July 1, 1916; Lance Corporal, Oct. 27, 1916; Invalided to England, Acting Corporal, Jan. 17, 1917; Returned to B. E. F., Nov. 6, 1917; Wounded, Marcoing, Nov. 20, 1917; Demobilized, St. John's, Feb. 15, 1919.

John Joseph Kelly   Reg. No. 188

Enlisted, Sept. 3, 1914; British Mediterranean Expeditionary Force, Aug. 20, 1915; Evacuated Suvla, sick, Oct. 5, 1915; Invalided to England, Dec. 12, 1915; British Expeditionary Force, Jan. 31, 1917, Wounded, Elverdinghe, Sept. 28, 1917; Evacuated to Hospital; Rejoined Battalion in the field, Oct. 29, 1917; Wounded, Marcoing, Nov. 20, 1917; Invalided to England, Nov. 23, 1917; Returned to Newfoundland on furlough, July 21, 1918; Demobilized, St. John's, April 3, 1919.

Michael Francis Kelly   Reg. No. 148

Enlisted, Sept. 3, 1914; Lance Corporal, June 19, 1915; Corporal, Oct. 29, 1915; British Mediterranean Expeditionary Force, Nov. 14, 1915; British Expeditionary Force, March 14, 1916; Sergeant, June 11, 1916; Killed in action, Beaumont Hamel, July 1, 1916.

Thomas Joseph Kelly   Reg. No. 178

Enlisted, Sept. 13, 1914; British Mediterranean Expeditionary Force, Aug. 20, 1915; Evacuated Suvla Bay, sick, Oct. 9, 1915; Invalided to England, Nov. 6, 1915; British Expeditionary Force, March 28, 1916; Killed in action, Beaumont Hamel, July 1, 1916.

LEO TERRENCE KENNEDY Reg. No. 224

Enlisted, Sept. 2, 1914; British Mediterranean Expeditionary Force, Aug. 20, 1915; Evacuated Suvla, sick, Oct. 6, 1915; Invalided to England, Nov. 22, 1915; Attached to 2nd Battalion, Ayr, Jan. 8, 1916; British Expeditionary Force, Aug. 24, 1916; Wounded, Ypres, Sept. 8, 1916; Evacuated to England, Sept. 13, 1916; Attached to 2nd Battalion, Oct. 23, 1916; Returned to B. E. F., March 25, 1917; Wounded, Marcoing, Dec. 4, 1917; Invalided to England, Dec. 8, 1917; Attached to Depot, 2nd Battalion, Jan. 6, 1918; Returned to Newfoundland, Dec. 12, 1918; Demobilized, St. John's, Jan. 31, 1919.

MICHAEL FRANCIS KENNEDY Reg. No. 355

Enlisted, Sept. 2, 1914; British Mediterranean Expeditionary Force, Aug. 20, 1915; Evacuated Suvla, sick, Dec. 21, 1915; Rejoined Battalion, Suez, Jan. 31, 1916; British Expeditionary Force, March 14, 1916; Killed in action, Beaumont Hamel, July 1, 1916.

WILLIAM P. KENNETH Reg. No. 127

Enlisted, Sept. 7, 1914; Struck off Strength, Newton on Ayr, time expired, Oct. 22, 1915.

19 14

ROBERT KERSHAW   Reg. No. 406

Enlisted, Sept. 3, 1914; Sergeant, Sept. 21, 1914; Company Quarter-master Sergeant, July 31, 1915; British Mediterranean Expeditionary Force, Aug. 20, 1915; Evacuated Suvla, sick, Oct. 21, 1915; Admitted to Hospital, Alexandria, Oct. 26, 1915; Invalided to England, Dec. 26, 1915; Attached to Depot, Ayr, April 3, 1916; Company Sergeant Major, April 5, 1916; 2nd Lieutenant, May 29, 1917; Returned to B. E. F., Dec. 18, 1917; Wounded, Belgium, March 9, 1918; Died of wounds, March 9, 1918.

STANLEY S. KIRBY   Reg. No. 242

Enlisted, Sept. 2, 1914; British Mediterranean Expeditionary Force, Aug. 20, 1915; Evacuated Suvla, sick, Oct. 31, 1915; Invalided to England, Dec. 6, 1915; Attached to Depot, Ayr, March 9, 1916; British Expeditionary Force, March 28, 1916; Wounded, Beaumont Hamel, July 1, 1916; Invalided to England, July 3, 1916; Attached to Depot, Ayr, Feb. 1, 1917; Returned to B. E. F., Aug. 5, 1917; Wounded, Marcoing, Dec. 1, 1917; Invalided to England, Dec. 12, 1917; Attached to Depot, Ayr, June 21, 1918; Embarked for Newfoundland on furlough, July 21, 1918; Discharged, St. John's, medically unfit, Nov. 25, 1918.

GEORGE SAMUEL KNIGHT   Reg. No. 309

Enlisted, Sept. 7, 1914; British Mediterranean Expeditionary Force, Aug. 20, 1915; Killed in action, Suvla Bay, Dec. 2, 1915.

19 NEWFOUNDLAND 14

Francis Herbert Knight   Reg. No. 287

Enlisted, Sept. 8, 1914; Lance Corporal, April 15, 1915; 2nd Lieutenant, April 22, 1915; British Mediterranean Expeditionary Force, Aug. 20, 1915; Lieutenant, Jan. 1, 1916; British Expeditionary Force, March 14, 1916; Wounded, Beaumont Hamel, July 1, 1916; Invalided to England, July 11, 1916; Returned to Newfoundland, July 20, 1916; Retired, Dec. 22, 1916.

William Knight   Reg. No. 373

Enlisted, Sept. 7, 1914; British Mediterranean Expeditionary Force, Aug. 20, 1915; Admitted to Hospital, Cairo, Jan. 20, 1916; British Expeditionary Force, May 8, 1916; Joined Battalion, June 9, 1916; Killed in action, Beaumont Hamel, July 1, 1916.

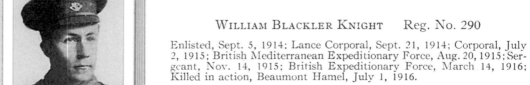

William Blackler Knight   Reg. No. 290

Enlisted, Sept. 5, 1914; Lance Corporal, Sept. 21, 1914; Corporal, July 2, 1915; British Mediterranean Expeditionary Force, Aug. 20, 1915; Sergeant, Nov. 14, 1915; British Expeditionary Force, March 14, 1916; Killed in action, Beaumont Hamel, July 1, 1916.

19 14

ROLAND STEPHEN LACEY   Reg. No. 77

Enlisted, Sept. 4, 1914; British Mediterranean Expeditionary Force, Aug. 20, 1915; Lance Corporal, February 3, 1916; British Expeditionary Force, March 23, 1916; Wounded, Beaumont Hamel, July 1, 1916; Repatriated to Newfoundland, June 6, 1917; Discharged, St. John's, medically unfit, July 11, 1917.

EDWARD LAHEY   Reg. No. 259

Enlisted, Sept. 2, 1914; British Mediterranean Expeditionary Force, Aug. 20, 1915; British Expeditionary Force, March 14, 1916; Lance Corporal, Aug. 11, 1916; Corporal, Sept. 28, 1916; Evacuated to Hospital, Nov. 14, 1916; Evacuated to England, Nov. 15, 1916; Attached to Depot, Ayr, Feb. 24, 1917; Embarked for Newfoundland, March 23, 1917; Discharged, St. John's, medically unfit, May 9, 1917.

ROBERT JOSEPH LAHEY   Reg. No. 254

Enlisted, Sept. 2, 1914; British Mediterranean Expeditionary Force, Aug. 20, 1915; Wounded, Suvla, Nov. 28, 1915; Rejoined Battalion Suez, Jan. 16, 1916; British Expeditionary Force, March 14, 1916; Killed in action, Beaumont Hamel, July 1, 1916.

THE BAND

1914

James Lambert   Reg. No. 387

Enlisted, Sept. 7, 1914; British Mediterranean Expeditionary Force, Aug. 20, 1915; Lance Corporal, Nov. 14, 1915; British Expeditionary Force, March 14, 1916; Wounded, Beaumont Hamel, July 1, 1916; Invalided to England, July 3, 1916; Attached to Depot, Ayr, Aug. 11, 1916; Attached to Pay and Record Office, London, Aug. 17, 1916; Acting Corporal, Dec. 23, 1916; Acting Staff Sergeant, Nov. 24, 1917; Acting Quartermaster Sergeant, Nov. 23, 1918; Appointed Superintending Clerk, April 12, 1919; Acting Staff Sergeant Major, June 25, 1919; Awarded Meritorious Service Medal, June 3, 1919; Still on Strength.

George Langmead, Jr.   Reg. No. 14

Enlisted, Sept. 2, 1914; Sergeant, Sept. 21, 1914; Company Quartermaster Sergeant, July 31, 1915; British Mediterranean Expeditionary Force, Aug. 20, 1915; British Expeditionary Force, March 14, 1916; Wounded, Beaumont Hamel, July 1, 1916; Commission, 2nd Lieutenant, July 1, 1916; Invalided to England, July 4, 1916; British Expeditionary Force, March 12, 1917; Lieutenant, Nov. 1, 1917; Wounded, Mesnieres, Dec. 2, 1917; Died of wounds, Dec. 8, 1917.

Cyril Larner   Reg. No. 426

Enlisted, Sept. 2, 1914; Admitted to Hospital, Edinburgh, May 18, 1915; Discharged to duty, Sept. 18, 1915; Recommended for discharge, medically unfit, Oct. 7, 1915; Embarked for Newfoundland, Oct. 15, 1915; Discharged, St. John's, medically unfit, with effect, Oct. 15, 1915.

EDWARD JOSEPH LAWLOR   Reg. No. 477

Enlisted, Sept. 9, 1914; Struck off Strength, Newton-on-Ayr, Nov. 26, 1915.

THOMAS JOSEPH LAWLOR   Reg. No. 535

Enlisted, Sept. 16, 1914; Lance Corporal, Nov. 12, 1915; Acting Corporal, Dec. 5, 1915; Acting Sergeant, Armourer 2nd Battalion, Feb. 3, 1916; Confirmed to rank, April 27, 1918; Awarded Meritorious Service Medal, June 3, 1919; Demobilized in England, June 9, 1919.

FREDERICK LeGROW   Reg. No. 9

Enlisted, Sept. 2, 1914; British Mediterranean Expeditionary Force, Aug. 20, 1915; British Expeditionary Force, Sept. 7, 1917; Wounded, Broembeek, Oct. 9, 1917; Returned to British Expeditionary Force, April 4, 1918; Demobilized, St. John's, Feb. 15, 1919.

Frederick Pratt LeGrow   Reg. No. 404

Enlisted, Sept. 14, 1914; Lance Corporal, July 20, 1915; British Mediterranean Expeditionary Force, Aug. 20, 1915; Evacuated from Suvla, Dec. 3, 1915; Invalided to England, Dec. 24, 1915; Attached to Depot, Feb. 15, 1916; Sergeant, April 20, 1916; Acting Company Sergeant Major, Aug. 21, 1916; British Expeditionary Force, Oct. 3, 1916; Confirmed to rank, Nov. 20, 1917; Wounded, Marcoing, Nov. 20, 1917; Invalided to England, Nov. 28, 1917; Discharged from Hospital, July 25, 1918; Embarked for Newfoundland, July 27, 1918; Discharged, St. John's, medically unfit, Sept. 28, 1918; Reattached for special duty at Department of Militia, Feb. 1, 1919; Staff Sergeant Major, Feb. 1, 1919; Discharged, St. John's, July 2, 1919.

Roy Bennett Leseman   Reg. No. 220

Enlisted, Sept. 3, 1914; British Mediterranean Expeditionary Force, Aug. 20, 1915; Evacuated from Suvla, Oct. 12, 1915; Invalided to England, Oct. 27, 1915; Attached to Second Battalion, Jan. 3, 1916; Lance Corporal, Oct. 27, 1916; Acting Corporal, Nov. 16, 1916; Returned to Newfoundland, furlough, Jan. 27, 1918; Confirmed to rank, April 27, 1918; Embarked for United Kingdom, Oct. 19, 1918; Demobilized, United Kingdom, March 7, 1919.

Philip S. LeMessurier   Reg. No. 62

Enlisted, Sept. 2, 1914; British Mediterranean Expeditionary Force, Aug. 20, 1915; Wounded, Suvla, Nov. 23, 1915; Evacuated to England, Nov. 24, 1915; Lance Corporal, Feb. 3, 1916; Corporal, Aug. 11, 1916; Acting Sergeant, Nov. 16, 1916; Second Lieutenant, May 18, 1917; Returned to Newfoundland, furlough, July 21, 1918; Lieutenant, Nov. 18, 1918; Retired and placed on reserve of officers, June 17, 1919.

19 14

David Lewis   Reg. No. 96

Enlisted, Sept. 2, 1914; British Mediterranean Expeditionary Force, Aug. 20, 1915; Invalided to England, Dec. 25, 1915; British Expeditionary Force, Aug. 18, 1917; Embarked for Newfoundland, furlough, July 27, 1918; Demobilized, St. John's, Feb. 15, 1919.

John Lewis   Reg. No. 189

Enlisted, Sept. 3, 1914; British Mediterranean Expeditionary Force, Aug. 20, 1915; British Expeditionary Force, March 14, 1916; Wounded, Beaumont Hamel, July 1, 1916; Invalided to England, July 4, 1916; Discharged, United Kingdom, medically unfit, Feb. 23, 1918.

Harold Lidstone   Reg. No. 163

Enlisted, Sept. 3, 1914; British Mediterranean Expeditionary Force, Aug. 20, 1915; British Expeditionary Force, March 14, 1916; Evacuated to England, sick, Aug. 12, 1916; Lance Corporal, Jan. 17, 1917; Returned to British Expeditionary Force, April 25, 1917; Joined Battalion in Field, June 7, 1917; Corporal, Sept. 17, 1917; Awarded Military Medal, Sept. 17, 1917; Killed in action, Marcoing, Nov. 20, 1917.

Augustus Lilly   Reg. No. 194

Enlisted, Sept. 3, 1914; British Mediterranean Expeditionary Force, Nov. 14, 1915; British Expeditionary Force, March 14, 1916; Killed in action, Beaumont Hamel, July 1, 1916.

Frank Thomas Lind   Reg. No. 541

Enlisted, Sept. 16, 1914; British Mediterranean Expeditionary Force, Aug. 20, 1915; Evacuated from Suvla, Dec. 8, 1915; Admitted to Hospital, Malta, Jan. 18, 1916; Discharged to duty, March 4, 1916; British Expeditionary Force, March 4, 1916; Rejoined Battalion, April 15, 1916; Killed in action, Beaumont Hamel, July 1, 1916.

Samuel Thomas Lodge   Reg. No. 165

Enlisted, Sept. 2, 1914; British Mediterranean Expeditionary Force, Aug. 20, 1915; Killed in action, Suvla Bay, Oct. 1, 1915.

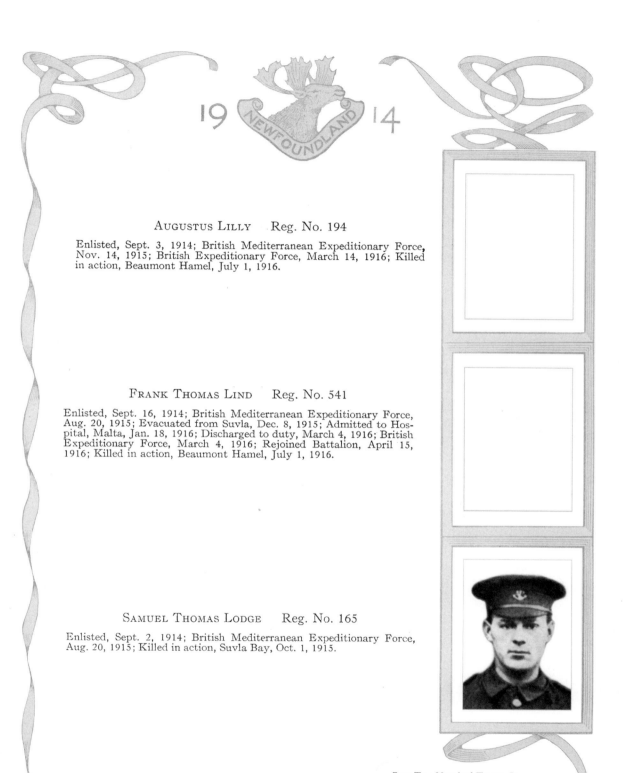

19 NEWFOUNDLAND 14

WILLIAM JOHN LONG   Reg. No. 48

Enlisted, Sept. 2, 1914; British Mediterranean Expeditionary Force, Aug. 20, 1915; Returned to Newfoundland, furlough, Jan. 13, 1916; Acting Sergeant, May 9, 1916; Acting Company Sergeant Major, June 9, 1916; 2nd Lieutenant, Nov. 1, 1916; Returned to England and attached to Depot, Ayr, July 27, 1916; British Expeditionary Force, May 12, 1917; Wounded, Marcoing, Nov. 20, 1917; Lieutenant, May 1, 1918; Retired and placed on reserve of officers, July 29, 1919.

JAMES NEWTON LOVEYS   Reg. No. 359

Enlisted, Sept. 11, 1914; British Mediterranean Expeditionary Force, Aug. 20, 1915; Evacuated from Suvla, Oct. 29, 1915; Invalided to England, Dec. 5, 1915; Attached to Depot, Ayr, Feb. 5, 1916; British Expeditionary Force, Jan. 31, 1917; Wounded, LesFosses Farm, April 23, 1917; Invalided to England, May 1, 1917; Attached to Depot, Ayr, July 7, 1917; Appointed Masseur, July 7, 1917; Lance Corporal July 24, 1917; Embarked for Newfoundland, furlough, July 21, 1918; Discharged, St. John's, medically unfit, Dec. 19, 1918.

GEORGE LUKINS   Reg. No. 544

Enlisted, Sept. 16, 1914; British Mediterranean Expeditionary Force, Aug. 20, 1915; British Expeditionary Force, March 14, 1916; Killed in action, Beaumont Hamel, July 1, 1916.

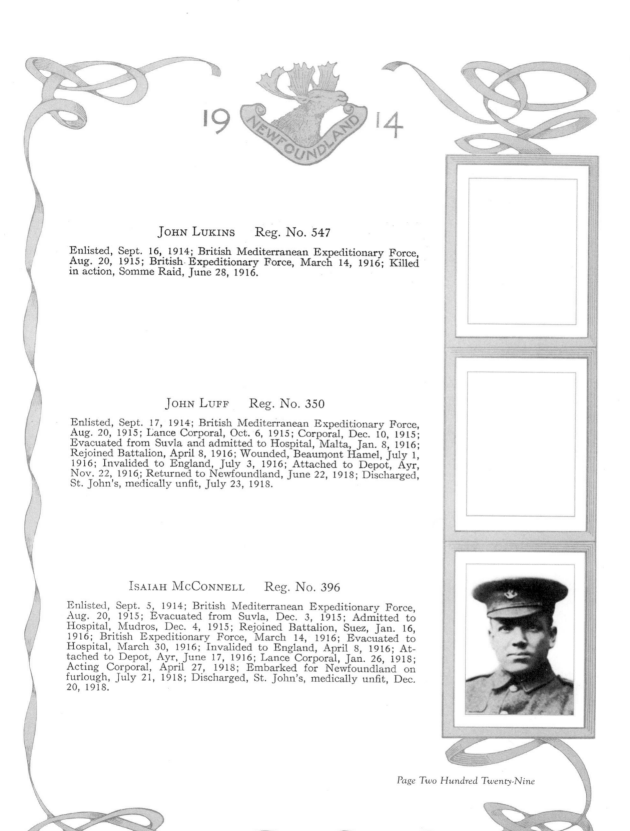

John Lukins   Reg. No. 547

Enlisted, Sept. 16, 1914; British Mediterranean Expeditionary Force, Aug. 20, 1915; British Expeditionary Force, March 14, 1916; Killed in action, Somme Raid, June 28, 1916.

John Luff   Reg. No. 350

Enlisted, Sept. 17, 1914; British Mediterranean Expeditionary Force, Aug. 20, 1915; Lance Corporal, Oct. 6, 1915; Corporal, Dec. 10, 1915; Evacuated from Suvla and admitted to Hospital, Malta, Jan. 8, 1916; Rejoined Battalion, April 8, 1916; Wounded, Beaumont Hamel, July 1, 1916; Invalided to England, July 3, 1916; Attached to Depot, Ayr, Nov. 22, 1916; Returned to Newfoundland, June 22, 1918; Discharged, St. John's, medically unfit, July 23, 1918.

Isaiah McConnell   Reg. No. 396

Enlisted, Sept. 5, 1914; British Mediterranean Expeditionary Force, Aug. 20, 1915; Evacuated from Suvla, Dec. 3, 1915; Admitted to Hospital, Mudros, Dec. 4, 1915; Rejoined Battalion, Suez, Jan. 16, 1916; British Expeditionary Force, March 14, 1916; Evacuated to Hospital, March 30, 1916; Invalided to England, April 8, 1916; Attached to Depot, Ayr, June 17, 1916; Lance Corporal, Jan. 26, 1918; Acting Corporal, April 27, 1918; Embarked for Newfoundland on furlough, July 21, 1918; Discharged, St. John's, medically unfit, Dec. 20, 1918.

PATRICK McDONALD   Reg. No. 230

Enlisted, Sept. 2, 1914; British Expeditionary Force, Dec. 12, 1916; Wounded, Broembeek, Oct. 9, 1917; Invalided to England, Oct. 19, 1917; Attached to Depot, Ayr, Nov. 28, 1917; Lance Corporal, Jan. 11, 1918; Awarded Military Medal, Jan. 14, 1918; Acting Corporal, March 19, 1918; Returned to Newfoundland, furlough, July 21, 1918; Embarked for United Kingdom, Oct. 19, 1918; Demobilized, United Kingdom, March 6, 1919.

JOHN PATRICK MacDONNELL   Reg. No. 582

Enlisted, Sept. 22, 1914; British Mediterranean Expeditionary Force, Aug. 20, 1915; Evacuated from Suvla, Oct. 20, 1915; Admitted 17th General Hospital, Alexandria, Oct. 25, 1915; Died of Dysentery, Oct. 29, 1915.

JAMES McGRATH   Reg. No. 104

Enlisted, Sept. 6, 1914; British Mediterranean Expeditionary Force, Aug. 20, 1915; Evacuated to England, Dec. 26, 1915; Returned to Newfoundland, furlough, July 10, 1917; Attached to Department of Militia, Nov. 1, 1917; Still on Strength.

Thomas Bernard McGrath   Reg. No. 128

Enlisted, Sept. 6, 1914; British Mediterranean Expeditionary Force, Nov. 14, 1915; British Expeditionary Force, March 14, 1916; Wounded, Beaumont Hamel, July 1, 1916; Evacuated to England, July 4, 1916; Returned to Newfoundland, furlough, Oct. 10, 1916; Lance Corporal, April 24, 1917; Acting Corporal, June 14, 1917; Embarked for United Kingdom, Aug. 4, 1917; Acting Sergeant, Sept. 9, 1917; Transferred to Forestry Company, Sept. 20, 1917; Second Lieutenant in Forestry Company, Feb. 1, 1918; Retired, Feb. 25, 1919.

Andrew Joseph McKay   Reg. No. 572

Enlisted, Sept. 17, 1914; British Mediterranean Expeditionary Force, Aug. 20, 1915; British Expeditionary Force, March 14, 1916; Wounded, Beaumont Hamel, July 1, 1916; Admitted 8th Stationary Hospital, Wimereux, July 3, 1916; Died of wounds, July 12, 1916.

John J. Mackey   Reg. No. 278

Enlisted, Sept. 8, 1914; British Mediterranean Expeditionary Force Sept. 20, 1915; Admitted Hospital, Mudros, Dec. 20, 1915; Rejoined Battalion, March 1, 1916; British Expeditionary Force, March 14, 1916; Wounded, Beaumont Hamel, July 1, 1916; Invalided to England, July 4, 1916; Returned to British Expeditionary Force, March 25, 1917; Admitted to Hospital, Rouen, April 16, 1917; Rejoined Battalion, June 11, 1917; Wounded, Steenbeke, Aug. 16, 1917; Invalided to England, Aug. 21, 1917; Attached to Depot, Ayr, Nov. 27, 1917; Repatriated to Newfoundland, Jan. 30, 1919; Demobilized, St. John's March 14, 1919.

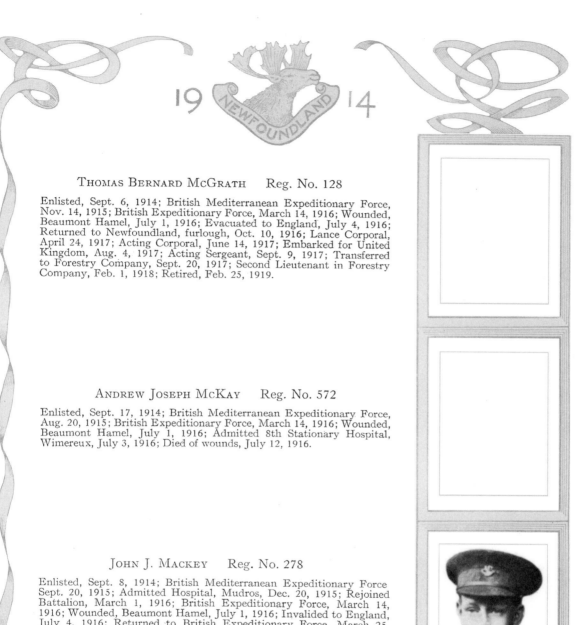

NEIL McLELLAN   Reg. No. 50

Enlisted, Sept. 2, 1914; Attached to Pay and Record Office, London, Feb. 5, 1915; Corporal, Sept. 4, 1915; Acting Staff Sergeant, June 10, 1916; Reverts to ranks at own request to proceed on Active Service, August 12, 1916; Lance Corporal, Sept. 9, 1916; British Expeditionary Force, Oct. 3, 1916; Corporal, Nov. 1, 1917; Prisoner of War, Wounded, Captured at Mesnieres, Dec. 3, 1917; Repatriated to England via Copenhagen, Dec. 16, 1918; Demobilized, St. John's, Aug. 11, 1919.

ERNEST FREDERICK McLEOD   Reg. No. 24

Enlisted, Sept. 2, 1914; British Mediterranean Expeditionary Force, Aug. 20, 1915; British Expeditionary Force, March 14, 1916; Invalided to England, Oct. 8, 1917; Demobilized, March 13, 1919.

NORMAN A. McLEOD   Reg. No. 158

Enlisted, Sept. 5, 1914; Sergeant, Sept. 21, 1914; British Mediterranean Expeditionary Force, Aug. 20, 1915; Company Quartermaster Sergeant, Nov. 14, 1915; Wounded, Suvla, Dec. 1, 1915; Evacuated to England, April 7, 1916; Returned to Newfoundland, furlough, June 29, 1916; Returned to England, Sept. 30, 1916; British Expeditionary Force, April 23, 1917; Wounded, Marcoing, Nov. 20, 1917; Evacuated to England, Dec. 8, 1917; 2nd Lieutenant, May 1, 1918; Lieutenant, May 1, 1918; Returned to Newfoundland, May 22, 1919; Retired and placed on Reserve of Officers, July 5, 1919.

Hector McNeil   Reg. No. 31

Enlisted, Sept. 2, 1914; Regimental Quartermaster Sergeant, Sept. 21, 1914; British Mediterranean Expeditionary Force, Aug. 20, 1915; British Expeditionary Force, March 14, 1916; Acting Quartermaster, July 12, 1916; Hon. Lieutenant Quartermaster, Nov. 26, 1916; Captain Quartermaster, July 23, 1918; Embarked for Newfoundland, furlough, July 24, 1918; Returned to United Kingdom, Nov. 27, 1918; Returned to British Expeditionary Force, Dec. 8, 1918; Mentioned in Despatches, March 16, 1919; Awarded O. B. E., June 3, 1919; Still on Strength.

Donald Fraser McNeill   Reg. No. 411

Enlisted, Sept. 8, 1914; British Mediterranean Expeditionary Force, Aug. 20, 1915; Evacuated from Suvla, Nov. 26, 1915; Invalided to England, Jan. 3, 1916; Attached to Depot, Ayr, Feb. 3, 1916; Wounded, Beaumont Hamel, July 1, 1916; Admitted 19th Casualty Clearing Station, July 2, 1916; Died of Wounds, July 6, 1916.

William Robert McNiven   Reg. No. 279

Enlisted, Sept. 7, 1914; British Mediterranean Expeditionary Force, Aug. 20, 1915; Evacuated from Suvla, Oct. 2, 1915; Rejoined Battalion, Jan. 26, 1916; British Expeditionary Force, March 14, 1916; Killed in action, Beaumont Hamel, July 1, 1916.

SYLVESTER MADDEN   Reg. No. 149

Enlisted, Sept. 7, 1914; British Mediterranean Expeditionary Force, Aug. 20, 1915; Evacuated to England, Jan. 24, 1916; Returned to Newfoundland, furlough, Sept. 8, 1916; Attached to Depot for duty, Jan. 5, 1917; Demobilized, St. John's, Feb. 25, 1919.

HENRY MORTON MADDICK   Reg. No. 140

Enlisted, Sept. 4, 1914; Lance Corporal, June 19, 1915; British Mediterranean Expeditionary Force, Aug. 20, 1915; Corporal, Nov. 15, 1915; Sergeant, Feb. 27, 1916; British Expeditionary Force, March 14, 1916; 2nd Lieutenant, June 11, 1916; Wounded, Beaumont Hamel, July 1, 1916; Evacuated to England, July 10, 1916; Repatriated to Newfoundland, Dec. 15, 1916; Retired, May 23, 1917; Placed on active list for duty at Department of Militia, Dec. 11, 1917; Lieutenant, Jan. 1, 1918; Captain, June 1, 1919.

MICHAEL MADDIGAN   Reg. No. 47

Enlisted, Sept. 2, 1914; British Mediterranean Expeditionary Force, Aug. 20, 1915; British Expeditionary Force, March 14, 1916; Wounded, Monchy, April 14, 1917; Invalided to England; Returned to B. E. F., Feb. 18, 1918; Transferred to England, "Permanent Base", March 8, 1918; Discharged, medically unfit, Sept. 28, 1918.

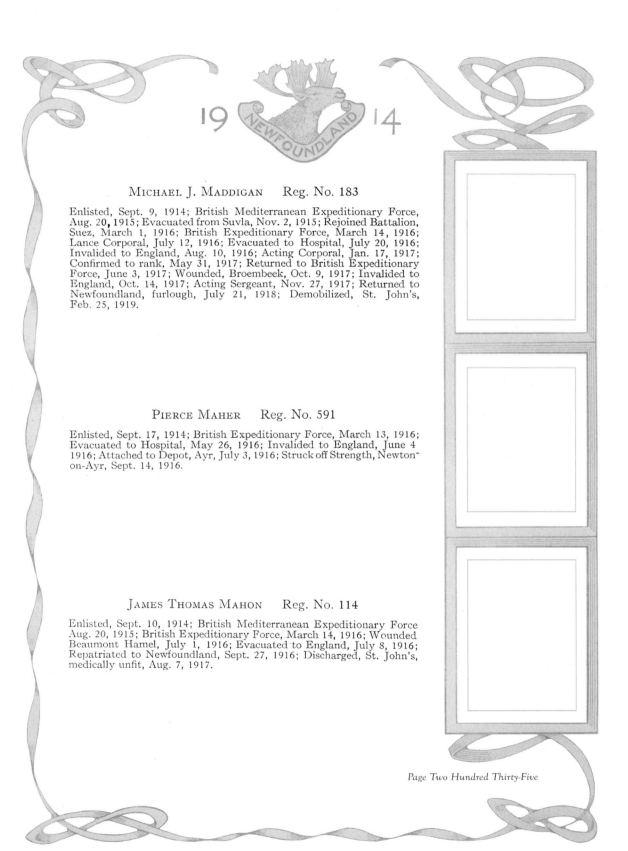

Michael J. Maddigan   Reg. No. 183

Enlisted, Sept. 9, 1914; British Mediterranean Expeditionary Force, Aug. 20, 1915; Evacuated from Suvla, Nov. 2, 1915; Rejoined Battalion, Suez, March 1, 1916; British Expeditionary Force, March 14, 1916; Lance Corporal, July 12, 1916; Evacuated to Hospital, July 20, 1916; Invalided to England, Aug. 10, 1916; Acting Corporal, Jan. 17, 1917; Confirmed to rank, May 31, 1917; Returned to British Expeditionary Force, June 3, 1917; Wounded, Broembeek, Oct. 9, 1917; Invalided to England, Oct. 14, 1917; Acting Sergeant, Nov. 27, 1917; Returned to Newfoundland, furlough, July 21, 1918; Demobilized, St. John's, Feb. 25, 1919.

Pierce Maher   Reg. No. 591

Enlisted, Sept. 17, 1914; British Expeditionary Force, March 13, 1916; Evacuated to Hospital, May 26, 1916; Invalided to England, June 4 1916; Attached to Depot, Ayr, July 3, 1916; Struck off Strength, Newton-on-Ayr, Sept. 14, 1916.

James Thomas Mahon   Reg. No. 114

Enlisted, Sept. 10, 1914; British Mediterranean Expeditionary Force Aug. 20, 1915; British Expeditionary Force, March 14, 1916; Wounded Beaumont Hamel, July 1, 1916; Evacuated to England, July 8, 1916; Repatriated to Newfoundland, Sept. 27, 1916; Discharged, St. John's, medically unfit, Aug. 7, 1917.

Allan W. Mallam   Reg. No. 413

Enlisted, Sept. 7, 1914; Struck off Strength, Newton-on-Ayr, Oct. 15, 1915.

Joseph Francis Maloney   Reg. No. 385

Enlisted, Sept. 7, 1914; Lance Corporal, Nov. 4, 1915; British Mediterranean Expeditionary Force, Nov. 14, 1915; Evacuated Suvla, sick, Jan. 4, 1916; Invalided to England, Jan. 24, 1916; Attached to Depot, Ayr, March 4, 1916; Repatriated to Newfoundland, May 18, 1917; Discharged, St. John's, medically unfit, June 20, 1917.

Augustus Joseph Manning   Reg. No. 177

Enlisted, Sept. 3, 1914; Lance Corporal, Sept. 21, 1914; Corporal, April 23, 1915; British Mediterranean Expeditionary Force, Aug. 20, 1915; Sergeant, Sept. 26, 1915; Evacuated from Suvla, Nov. 1, 1915; Rejoined Battalion, Suez, Jan. 26, 1916; British Expeditionary Force, March 14, 1916; Killed in action, Somme, June 1, 1916.

1914

PETER MANSFIELD   Reg. No. 85

Enlisted, Sept. 7, 1914; Embarked for United Kingdom, Oct. 24, 1914; Lance Corporal, Dec. 5, 1915; British Expeditionary Force, March 28, 1916; Invalided to England, Oct. 12, 1916; Acting Corporal, Jan. 17, 1917; Embarked for Newfoundland, June 6, 1917; Discharged, St. John's, medically unfit, March 26, 1918.

WILLIAM MANSTON   Reg. No. 327

Enlisted, Sept. 8, 1914; Lance Corporal, Sept. 26, 1914; Corporal, April 23, 1915; Sergeant, July 10, 1915; British Mediterranean Expeditionary Force, Aug. 20, 1915; Evacuated from Suvla, Dec. 6, 1915; Invalided to England, Dec. 26, 1915; Repatriated to Newfoundland, March 23, 1916; Attached to Depot, April 10, 1916; Discharged, St. John's, medically unfit, Sept. 12, 1916.

WILLIS MANUEL   Reg. No. 272

Enlisted, Sept. 2, 1914; Lance Corporal, Nov. 4, 1915; British Mediterranean Expeditionary Force, Nov. 14, 1915; Admitted Hospital, Suez, Feb. 26, 1916; Discharged to Base Depot, Alexandria, March 31, 1916; Rejoined Battalion, France, May 9, 1916; Wounded, Beaumont Hamel, July 1, 1916; Invalided to England, July 4, 1916; Repatriated to Newfoundland, Sept. 13, 1917; Discharged, St. John's, medically unfit, Feb. 16, 1918.

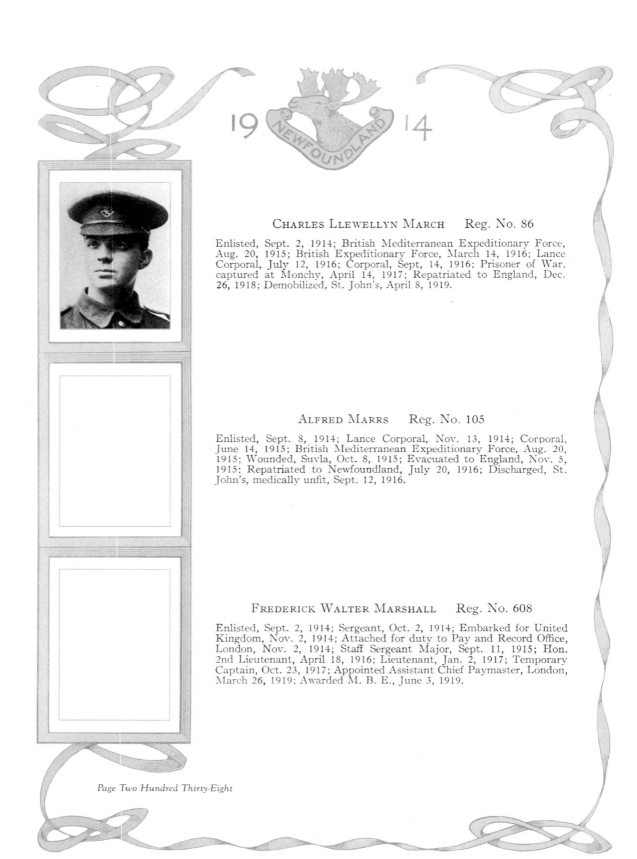

CHARLES LLEWELLYN MARCH   Reg. No. 86

Enlisted, Sept. 2, 1914; British Mediterranean Expeditionary Force, Aug. 20, 1915; British Expeditionary Force, March 14, 1916; Lance Corporal, July 12, 1916; Corporal, Sept, 14, 1916; Prisoner of War, captured at Monchy, April 14, 1917; Repatriated to England, Dec. 26, 1918; Demobilized, St. John's, April 8, 1919.

ALFRED MARRS   Reg. No. 105

Enlisted, Sept. 8, 1914; Lance Corporal, Nov. 13, 1914; Corporal, June 14, 1915; British Mediterranean Expeditionary Force, Aug. 20, 1915; Wounded, Suvla, Oct. 8, 1915; Evacuated to England, Nov. 5, 1915; Repatriated to Newfoundland, July 20, 1916; Discharged, St. John's, medically unfit, Sept. 12, 1916.

FREDERICK WALTER MARSHALL   Reg. No. 608

Enlisted, Sept. 2, 1914; Sergeant, Oct. 2, 1914; Embarked for United Kingdom, Nov. 2, 1914; Attached for duty to Pay and Record Office, London, Nov. 2, 1914; Staff Sergeant Major, Sept. 11, 1915; Hon. 2nd Lieutenant, April 18, 1916; Lieutenant, Jan. 2, 1917; Temporary Captain, Oct. 23, 1917; Appointed Assistant Chief Paymaster, London, March 26, 1919; Awarded M. B. E., June 3, 1919.

1914

CHARLES P. MARTIN   Reg. No. 192

Enlisted, Sept. 3, 1914; British Mediterranean Expeditionary Force, Aug. 20, 1915; Wounded, Suvla, Nov. 1, 1915; Discharged to duty, Dec. 20, 1915; British Expeditionary Force, March 18, 1916; Rejoined Battalion, April 15, 1916; Lance Corporal, Aug. 8, 1916; Corporal, Nov. 23, 1916; Prisoner of War, captured at Monchy, April 14, 1917; Repatriated to England, Dec. 31, 1918; Returned to Newfoundland, March 12, 1919; Demobilized, St. John's, April 21, 1919; Reattested for duty, Depot, May 27, 1919; Demobilized Aug. 30, 1919.

ERIC S. MARTIN   Reg. No. 616

Enlisted, Oct. 2, 1914; British Mediterranean Expeditionary Force, Aug. 20, 1915; Wounded, Suvla, Oct. 17, 1915; Admitted Hospital, Cairo, Oct. 24, 1915; Rejoined Battalion, Suez, March 1, 1916; British Expeditionary Force, March 14, 1916; Killed in action, Beaumont Hamel, July 1, 1916.

ROBERT BERKLEY MARTIN   Reg. No. 499

Enlisted, Sept. 19, 1914; British Mediterranean Expeditionary Force, Aug. 20, 1915; Evacuated Suvla, sick, Oct. 5, 1915; Admitted Hospital, Alexandria, Oct. 10, 1915; Invalided to England, Dec. 6, 1915; Attached to Depot, Ayr, Feb. 2, 1916; Lance Corporal, March 30, 1916; Acting Corporal, Jan. 17, 1917; British Expeditionary Force, Feb. 8, 1918; Rejoined Battalion, Feb. 20, 1918; Evacuated to Hospital, Feb. 26, 1918; Rejoined Battalion, May 4, 1918; Embarked for Newfoundland, furlough, July 27, 1918; Demobilized, Feb. 15, 1919.

CHURCH LADS BRIGADE GROUP

19 14

RONALD MARTIN   Reg. No. 75

Enlisted, Sept. 2, 1914; British Mediterranean Expeditionary Force, Aug. 20, 1915; Invalided to England, Jan. 2, 1916; Attached for duty to Pay and Record Office, London, June 16, 1916; Acting Corporal, Dec. 23, 1916; Acting Sergeant, Nov. 24, 1917; Acting Staff Sergeant, Dec. 21, 1918.

HAROLD WALTER MATTHEWS   Reg. No. 358

Enlisted, Sept. 5, 1914; British Mediterranean Expeditionary Force, Aug. 20, 1915; Evacuated from Suvla, Dec. 1, 1915; Invalided to England, Dec. 26, 1915; Embarked for Newfoundland, Sept, 5, 1916; Discharged, St. John's, medically unfit, Feb. 3, 1917.

THOMAS MOULAND   Reg. No. 488

Enlisted, Sept. 11, 1914; British Mediterranean Expeditionary Force, Aug. 20, 1915; Wounded, Cape Helles, Jan. 7, 1916; Admitted Hospital, Malta, Jan. 13, 1916; Invalided to England, May 12, 1916; Admitted St. Dunstan's Hospital for the Blind, Aug. 19, 1916; Discharged, United Kingdom, medically unfit, June 15, 1917.

WILLIAM MAY   Reg. No. 351

Enlisted, Sept. 4, 1914; British Mediterranean Expeditionary Force, Aug. 20, 1915; Evacuated from Suvla, Nov. 11, 1915; Discharged from duty, Feb. 11, 1916; Readmitted to Hospital, Feb. 17, 1916; Invalided to England, April 23, 1916; Attached to Depot, Ayr, Aug. 3, 1916; British Expeditionary Force, Aug. 5, 1917; Admitted Hospital, Dec. 23, 1917; Rejoined Battalion, April 2, 1918; Admitted Hospital, May 2, 1918; Invalided to England, May 15, 1918; Discharged for duty, July 11, 1918; Embarked for Newfoundland, furlough, July 21, 1918; Demobilized, St. John's, Feb. 15, 1919.

CONSTANTINE MAYER   Reg. No. 175

Enlisted, Sept. 3, 1914; Struck off Strength, Newton-on-Ayr, Oct. 15, 1915, time expired.

ALLAN MOYES   Reg. No. 546

Enlisted, Sept. 16, 1914; British Mediterranean Expeditionary Force, Aug. 20, 1915; Admitted Hospital, Alexandria, Oct. 27, 1915; Rejoined Battalion, Suez, Jan. 31, 1916; Admitted Hospital, Suez, Feb. 27, 1916; Rejoined Battalion, March 4, 1916; British Expeditionary Force, March 14, 1916; Killed in action, Beaumont Hamel, July 1, 1916.

Frederick Courtney Mellor   Reg. No. 91

Enlisted, Sept. 2, 1914; 2nd Lieutenant, April 22, 1915; Lieutenant, Oct. 16, 1915; British Expeditionary Force, March 23, 1916; Killed in action, Beaumont Hamel, July 1, 1916.

Albert Mercer   Reg. No. 264

Enlisted, Sept. 2, 1914; British Mediterranean Expeditionary Force, Aug. 20, 1915; Evacuated from Suvla, Oct. 11, 1915; Rejoined Battalion, Suez, Jan. 31, 1916; British Expeditionary Force, March 14, 1916; Wounded, Beaumont Hamel, July 1, 1916; Invalided to England, July 4, 1916; Attached to Depot, Ayr, Aug. 11, 1916; British Expeditionary Force, Feb. 10, 1917; Rejoined Battalion in field, June 19, 1917; Wounded, Steenbeke, Aug. 16, 1917; Invalided to England, Aug. 25, 1917; Repatriated to Newfoundland, Feb. 23, 1918; Discharged, St John's, medically unfit, April 10, 1918.

Frederick Mercer   Reg. No. 159

Enlisted, Sept. 2, 1914; Corporal, Sept. 21, 1914; Sergeant, Aug. 14, 1915; British Mediterranean Expeditionary Force, Aug. 20, 1915; British Expeditionary Force, March 14, 1916; Wounded, Beaumont Hamel, July 1, 1916; Evacuated to England, July 5, 1916; Returned to Newfoundland, furlough, Oct. 28, 1916; Returned to England, Jan. 21, 1917; Returned to British Expeditionary Force, July 25, 1918; Wounded, Ledgeham, Oct. 14, 1918; Company Sergeant Major, Dec. 4, 1918; Mentioned in Despatches of Sir Douglas Haig, March 16, 1919; Transferred to England, April 23, 1919; Returned to Newfoundland, May 22, 1919; Demobilized, St. John's, June 29, 1919.

Albert Edward Metcalfe   Reg. No. 256

Enlisted, Sept. 2, 1914; British Mediterranean Expeditionary Force, Aug. 20, 1915; Evacuated from Suvla, Oct. 21, 1915; Rejoined Battalion, Suez, March 7, 1916; British Expeditionary Force, March 14, 1916; Wounded, Beaumont Hamel, July 1, 1916; Invalided to England, July 3, 1916; Repatriated to Newfoundland, Oct. 28, 1916; Discharged, St. John's, medically unfit, April 4, 1917.

James Mifflin   Reg. No. 419

Enlisted, Sept. 3, 1914; Lance Corporal, June 14, 1915; British Mediterranean Expeditionary Force, Aug. 20, 1915; Evacuated from Suvla, Oct. 17, 1915; Invalided to England, Nov. 1, 1915; Corporal, April 20, 1916; Attached to Depot, Ayr, April 28, 1916; Acting Sergeant, Aug. 11, 1916; 2nd Lieutenant, Nov. 1, 1916; British Expeditionary Force, April 23, 1917; Lieutenant, March 18, 1918; Wounded, Haslar Camp, Belgium, March 27, 1918; Awarded Military Cross, March 29, 1918; Invalided to England, April 3, 1918; Discharged from Hospital, June 22, 1918; Embarked for Newfoundland, furlough, July 21, 1918; Returned to United Kingdom, Oct. 19, 1918; Returned to British Expeditionary Force, Nov. 19, 1918; Rejoined Battalion, Nov. 26, 1918; Embarked for Newfoundland, May 22, 1919; Retired and placed on Reserve of Officers, June 20, 1919.

Victor William Miles   Reg. No. 214

Enlisted, Sept. 8, 1914; Sergeant, Sept. 21, 1914; Company Quartermaster Sergeant, May 6, 1915; Evacuated from Suvla, Oct. 11, 1915; Rejoined Battalion, Suez, Jan. 26, 1916; Acting Company Sergeant Major, May 29, 1916; Confirmed to rank, June 11, 1916; Killed in action, Beaumont Hamel, July 1, 1916.

19 14

BENJAMIN MILLER   Reg. No. 300

Enlisted, Sept. 8, 1914; British Mediterranean Expeditionary Force, Aug. 20. 1915; Evacuated from Suvla, Dec. 2, 1915; Invalided to England, Jan. 12, 1916; Attached to Depot, Ayr, March 13, 1916; British Expeditionary Force, March 28, 1916; Rejoined Battalion, April 15, 1916; Lance Corporal, Aug. 11, 1916; Wounded, Gueudecourt, Oct. 12, 1916; Invalided to England, Oct. 22, 1916; Attached to Depot, Ayr, Jan. 19, 1917; Returned to British Expeditionary Force, April 25, 1917; Rejoined Battalion, June 7, 1917; Corporal, June 14, 1917; Killed in action, Broembeek, Oct. 9, 1917.

GEORGE MILLER   Reg. No. 587

Enlisted, Sept. 24, 1914; British Mediterranean Expeditionary Force, Nov. 14, 1915; British Expeditionary Force, March 14, 1916; Killed in action, Beaumont Hamel, July 1, 1916.

WILLIAM MILLER   Reg. No. 107

Enlisted, Sept. 2, 1914; British Mediterranean Expeditionary Force, Aug. 20, 1915; Wounded, Suvla, Oct. 17, 1915; Died of Wounds and buried at sea, Hospital Ship "Galeka," Oct. 18, 1915.

JOSEPH MILLEY   Reg. No. 85

Enlisted, Sept. 7, 1914; British Mediterranean Expeditionary Force, Aug. 20, 1915; Evacuated to England, Jan. 3, 1916; Returned to Newfoundland, Jan. 26, 1917; Demobilized, St. John's, April 5, 1919.

JAMES WILLIAM MOORE   Reg. No. 529

Enlisted, Sept. 15, 1914; British Mediterranean Expeditionary Force, Aug. 20, 1915; Wounded, Suvla, Nov. 29, 1915; Admitted Hospital, Malta, Dec. 7, 1915; Joined Base Depot, Alexandria, March 9, 1916; British Expeditionary Force, March 18, 1916; Rejoined Battalion, April 15, 1916; Wounded, Gueudecourt, Oct. 12, 1916; Invalided to England, Oct. 20, 1916; Repatriated to Newfoundland, May 30, 1918; Discharged, St. John's, medically unfit, July 9, 1918.

HARRISON MOORES   Reg. No. 218

Enlisted, Sept. 7, 1914; British Mediterranean Expeditionary Force, Aug. 20, 1915; British Expeditionary Force, March 14, 1916; Wounded, Beaumont Hamel, July 1, 1916; Invalided to England, July 4, 1916; Attached Depot, Second Battalion, Aug. 25, 1916; Returned to Newfoundland, furlough, July 27, 1918; Demobilized, St. John's, March 19, 1919.

John Edgar Morris   Reg. No. 120

Enlisted, Sept. 8, 1914; Struck off Strength, Newton-on-Ayr, Oct. 15, 1915, time expired.

Kenneth Morris   Reg. No. 412

Enlisted, Sept. 8, 1914; British Mediterranean Expeditionary Force, Aug. 20, 1915; Evacuated from Suvla, Nov. 26, 1915; Invalided to England, Jan. 3, 1916; Attached to Depot, Ayr, March 7, 1916; British Expeditionary Force, March 28, 1916; Rejoined Battalion, April 15, 1916; Killed in action, Beaumont Hamel, July 1, 1916.

Michael William Morrissey   Reg. No. 427

Enlisted, Sept. 2, 1914; British Mediterranean Expeditionary Force, Nov. 14, 1915; British Expeditionary Force, March 14, 1916; Evacuated to Hospital, April 5, 1916; Invalided to England, April 8, 1916; Attached to Depot, Ayr, May 19, 1916; Repatriated to Newfoundland, Sept. 8, 1916; Discharged, St. John's, medically unfit, Feb. 1, 1918.

Thomas Patrick Morrissey   Reg. No. 211

Enlisted, Sept. 3, 1914; British Mediterranean Expeditionary Force, Aug. 20, 1915; Corporal, Feb. 27, 1916; Accidentally wounded, March 15, 1916; Invalided to England, April 24, 1916; Attached to Depot, Ayr, July 20, 1916; Acting Sergeant, Sept. 12, 1916; Confirmed to rank, April 27, 1918; Returned to Newfoundland for duty, May 13, 1918; Embarked for United Kingdom, Aug. 8, 1918; Returned to Newfoundland, Jan. 30, 1919; Demobilized, St. John's, April 28, 1919.

Edgar Page Motty   Reg. No. 446

Enlisted, Sept. 8, 1914; British Mediterranean Expeditionary Force Aug. 20, 1915; Evacuated from Suvla, Dec. 7, 1915; Rejoined Battalion, Suez, Jan. 16, 1916; British Expeditionary Force, March 14, 1916; Wounded, Monchy, April 14, 1917; Invalided to England, April 19, 1917; Attached to Depot, Ayr, Aug. 17, 1917; Returned to British Expeditionary Force, Feb. 18, 1918; Embarked for Newfoundland, furlough, July 27, 1918; Discharged, St. John's, medically unfit, Dec. 7, 1918.

Abraham Thomas Mullett   Reg. No. 437

Enlisted, Sept. 8, 1914; British Mediterranean Expeditionary Force Aug. 20, 1915; British Expeditionary Force, March 14, 1916; Evacuated to Hospital, Feb. 7, 1917; Rejoined Battalion, May 7, 1917; Embarked for Newfoundland, furlough, July 27, 1918; Discharged, St. John's, medically unfit, Feb. 15, 1919.

FRANK MULLINS   Reg. No. 525

Enlisted, Sept. 16, 1914; Struck off Strength, Newton-on-Ayr, Oct. 15, 1915, time expired.

BERNARD MURPHY   Reg. No. 530

Enlisted, Sept. 16, 1914; British Mediterranean Expeditionary Force, Aug. 20, 1915; Evacuated from Suvla, Nov. 4, 1915; Admitted Hospital, Malta, Nov. 10, 1915; Invalided to England, Feb. 12, 1916; Admitted 3rd London General Hospital, Wandsworth, Feb. 25, 1916; British Expeditionary Force, June 3, 1917; Attached to Depot, Ayr, Nov. 23, 1916; Rejoined Battalion, May 19, 1918; Embarked for Newfoundland, furlough, July 27, 1918; Demobilized, St. John's, April 1, 1919.

EDWARD JOSEPH MURPHY   Reg. No. 112

Enlisted, Sept. 4, 1914; British Mediterranean Expeditionary Force, Aug. 20, 1915; Evacuated to England, Nov. 16, 1915; British Expeditionary Force, March 28, 1916; Killed in action, Beaumont Hamel, July 1, 1916.

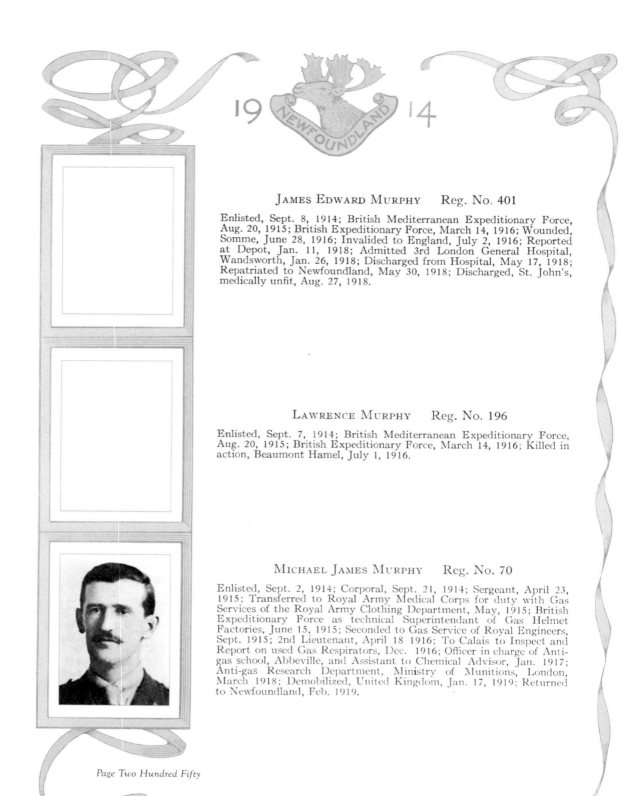

James Edward Murphy   Reg. No. 401

Enlisted, Sept. 8, 1914; British Mediterranean Expeditionary Force, Aug. 20, 1915; British Expeditionary Force, March 14, 1916; Wounded, Somme, June 28, 1916; Invalided to England, July 2, 1916; Reported at Depot, Jan. 11, 1918; Admitted 3rd London General Hospital, Wandsworth, Jan. 26, 1918; Discharged from Hospital, May 17, 1918; Repatriated to Newfoundland, May 30, 1918; Discharged, St. John's, medically unfit, Aug. 27, 1918.

Lawrence Murphy   Reg. No. 196

Enlisted, Sept. 7, 1914; British Mediterranean Expeditionary Force, Aug. 20, 1915; British Expeditionary Force, March 14, 1916; Killed in action, Beaumont Hamel, July 1, 1916.

Michael James Murphy   Reg. No. 70

Enlisted, Sept. 2, 1914; Corporal, Sept. 21, 1914; Sergeant, April 23, 1915; Transferred to Royal Army Medical Corps for duty with Gas Services of the Royal Army Clothing Department, May, 1915; British Expeditionary Force as technical Superintendant of Gas Helmet Factories, June 15, 1915; Seconded to Gas Service of Royal Engineers, Sept. 1915; 2nd Lieutenant, April 18 1916; To Calais to Inspect and Report on used Gas Respirators, Dec. 1916; Officer in charge of Anti-gas school, Abbeville, and Assistant to Chemical Advisor, Jan. 1917; Anti-gas Research Department, Ministry of Munitions, London, March 1918; Demobilized, United Kingdom, Jan. 17, 1919; Returned to Newfoundland, Feb. 1919.

19 14

Walter L. Murphy   Reg. No. 407

Enlisted, Sept. 8, 1914; British Mediterranean Expeditionary Force, Aug. 20, 1915; Admitted, 1st Stationary Hospital, Mudros, Sept. 27, 1915; Died of dysentery, Sept. 29, 1915.

Alfred Seymour Murray   Reg. No. 39

Enlisted, Sept. 2, 1914; British Mediterranean Expeditionary Force, Aug. 20, 1915; Evacuated from Suvla, Dec. 1, 1915; Discharged to Base Depot, Alexandria, March 3, 1916; British Expeditionary Force, March 18, 1916; Admitted to Hospital, Rouen, April 4, 1916; Transferred to England, April 11, 1916; Attached to Depot, Ayr, May 2, 1916; Lance Corporal, Jan. 29, 1917; Corporal, April 27, 1918; Embarked for Newfoundland, furlough, July 21, 1918; Demobilized, St. John's, Feb. 15, 1919.

Matthew Joseph Myler   Reg. No. 548

Enlisted, Sept. 16, 1914; Struck off Strength, Newton-on-Ayr, Oct. 15, 1915, time expired.

John Myrick   Reg. No. 99

Enlisted, Sept. 2, 1914; British Mediterranean Expeditionary Force, Aug. 20, 1915; Evacuated to Hospital, Dec. 1, 1915; Died 3rd Canadian Stationary Hospital, Mudros, Dec. 10, 1915.

Edward George Nauftall

Enlisted, Sept. 2, 1914; British Mediterranean Expeditionary Force, Aug. 20, 1915; Evacuated to England, Dec. 2, 1915; Returned to Newfoundland, furlough, Aug. 3, 1916; British Expeditionary Force, Sept. 7, 1917; Evacuated to Hospital, Sept. 26, 1918; Died 3rd Australian Casualty Clearing Station, Sept. 29, 1918.

William John Neville   Reg. No. 376

Enlisted, Sept. 8, 1914; British Mediterranean Expeditionary Force, Aug. 20, 1915; British Expeditionary Force, March 14, 1916; Wounded, Beaumont Hamel, July 1, 1916; Invalided to England, July 4, 1916; Attached to Depot, Ayr, Aug. 8, 1916; Returned to British Expeditionary Force, Nov. 30, 1916; Rejoined Battalion, Dec. 12, 1916; Killed in action, Monchy, April 14, 1917.

WILLIAM THOMAS NEWELL   Reg. No. 520

Enlisted, Sept. 15, 1914; British Mediterranean Expeditionary Force, Aug. 20, 1915; Served with First Composite Battalion on Western Egyptian Frontier, Dec. 1915 to Feb. 1916; British Expeditionary Force, March 2, 1916; Embarked for Newfoundland, furlough, July 27, 1918; Demobilized, St. John's, March 17, 1919.

ALBERT STANLEY NEWMAN   Reg. No. 36

Enlisted, Sept. 2, 1914; Lance Corporal, Sept. 21, 1914; Corporal, Oct. 3, 1914; Sergeant, April 21, 1915; British Mediterranean Expeditionary Force, Aug. 20, 1915; Admitted to Hospital, Malta, Dec. 2, 1915; Invalided to England, March 26, 1916; Attached to Depot, Ayr, June 25, 1916; Returned to Newfoundland, furlough, July 3, 1916; Attached to Depot, Ayr, April 30, 1917; 2nd Lieutenant, May 18, 1917; British Expeditionary Force, Dec. 17, 1917; Wounded, Kieberg Ridge, Oct. 25, 1918; Invalided to England, Nov. 10, 1918; Lieutenant, Nov. 18, 1918; Rejoined Battalion in Field, Dec. 19, 1918; Acting Captain, Feb. 12, 1919; Transferred to United Kingdom, April 23, 1919; Embarked for Newfoundland, May 20, 1919; Retired, June 6, 1919.

ARCHIBALD M. NEWMAN   Reg. No. 487

Enlisted, Sept. 11, 1914; British Mediterranean Expeditionary Force, Aug. 20, 1915; Wounded, Suvla, Nov. 1, 1915; Admitted Hospital, Cairo, Nov. 5, 1915; British Expeditionary Force, April 3, 1916; Rejoined Battalion, April 8, 1916; Wounded, Beaumont Hamel, July 1, 1916; Died of wounds, 29th Casualty Clearing Station, July 3, 1916.

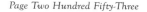

1914

NEWFOUNDLAND

JOHN E. B. NICHOL   Reg. No. 129

Enlisted, Sept. 9, 1914; British Mediterranean Expeditionary Force, Aug. 20, 1915; British Expeditionary Force, April 26, 1916; Wounded, Beaumont Hamel, July 1, 1916; Lance Corporal, Sept. 17, 1917; Wounded, Marcoing, Nov. 20, 1917; Evacuated to England, Dec. 5, 1917; Awarded Military Medal, Jan. 14, 1918; Repatriated to Newfoundland, July 21, 1918; Discharged, St. John's, medically unfit, Aug. 22, 1918.

JOHN NICHOLLE   Reg. No. 435

Enlisted, Sept. 7, 1914; British Mediterranean Expeditionary Force, Aug. 20, 1915; Evacuated from Suvla, Dec. 2, 1915; Invalided to England, Jan. 17, 1916; Attached to Depot, Ayr, June 17, 1916; British Expeditionary Force, Sept. 14, 1917; Wounded, Marcoing, Nov. 20, 1917; Joined Base Depot, Rouen, Nov. 29, 1917; Rejoined Battalion, Dec. 11, 1917; Embarked for Newfoundland, furlough, July 27, 1918; Demobilized, St. John's, Feb. 15, 1919.

JOHN FRANCIS NICOL   Reg. No. 336

Enlisted, Sept. 5, 1914; British Mediterranean Expeditionary Force, Aug. 20, 1915; Evacuated from Suvla, Oct. 13, 1915; Invalided to England, Dec. 4, 1915; Attached to Depot, Ayr, March 14, 1916; British Expeditionary Force, March 28, 1916; Rejoined Battalion, in the field, April 15, 1916; Embarked for Newfoundland, furlough July 27, 1918; Demobilized, St. John's, March 28, 1919.

LLEWELLYN NORMAN   Reg. No. 425

Enlisted, Sept. 3, 1914; British Mediterranean Expeditionary Force, Aug. 20, 1915; Evacuated from Suvla Nov. 30, 1915; Admitted Hospital, Malta, Dec. 3, 1915; Rejoined Battalion, Suez, Jan. 31, 1916; British Expeditionary Force, March 14, 1916; Evacuated to Hospital, May 7, 1916; Rejoined Battalion, July 12, 1916; Evacuated to Hospital, Oct. 1, 1916; Invalided to England, Nov. 2, 1916; Attached to Depot, Ayr, Jan. 17, 1917; Appointed Masseur, June 24, 1917; Embarked for Newfoundland, furlough July 21, 1918; Attached to Department of Militia for duty, Nov. 27, 1918; Corporal, April 1, 1919; Demobilized, St. John's, Aug. 1, 1919.

WILLIAM LEONARD NORRIS   Reg. No. 101

Enlisted, Sept. 2, 1914; British Mediterranean Expeditionary Force, Aug. 20, 1915; Evacuated from Suvla, Oct. 14, 1915; Invalided to England, Nov. 28, 1915; Attached to Depot, Ayr, May 9, 1916; British Expeditionary Force, March 1, 1917; Reattached to Depot, Ayr, April 18, 1917; Returned to British Expeditionary Force, July 1, 1918; Returned to Newfoundland, furlough, July 27, 1918; Demobilized, St. John's, Jan. 24, 1919.

FREDERICK THOMAS NOSEWORTHY   Reg. No. 527

Enlisted, Sept. 16, 1914; British Mediterranean Expeditionary Force. Aug. 20, 1915; Served with 1st Composite Battalion, W. E. F., Dec, 1915 to Feb. 1916; Evacuated to Hospital, Dec. 19, 1915; Discharged to duty, Jan. 20, 1916; Rejoined Battalion, Suez, Feb. 22, 1916; British Expeditionary Force, March 2, 1916; Evacuated to Hospital, May 20, 1917; Rejoined Battalion, July 2, 1917; Wounded, Marcoing, Nov. 20, 1917; Invalided to England, Nov. 26, 1917; Attached Depot, Winchester, Jan. 27, 1918; Embarked for Newfoundland, furlough, July 21, 1918; Discharged, St. John's, medically unfit, Dec. 5, 1918.

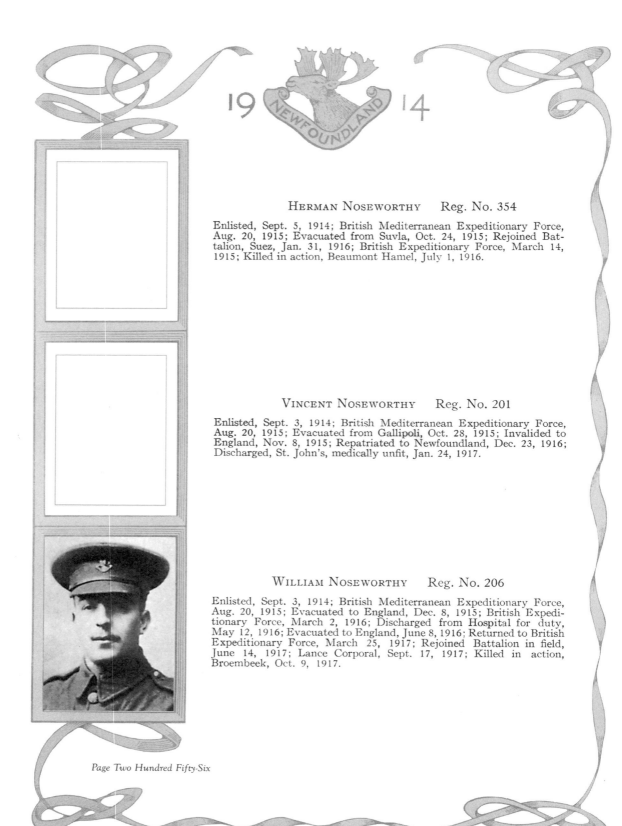

HERMAN NOSEWORTHY   Reg. No. 354

Enlisted, Sept. 5, 1914; British Mediterranean Expeditionary Force, Aug. 20, 1915; Evacuated from Suvla, Oct. 24, 1915; Rejoined Battalion, Suez, Jan. 31, 1916; British Expeditionary Force, March 14, 1915; Killed in action, Beaumont Hamel, July 1, 1916.

VINCENT NOSEWORTHY   Reg. No. 201

Enlisted, Sept. 3, 1914; British Mediterranean Expeditionary Force, Aug. 20, 1915; Evacuated from Gallipoli, Oct. 28, 1915; Invalided to England, Nov. 8, 1915; Repatriated to Newfoundland, Dec. 23, 1916; Discharged, St. John's, medically unfit, Jan. 24, 1917.

WILLIAM NOSEWORTHY   Reg. No. 206

Enlisted, Sept. 3, 1914; British Mediterranean Expeditionary Force, Aug. 20, 1915; Evacuated to England, Dec. 8, 1915; British Expeditionary Force, March 2, 1916; Discharged from Hospital for duty, May 12, 1916; Evacuated to England, June 8, 1916; Returned to British Expeditionary Force, March 25, 1917; Rejoined Battalion in field, June 14, 1917; Lance Corporal, Sept. 17, 1917; Killed in action, Broembeek, Oct. 9, 1917.

Michael Joseph Nugent   Reg. No. 428

Enlisted, Sept. 2, 1914; Lance Corporal, Nov. 13, 1914; Corporal, April 21, 1915; Sergeant, July 10, 1915; British Mediterranean Expeditionary Force, Aug. 20, 1915; Evacuated from Suvla, Dec. 23, 1915; Discharged to Base, Alexandria, Jan. 3, 1916; Admitted Hospital, Cairo, Feb. 10, 1916; Discharged to Base, Alexandria, June 10, 1916; British Expeditionary Force, June 26, 1916; Classified "Permanent Base" at Base Depot, Rouen, July 17, 1916; Transferred to England, July 24, 1916; Attached to Depot, Ayr, Aug. 6, 1916; Embarked for Newfoundland, Aug. 23, 1916; 2nd Lieutenant, Oct. 9, 1917; Embarked for United Kingdom, Dec. 31, 1917; Returned to British Expeditionary Force, Nov. 19, 1918; Rejoined Battalion, Nov. 27, 1918; Lieutenant, April 9, 1919; Embarked for Newfoundland, May 22, 1919; Retired, June 17, 1919.

Bertram William Oake   Reg. No. 539

Enlisted, Sept. 16, 1914; Struck off Strength, Newton-on-Ayr, Oct. 15, 1915, time expired.

John Joseph Oakley   Reg. No. 392

Enlisted, Sept. 7, 1914; Lance Corporal, Sept. 21, 1914; Corporal, April 23, 1915; British Mediterranean Expeditionary Force, Aug. 20, 1915; Evacuated from Suvla, Nov. 20, 1915; Invalided to England, Jan. 3, 1916; Attached to Depot, Ayr, Feb. 24, 1916; Sergeant, Feb. 24, 1916; British Expeditionary Force, March 1, 1917; Rejoined Depot, Ayr, April 18, 1917; Returned to British Expeditionary Force, July 1, 1918; Attached to Depot, Winchester, Oct. 11, 1918; Embarked for Newfoundland, Jan. 30, 1919; Demobilized, St. John's, March 6, 1919.

"BOWRING'S GROUP"

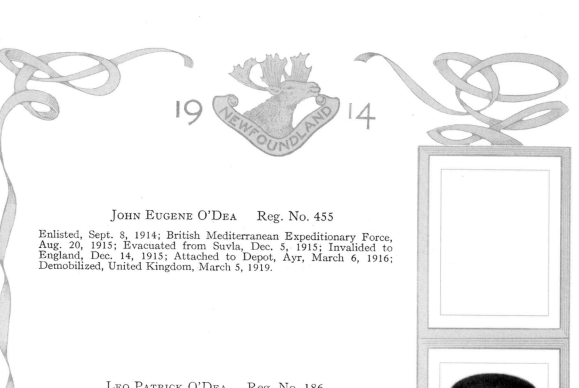

John Eugene O'Dea   Reg. No. 455

Enlisted, Sept. 8, 1914; British Mediterranean Expeditionary Force, Aug. 20, 1915; Evacuated from Suvla, Dec. 5, 1915; Invalided to England, Dec. 14, 1915; Attached to Depot, Ayr, March 6, 1916; Demobilized, United Kingdom, March 5, 1919.

Leo Patrick O'Dea   Reg. No. 186

Enlisted, Sept. 4, 1914; British Mediterranean Expeditionary Force, Aug. 20, 1915; British Expeditionary Force, March 14, 1916; Wounded, Beaumont Hamel, July 1, 1916; Invalided to England, July 4, 1916; Returned to British Expeditionary Force, March 25, 1917; Lance Corporal, April 16, 1917; Wounded, Mesnieres, Nov. 30, 1917; Invalided to England, Dec. 7, 1917; Acting Corporal, March 6, 1918; Acting Sergeant, May 29, 1918; Returned to Newfoundland, furlough, July 21, 1918; Demobilized, St. John's, Feb. 15, 1919.

Albert O'Driscoll   Reg. No. 551

Enlisted, Sept. 16, 1914; British Mediterranean Expeditionary Force, Aug. 20, 1915; Evacuated from Suvla, Oct. 16, 1915; Invalided to England, Nov. 19, 1915; Attached to Depot, Ayr, Feb. 2, 1916; British Expeditionary Force, March 28, 1916; Killed in action, Beaumont Hamel, July 1, 1916.

CHARLES CUNNINGHAM OKE   Reg. No. 60

Enlisted, Sept. 2, 1914; Corporal, Sept. 21, 1914; Sergeant, Oct. 3, 1914; Company Quartermaster Sergeant, July 10, 1915; British Mediterranean Expeditionary Force, Aug. 20, 1915; Repatriated to Newfoundland for discharge, July 20, 1916; Discharged, medically unfit, Jan. 31, 1917; Reattested for special duty at Department of Militia, Nov. 1, 1917; Acting Staff Sergeant Major, Nov. 1, 1917; Hon. 2nd Lieutenant, Sept. 1, 1918; Retired and placed on Reserve of Officers, Dec. 31, 1918.

HARRIS B. OKE   Reg. No. 565

Enlisted, Sept. 16, 1914; Struck off Strength, on transfer to Commissioned Rank of Royal Scots, Nov. 10, 1915.

PATRICK JOSEPH O'KEEFE   Reg. No. 479

Enlisted, Sept. 9, 1914; British Mediterranean Expeditionary Force, Aug. 20, 1915; Evacuated from Suvla, Oct. 14, 1915; Invalided to England, Dec. 26, 1915; Attached to Depot, Ayr, Feb. 24, 1916; Embarked for Newfoundland, Sept. 8, 1916; Discharged, St. John's, medically unfit, July 31, 1917.

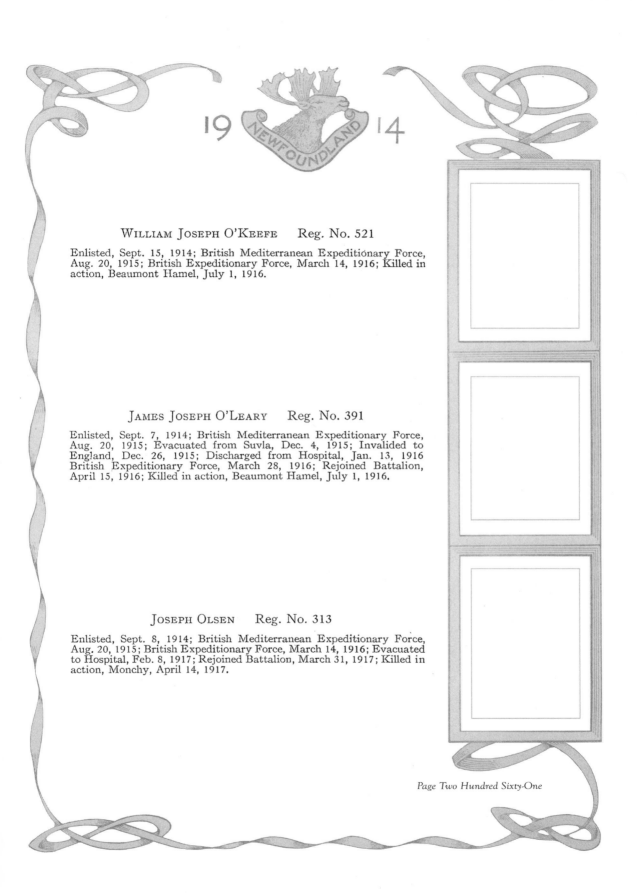

WILLIAM JOSEPH O'KEEFE Reg. No. 521

Enlisted, Sept. 15, 1914; British Mediterranean Expeditionary Force, Aug. 20, 1915; British Expeditionary Force, March 14, 1916; Killed in action, Beaumont Hamel, July 1, 1916.

JAMES JOSEPH O'LEARY Reg. No. 391

Enlisted, Sept. 7, 1914; British Mediterranean Expeditionary Force, Aug. 20, 1915; Evacuated from Suvla, Dec. 4, 1915; Invalided to England, Dec. 26, 1915; Discharged from Hospital, Jan. 13, 1916 British Expeditionary Force, March 28, 1916; Rejoined Battalion, April 15, 1916; Killed in action, Beaumont Hamel, July 1, 1916.

JOSEPH OLSEN Reg. No. 313

Enlisted, Sept. 8, 1914; British Mediterranean Expeditionary Force, Aug. 20, 1915; British Expeditionary Force, March 14, 1916; Evacuated to Hospital, Feb. 8, 1917; Rejoined Battalion, March 31, 1917; Killed in action, Monchy, April 14, 1917.

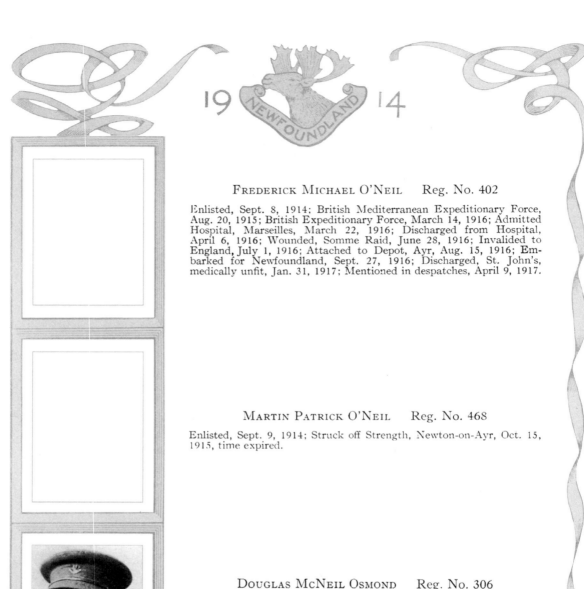

FREDERICK MICHAEL O'NEIL   Reg. No. 402

Enlisted, Sept. 8, 1914; British Mediterranean Expeditionary Force, Aug. 20, 1915; British Expeditionary Force, March 14, 1916; Admitted Hospital, Marseilles, March 22, 1916; Discharged from Hospital, April 6, 1916; Wounded, Somme Raid, June 28, 1916; Invalided to England, July 1, 1916; Attached to Depot, Ayr, Aug. 15, 1916; Embarked for Newfoundland, Sept. 27, 1916; Discharged, St. John's, medically unfit, Jan. 31, 1917; Mentioned in despatches, April 9, 1917.

MARTIN PATRICK O'NEIL   Reg. No. 468

Enlisted, Sept. 9, 1914; Struck off Strength, Newton-on-Ayr, Oct. 15, 1915, time expired.

DOUGLAS McNEIL OSMOND   Reg. No. 306

Enlisted, Sept. 4, 1914; British Mediterranean Expeditionary Force, Aug. 20, 1915; Evacuated from Suvla, Oct. 10, 1915; Invalided to England, Nov. 22, 1915; Attached to Depot, Ayr, Jan. 19, 1916; Lance Corporal, Feb. 3, 1916; British Expeditionary Force, March 13, 1916; Rejoined Battalion, April 8, 1916; Wounded, Beaumont Hamel, July 1, 1916; Died of Wounds, 29th Casualty Clearing Station, July 8, 1916.

19 14

FRANK O'TOOLE   Reg. No. 365

Enlisted, Sept. 8, 1914; Lance Corporal, April 17, 1915; Corporal, July 27, 1915; British Mediterranean Expeditionary Force, Aug. 20, 1915; Sergeant, Nov. 14, 1915; Wounded, Suvla, Nov. 14, 1915; Invalided to England, Dec. 31, 1915; Attached to Depot, Ayr, Feb. 1, 1916; 2nd Lieutenant, Nov. 1, 1916; British Expeditionary Force, May 4, 1917; Wounded, Broembeek, Oct. 9, 1917; Died of Wounds at 4th Casualty Clearing Station, Oct. 12, 1917.

ALEXANDER EDWARD PARSONS   Reg. No. 585

Enlisted, Sept. 22, 1914; British Mediterranean Expeditionary Force, Aug. 20, 1915; Evacuated from Suvla, Oct. 29, 1915; Admitted 6th Stationary Hospital, Mudros, Oct. 31, 1915; Discharged to duty, Nov. 26, 1915; Lance Corporal, Feb. 27, 1916; Rejoined Battalion, March 1, 1916; British Expeditionary Force, March 14, 1916; Evacuated to Hospital, April 28, 1916; Invalided to England, May 9, 1916; Repatriated to Newfoundland, June 22, 1916; Discharged, St. John's, medically unfit, March 20, 1917.

WILLIAM JOHN PARSONS   Reg. No. 438

Enlisted, Sept. 8, 1914; British Mediterranean Expeditionary Force, Aug. 20, 1915; Evacuated to Hospital, Suez, Feb. 21, 1916; Discharged to duty, March 4, 1916; British Expeditionary Force, March 14, 1916; Wounded, Steenbeke, Aug. 14, 1917; Invalided to England, Aug. 18, 1917; Attached to Depot, Ayr, Nov. 10, 1917; Transferred to Foresters, Jan. 4, 1918; Sergeant, Dec. 21, 1918; Reattached to Second Battalion, May 29, 1919; Embarked for Newfoundland, June 24, 1919; Demobilized, St. John's, Aug. 22, 1919.

Neil Patrick   Reg. No. 51

Enlisted, Sept. 2, 1914; Lance Corporal, June 14, 1915; British Mediterranean Expeditionary Force, Aug. 20, 1915; Corporal, Feb. 27, 1916; British Expeditionary Force, March 14, 1916; Wounded, Beaumont Hamel, July 1, 1916; Acting Sergeant, Sept. 2, 1916; Acting Company Sergeant Major, Nov. 30, 1916; Rank confirmed, Nov. 30, 1916; Returned to British Expeditionary Force, Aug. 5, 1917; Wounded, Marcoing, Nov. 20, 1917; Returned to Newfoundland on duty, May 13, 1918; Demobilized, St. John's, March 1, 1919.

Reginald Grant Patterson   Reg. No. 504

Enlisted, Sept. 7, 1914; Lance Corporal, Jan. 30, 1915; 2nd Lieutenant, April 22, 1915; Lieutenant, Oct. 16, 1915; British Mediterranean Expeditionary Force, Nov. 14, 1915; British Expeditionary Force, March 14, 1916; Wounded, Beaumont Hamel, July 1, 1916; Invalided to England, July 4, 1916; Attached to Depot, Ayr, Aug. 10, 1916; Returned to British Expeditionary Force, Awarded Military Cross, Sept. 26, 1917 Awarded Bar to Military Cross, Nov. 20, 1917; Wounded Ledgeham, Oct. 14, 1918; Invalided to England, Oct. 18, 1918; Attached to Depot, Winchester, Feb. 14, 1919; Embarked for Newfoundland, Feb. 15, 1919; Retired, St. John's, March 18, 1919.

George Paver   Reg. No. 534

Enlisted, Sept. 4, 1914; Regimental Sergeant Major, Sept. 21, 1914; British Mediterranean Expeditionary Force, Aug. 20, 1915; Admitted 5th Canadian Stationary Hospital, Cairo, Sept. 12, 1915; Discharged from Hospital, Oct. 17, 1915; Rejoined Battalion, Suez, Jan. 31, 1916; British Expeditionary Force, March 14, 1916; Evacuated to Hospital, April 1, 1916; Classified "P. B." at Base Depot, Rouen, April 4, 1916; Transferred to England, April 27, 1916; Attached to Depot, Ayr, June 14, 1916; Embarked for Newfoundland, July 20, 1916; Discharged, St. John's, medically unfit, Dec. 11, 1916.

1914

Chesley Morton Peet   Reg. No. 235

Enlisted, Sept. 4, 1914; British Mediterranean Expeditionary Force, Aug. 20, 1915; Evacuated from Suvla, Dec. 6, 1915; Invalided to England, Jan. 13, 1916; Attached to Depot, Ayr, Feb. 28, 1916; British Expeditionary Force, March 1, 1917; Returned to England, April 18, 1917; Returned to British Expeditionary Force, July 1, 1918; Embarked for Newfoundland, furlough, July 27, 1918; Discharged, St. John's, medically unfit, Dec. 7, 1918.

Arthur Nicholas Penney   Reg. No. 229

Enlisted, Sept. 2, 1914; British Mediterranean Expeditionary Force, Aug. 20, 1915; British Expeditionary Force, March 14, 1916; Wounded, Beaumont Hamel, July 1, 1916; Invalided to England, July 3, 1916; Attached Second Battalion, Sept. 16, 1916; Acting Sergeant, Feb. 27, 1916; Confirmed to Rank, Jan. 11, 1918; Returned to Newfoundland, furlough, July 21, 1918; Demobilized, St. John's, April 14, 1919.

Robert Penney   Reg. No. 559

Enlisted, Sept. 16, 1914; British Expeditionary Force, July 16, 1916; Evacuated to Hospital, Oct. 21, 1916; Invalided to England, Nov. 7, 1916; Repatriated to Newfoundland, May 4, 1917; Discharged, St. John's, medically unfit, June 6, 1917.

Arthur Joseph Penny   Reg. No. 6

Enlisted, Sept. 2, 1914; Lance Corporal, Sept. 21, 1914; Corporal, Nov. 13, 1914; Sergeant, April 23, 1915; British Mediterranean Expeditionary Force, Aug. 20, 1915; Acting Company Sergeant Major, Feb. 11, 1916; British Expeditionary Force, Oct. 3, 1916; Missing, believed killed, Monchy, April 14, 1917.

Thomas Avery Perry   Reg. No. 423

Enlisted, Sept. 3, 1914; British Mediterranean Expeditionary Force, Aug. 20, 1915; British Expeditionary Force, March 14, 1916; Wounded, Beaumont Hamel, July 1, 1916; Admitted 10th General Hospital, Rouen, July 4, 1916; Rejoined Battalion, July 21, 1916; Wounded, Gueudecourt, Oct. 12, 1916; Admitted to 8th General Hospital, Rouen, Oct. 14, 1916; Rejoined Battalion, Nov. 13, 1916; Evacuated to Hospital, Feb. 8, 1917; Invalided to England, Feb. 26, 1917; Attached to Depot, Ayr, April 10, 1917; Embarked for Newfoundland, April 20, 1917; Discharged, St. John's, medically unfit, May 30, 1917.

Walter James Petrie   Reg. No. 566

Enlisted, Sept. 19, 1914; Struck off Strength, Newton-on-Ayr, Oct. 15 1915, time expired.

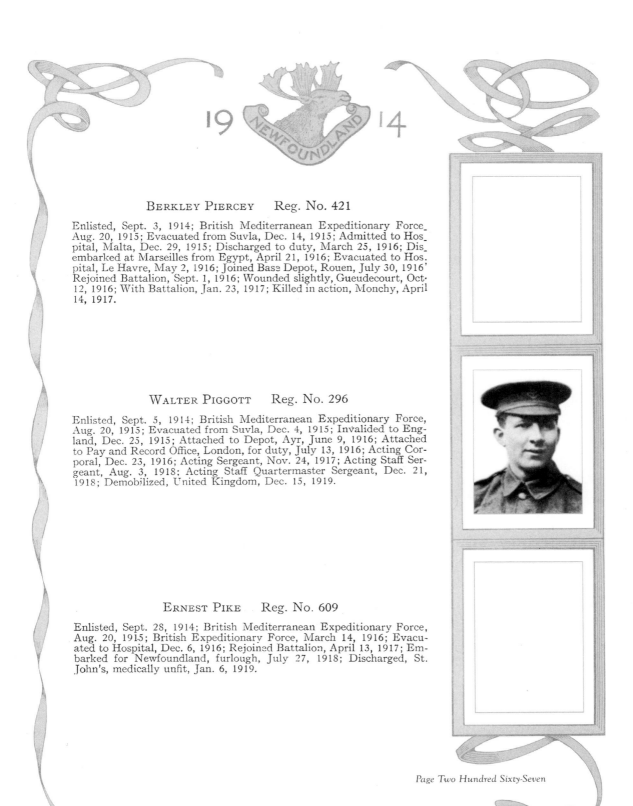

19 NEWFOUNDLAND 14

BERKLEY PIERCEY   Reg. No. 421

Enlisted, Sept. 3, 1914; British Mediterranean Expeditionary Force, Aug. 20, 1915; Evacuated from Suvla, Dec. 14, 1915; Admitted to Hospital, Malta, Dec. 29, 1915; Discharged to duty, March 25, 1916; Disembarked at Marseilles from Egypt, April 21, 1916; Evacuated to Hospital, Le Havre, May 2, 1916; Joined Base Depot, Rouen, July 30, 1916; Rejoined Battalion, Sept. 1, 1916; Wounded slightly, Gueudecourt, Oct. 12, 1916; With Battalion, Jan. 23, 1917; Killed in action, Monchy, April 14, 1917.

WALTER PIGGOTT   Reg. No. 296

Enlisted, Sept. 5, 1914; British Mediterranean Expeditionary Force, Aug. 20, 1915; Evacuated from Suvla, Dec. 4, 1915; Invalided to England, Dec. 25, 1915; Attached to Depot, Ayr, June 9, 1916; Attached to Pay and Record Office, London, for duty, July 13, 1916; Acting Corporal, Dec. 23, 1916; Acting Sergeant, Nov. 24, 1917; Acting Staff Sergeant, Aug. 3, 1918; Acting Staff Quartermaster Sergeant, Dec. 21, 1918; Demobilized, United Kingdom, Dec. 15, 1919.

ERNEST PIKE   Reg. No. 609

Enlisted, Sept. 28, 1914; British Mediterranean Expeditionary Force, Aug. 20, 1915; British Expeditionary Force, March 14, 1916; Evacuated to Hospital, Dec. 6, 1916; Rejoined Battalion, April 13, 1917; Embarked for Newfoundland, furlough, July 27, 1918; Discharged, St. John's, medically unfit, Jan. 6, 1919.

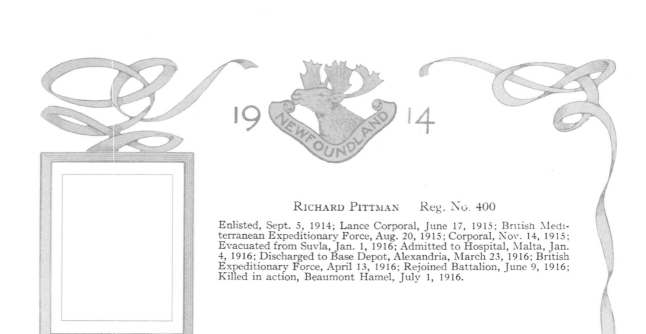

RICHARD PITTMAN   Reg. No. 400

Enlisted, Sept. 5, 1914; Lance Corporal, June 17, 1915; British Mediterranean Expeditionary Force, Aug. 20, 1915; Corporal, Nov. 14, 1915; Evacuated from Suvla, Jan. 1, 1916; Admitted to Hospital, Malta, Jan. 4, 1916; Discharged to Base Depot, Alexandria, March 23, 1916; British Expeditionary Force, April 13, 1916; Rejoined Battalion, June 9, 1916; Killed in action, Beaumont Hamel, July 1, 1916.

DAVID POWER   Reg. No. 310

Enlisted, Sept. 2, 1914; British Mediterranean Expeditionary Force, Aug. 20, 1915; British Expeditionary Force, March 14, 1916; Evacuated to Hospital, July 15, 1917; Rejoined Battalion, Oct. 14, 1917; Wounded, Mesnieres, Dec. 3, 1917; Invalided to England, Dec. 9, 1917; Attached to Depot, Ayr, Feb. 18, 1918; Embarked for Newfoundland, furlough, July 21, 1918; Demobilized, St. John's, Feb. 15, 1919.

ARTHUR MILLIGAN PRATT   Reg. No. 522

Enlisted, Sept. 16, 1914; British Mediterranean Expeditionary Force, Aug. 20, 1915; British Expeditionary Force, March 14, 1916; Wounded, Beaumont Hamel, July 1, 1916; Invalided to England, July 7, 1916; Attached to Depot, Ayr, Oct. 16, 1916; Returned to British Expeditionary Force, June 3, 1917; Admitted to Hospital, Rouen, June 21, 1917; Discharged to duty, Sept. 28, 1917; Evacuated to Hospital, April 7, 1918; Discharged to duty, July 11, 1918; Embarked for Newfoundland, furlough, July 27, 1918; Discharged, St. John's, medically unfit, Nov. 25, 1918.

ARTHUR PURCHASE   Reg. No. 540

Enlisted, Sept. 16, 1914; Struck off Strength, Newton-on-Ayr, Oct. 15, 1915, time expired.

GEORGE ALBERT RAINES   Reg. No. 381

Enlisted, Sept. 2, 1914; British Mediterranean Expeditionary Force, Aug. 20, 1915; Evacuated from Suvla, Oct. 14, 1915; Invalided to England, July 6, 1916; Attached to Depot, Ayr, Aug. 15, 1916; British Expeditionary Force, Oct. 24, 1916; Rejoined Battalion, Nov. 18, 1916; Evacuated to Hospital, Jan. 8, 1918; Rejoined Battalion, March 18, 1918; Embarked for Newfoundland, furlough, July 27, 1918; Demobilized, St. John's, Feb. 15, 1919.

HUBERT J. RANDELL   Reg. No. 94

Enlisted, Sept. 2, 1914; British Mediterranean Expeditionary Force, Aug. 20, 1915; British Expeditionary Force, March 28, 1916; Wounded, Beaumont Hamel, July 1, 1916; Embarked for Newfoundland, May 4, 1917; Discharged, St. John's, medically unfit, June 6, 1917; Attested for service in Newfoundland Forestry Corps, Dec. 28, 1917; Lance Corporal, Jan. 30, 1918; Corporal, March 28, 1918; Embarked for Overseas, March 28, 1918; Sergeant, Sept. 28, 1918; Embarked for Newfoundland, Feb. 1, 1919; Demobilized, St. John's, April 10, 1919.

John Joseph Reardigan   Reg. No. 72

Enlisted, Sept. 2, 1914; Lance Corporal, Nov. 15, 1914; Corporal, July 2, 1915; British Mediterranean Expeditionary Force, Aug. 20, 1915; Reverted to Ranks at own request, Sept. 15, 1915; British Expeditionary Force, March 14, 1916; Returned to Newfoundland, furlough, July 10, 1917; Discharged, St. John's, medically unfit, Aug. 2, 1918.

George Wilfred Rees   Reg. No. 388

Enlisted, Sept. 5, 1914; British Mediterranean Expeditionary Force, Aug. 20, 1915; Evacuated Suvla, Dec. 6, 1915; Invalided to England Jan. 3, 1916; Attached to Depot, Ayr, Feb. 2, 1916; British Expeditionary Force, Feb. 10, 1917; Evacuated to Hospital, March 8, 1917; Invalided to England, March 23, 1917; Attached to Depot, Ayr, Aug. 7, 1917; Repatriated to Newfoundland, Sept. 13, 1917; Discharged, St. John's, medically unfit, Feb. 1, 1918.

Henry Reid   Reg. No. 513

Enlisted, Sept. 21, 1914; British Mediterranean Expeditionary Force, Aug. 20, 1915; British Expeditionary Force, March 14, 1916; Wounded, Beaumont Hamel, July 1, 1916; Invalided to England, July 5, 1916; Attached to Depot, Ayr, Oct. 31, 1916; Embarked for Newfoundland, May 18, 1917; Discharged, St. John's, medically unfit, Aug. 28, 1917.

ROBERT BRUCE REID   Reg. No. 593

Enlisted, Sept. 8, 1914; Lance Corporal, Aug. 10, 1915; Second Lieutenant, Aug. 16, 1915; British Mediterranean Expeditionary Force, Aug. 20, 1915; British Expeditionary Force, May 14, 1916; Killed in action, Beaumont Hamel, July 1, 1916.

CHARLES JAMES RENOUF   Reg. No. 147

Enlisted, Sept. 2, 1914; Lance Corporal, March 23, 1915; British Mediterranean Expeditionary Force, Aug. 20, 1915; Corporal, Nov. 20, 1915; British Expeditionary Force, March 14, 1916; Wounded, Beaumont Hamel, July 1, 1916; Evacuated to England, July 3, 1916; Repatriated to Newfoundland, May 4, 1917; Discharged, St. John's, medically unfit, June 6, 1917.

ARTHUR JAMES RENDELL   Reg. No. 204

Enlisted, Sept. 3, 1914; British Mediterranean Expeditionary Force, Aug. 20, 1915; Lance Corporal, Dec. 1, 1915; British Expeditionary Force, March 14, 1916; Killed in action, Beaumont Hamel, July 1, 1916.

LEO T. RENDELL   Reg. No. 231

Enlisted, Sept. 2, 1914; British Mediterranean Expeditionary Force, Aug. 20, 1915; British Expeditionary Force, March 14, 1916; Wounded, Beaumont Hamel, July 1, 1916; Invalided to England, July 5, 1916, Attached to Second Battalion, Ayr, Oct. 30, 1916; Returned to British Expeditionary Force, Aug. 5, 1917; Rejoined Battalion in the Field, Aug. 28, 1917; Wounded, Broembeek, Oct. 9, 1917; Invalided to England, Oct. 12, 1917; Attached to Depot, Ayr, Jan. 22, 1918; Returned to Newfoundland, furlough, June 21, 1918; Demobilized, St. John's Feb. 15, 1919.

FINLAY McK. CAMPBELL RICHARDS   Reg. No. 8

Enlisted, Sept. 2, 1914; British Mediterranean Expeditionary Force Aug. 20, 1915; Wounded, Suvla, Nov. 1, 1915; British Expeditionary Force, March 14, 1916; Wounded, Beaumont Hamel, July 1, 1916; Invalided to England, Returned to British Expeditionary Force, Dec. 12, 1916; Lance Corporal, March 14, 1917; Prisoner of War, captured at Monchy, April 14, 1917; Repatriated to England, Dec. 25, 1918; Demobilized, St. John's, June 10, 1919.

WILLIAM WALTER RICHARDS   Reg. No. 41

Enlisted, Sept. 2, 1914; British Mediterranean Expeditionary Force, Aug. 20, 1915; British Expeditionary Force, March 14, 1916; Wounded, Beaumont Hamel, July 1, 1916; Invalided to England, July 5, 1916; Returned to British Expeditionary Force, March 25, 1917; Invalided to England, April 11, 1918; Demobilized, St. John's, Feb. 15, 1919.

19 **NEWFOUNDLAND** 14

FRANK RICHARDSON   Reg. No. 66

Enlisted, Sept. 2, 1914; British Mediterranean Expeditionary Force, Aug. 20, 1915; British Expeditionary Force, March 14, 1916; Lance Corporal, June 11, 1916; Invalided to England, July 5, 1916; Wounded, Beaumont Hamel, July 1, 1916; Corporal, Oct. 27, 1916; Returned to British Expeditionary Force, Dec. 30, 1916; Killed in action, Steenbeke, Aug. 16, 1917.

F. J. RICKETTS   Reg. No. 451

Enlisted, Sept. 11, 1914; Struck off Strength, Newton-on-Ayr, Oct. 15, 1915, time expired.

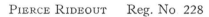

PIERCE RIDEOUT   Reg. No. 228

Enlisted, Sept. 2, 1914; British Mediterranean Expeditionary Force, Aug. 20, 1915; Admitted to Hospital, Lemnos, Sept. 20, 1915; Invalided to England, Oct. 20, 1915; Attached to Second Battalion, Jan. 19, 1916; British Expeditionary Force, March 28, 1916; Evacuated to Hospital, Oct. 21, 1916; Invalided to England, Nov. 15, 1916; Attached to Second Battalion, Jan. 15, 1917; Returned to British Expeditionary Force, Aug. 5, 1917; Evacuated to Hospital, Oct. 31, 1917; Invalided to England, Nov. 15, 1917; Died at 3rd London General Hospital, April 27, 1918.

FRANK ROBERTS   Reg. No. 383

Enlisted, Sept. 5, 1914; British Mediterranean Expeditionary Force, Aug. 20, 1915; Wounded, Suvla, Oct. 22, 1915; Died of wounds at 20th Casualty Clearing Station, Oct. 23, 1915.

FREDERICK GEORGE ROBERTS   Reg. No. 440

Enlisted, Sept. 8, 1914; British Mediterranean Expeditionary Force, Aug. 20, 1915; British Expeditionary Force, March 14, 1916; Wounded, Beaumont Hamel, July 1, 1916; Invalided to England, July 5, 1916; Discharged from Hospital, March 29, 1917; Attached to Depot, Ayr, April 5, 1917; Repatriated to Newfoundland, April 10, 1917; Discharged, St. John's, medically unfit, May 9, 1917.

WALTER GRAHAM ROBERTS   Reg. No. 368

Enlisted, Sept. 5, 1914; British Mediterranean Expeditionary Force, Aug. 20, 1915; Evacuated from Suvla, Dec. 1, 1915; Invalided to England, Jan. 16, 1916; Attached to Depot, Ayr, Sept. 13, 1916; Lance Corporal, May 21, 1917; Acting Corporal, Oct. 22, 1917; Attached to Pay and Record Office, London, for duty, March 9, 1918; Acting Sergeant, May 11, 1918; Embarked for Newfoundland, furlough, July 21, 1918; Demobilized, St. John's, Feb. 20, 1919.

Eric McKenzie Robertson   Reg. No. 497

Enlisted, Sept. 7, 1914; British Mediterranean Expeditionary Force, Aug. 20, 1915; Evacuated from Suvla, Oct. 29, 1915; Rejoined Battalion, Suez, Jan. 16, 1916; British Expeditionary Force, March 14, 1916; Wounded, Beaumont Hamel, July 1, 1916; Invalided to England, July 6, 1916; Attached to Depot, Ayr, Aug. 29, 1916; Embarked for Newfoundland, July 18, 1917; Discharged, St. John's, medically unfit, Aug. 28, 1917.

John Joseph Robinson   Reg. No. 480

Enlisted, Sept. 9, 1914; Lance Corporal, Sept. 21, 1914; Corporal, Jan. 5, 1915; Sergeant, July 10, 1915; British Mediterranean Expeditionary Force, Aug. 20, 1915; Evacuated from Suvla, Nov. 21, 1915; Admitted to Hospital, Malta, Nov. 27, 1915; Discharged to duty, Jan. 26, 1916; British Expeditionary Force, March 18, 1916; Wounded, Beaumont Hamel, July 1, 1916; Invalided to England, Aug. 24, 1916; Repatriated to Newfoundland, Sept. 27, 1916; Discharged, St. John's, medically unfit, Dec. 31, 1916.

Charles Dalton Rogers   Reg. No. 389

Enlisted, Sept. 5, 1914; British Mediterranean Expeditionary Force, Aug. 20, 1915; Admitted to Hospital, Suez, Feb. 16, 1916; Discharged to Base Depot, Alexandria, April 25, 1916; British Expeditionary Force, April 26, 1916; Invalided to England, June 17, 1916; Attached to Depot, Ayr, July 18, 1916; Returned to British Expeditionary Force, Oct. 3, 1916; Admitted to Hospital, Rouen, Jan. 15, 1917; Invalided to England, Feb. 15, 1917; Attached to Depot, Ayr, March 22, 1917; Returned to British Expeditionary Force, Aug. 5, 1917; Classified "P. B." at Rouen, Aug. 7, 1917; Transferred to England, Aug. 12, 1917; Attached to Depot, Ayr, Aug. 17, 1917; Embarked for Newfoundland, May 22, 1919; Demobilized, St. John's, June 29, 1919.

19 14

NEWFOUNDLAND

SONS OF ENGLAND

1914

EDWARD JOSEPH ROGERS   Reg. No. 355

Enlisted, Sept. 5, 1914; British Mediterranean Expeditionary Force,
Aug. 20, 1915; British Expeditionary Force, March 14, 1916; Killed in
action, Beaumont Hamel, July 1, 1916.

THOMAS EDWARD ROGERS   Reg. No. 394

Enlisted, Sept. 5, 1914; British Mediterranean Expeditionary Force,
Aug. 20, 1915; Evacuated from Suvla, Oct. 29, 1915; Admitted to
Hospital, Malta, Nov. 10, 1915; Rejoined Battalion, Suez, Jan. 26,
1916; British Expeditionary Force, March 14, 1916; Killed in action,
Gueudecourt, Oct. 12, 1916.

WILLIAM ROOST   Reg. No. 76

Enlisted, Sept. 2, 1914; British Mediterranean Expeditionary Force,
Aug. 20, 1915; British Expeditionary Force, March 14, 1916; Wounded,
Beaumont Hamel, July 1, 1916; Invalided to England, July 3, 1916;
Returned to British Expeditionary Force, Jan. 31, 1917; Killed in action,
Sailly-Saillisel, March 2, 1917.

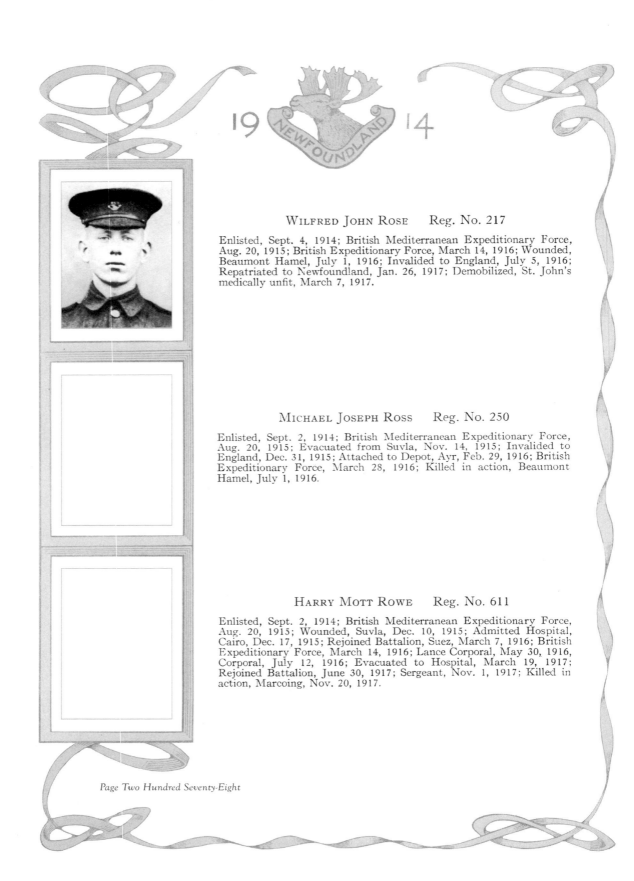

WILFRED JOHN ROSE   Reg. No. 217

Enlisted, Sept. 4, 1914; British Mediterranean Expeditionary Force, Aug. 20, 1915; British Expeditionary Force, March 14, 1916; Wounded, Beaumont Hamel, July 1, 1916; Invalided to England, July 5, 1916; Repatriated to Newfoundland, Jan. 26, 1917; Demobilized, St. John's medically unfit, March 7, 1917.

MICHAEL JOSEPH ROSS   Reg. No. 250

Enlisted, Sept. 2, 1914; British Mediterranean Expeditionary Force, Aug. 20, 1915; Evacuated from Suvla, Nov. 14, 1915; Invalided to England, Dec. 31, 1915; Attached to Depot, Ayr, Feb. 29, 1916; British Expeditionary Force, March 28, 1916; Killed in action, Beaumont Hamel, July 1, 1916.

HARRY MOTT ROWE   Reg. No. 611

Enlisted, Sept. 2, 1914; British Mediterranean Expeditionary Force, Aug. 20, 1915; Wounded, Suvla, Dec. 10, 1915; Admitted Hospital, Cairo, Dec. 17, 1915; Rejoined Battalion, Suez, March 7, 1916; British Expeditionary Force, March 14, 1916; Lance Corporal, May 30, 1916, Corporal, July 12, 1916; Evacuated to Hospital, March 19, 1917; Rejoined Battalion, June 30, 1917; Sergeant, Nov. 1, 1917; Killed in action, Marcoing, Nov. 20, 1917.

EDWARD CLAYTON ROWSELL   Reg. No. 571

Enlisted, Sept. 17, 1914; British Mediterranean Expeditionary Force, Aug. 20, 1915; British Expeditionary Force, March 14, 1916; Lance Corporal, May 18, 1916; Killed in action, Beaumont Hamel, July 1, 1916.

WILLIAM THOMAS RYALL   Reg. No. 53

Enlisted, Sept. 2, 1914; Lance Corporal, Sept. 21, 1914; Corporal, March 12, 1915; Sergeant, June 14, 1915; Company Sergeant Major, Oct. 14, 1915; 2nd Lieutenant, Nov. 27, 1915; British Expeditionary Force, June 5, 1916; Killed in action, Beaumont Hamel, July 1, 1916.

BERNARD RYAN   Reg. No. 123

Enlisted, Sept. 2, 1914; British Mediterranean Expeditionary Force, Aug. 20, 1915; British Expeditionary Force, March 18, 1916; Wounded Beaumont Hamel, July 1, 1916; Evacuated to England, July 5, 1916; Returned to British Expeditionary Force, Dec. 30, 1916; Killed in action, Monchy, April 14, 1917.

19 NEWFOUNDLAND 14

JOHN JOSEPH RYAN   Reg. No. 38

Enlisted, Sept. 2, 1914; British Mediterranean Expeditionary Force, Aug. 20, 1915; Wounded, Suvla, Nov. 11, 1915; Invalided to England, Nov. 28, 1915; Attached to Depot, Ayr, March 2, 1916; British Expeditionary Force, April 13, 1916; Wounded near Sonken Road, Nov. 30, 1916; Invalided to England, Dec. 6, 1916; Attached to Depot, Ayr, July 17, 1917; Embarked for Newfoundland, July 18, 1917; Discharged, St. John's, medically unfit. Feb. 6, 1918.

THOMAS BROWN RYAN   Reg. No. 260

Enlisted, Sept. 2, 1914; British Mediterranean Expeditionary Force, Aug. 20, 1915; British Expeditionary Force, March 14, 1916; Wounded, Gueudecourt, Oct. 12, 1916; Invalided to England, Nov. 8, 1916; Attached to Depot, Ayr, Jan. 26, 1917; Lance Corporal, Nov. 5, 1917; Acting Corporal, July 10, 1918; Returned to Newfoundland, furlough, July 21, 1918; Demobilized, St. John's, Feb. 15, 1919.

WILLIAM JOSEPH RYAN   Reg. No. 133

Enlisted, Sept. 7, 1914; Lance Corporal, Nov. 13, 1914; Corporal. July 2, 1915; British Mediterranean Expeditionary Force, Aug. 20, 1915; Evacuated, Suvla, Oct. 17, 1915; Admitted Hospital, Cairo, Oct. 21, 1915; Rejoined Battalion, Suez, March 7, 1916; British Expeditionary Force, March 14, 1916; Killed in action, Beaumont Hamel, July 1, 1916.

1914

PETER SAMSON   Reg. No. 267

Enlisted, Sept. 2, 1914; British Mediterranean Expeditionary Force, Aug. 20, 1915; Lance Corporal, Dec. 10, 1915; British Expeditionary Force, March 14, 1916; Evacuated to Hospital, March 28, 1916; Invalided to England, April 16, 1916; Returned to British Expeditionary Force, June 25, 1916; Corporal, Aug. 8, 1916; Sergeant, Sept. 14, 1916; Wounded, Gueudecourt, Oct. 12, 1916; Invalided to England, Oct. 19, 1916; Awarded Distinguished Conduct Medal, Dec. 11, 1916; Decorated with Croix de Guerre, May 1, 1917; Returned to British Expeditionary Force, June 11, 1917; Wounded, Steenbeke, Aug. 16, 1917; Invalided to England, Aug. 21, 1917; Returned to British Expeditionary Force, Dec. 5, 1917; Company Sergeant Major, Dec. 26, 1917; Returned to Newfoundland, furlough, July 27, 1918; Demobilized, St. John's, Feb, 15, 1919.

MICHAEL FRANCIS SEARS   Reg. No. 73

Enlisted, Sept. 2, 1914; British Mediterranean Expeditionary Force, Aug. 20, 1915; British Expeditionary Force, March 14, 1916; Returned to Newfoundland, March 23, 1917; Discharged, St. John's, medically unfit, Jan. 2. 1918.

HORATIUS SEAWARD   Reg. No. 172

Enlisted, Sept. 8, 1914; British Mediterranean Expeditionary Force, Aug. 20, 1915; Evacuated, Suvla, Nov. 24, 1915; Invalided to England, Nov. 24, 1915; British Expeditionary Force, Dec. 12, 1916; Killed in action, Steenbeke, Aug. 16. 1917.

WILLIAM BURTON SHAVE   Reg. No. 543

Enlisted, Sept. 16, 1914; British Mediterranean Expeditionary Force, Aug. 20, 1915; British Expeditionary Force, March 14, 1916; Wounded, Beaumont Hamel, July 1, 1916; Invalided to England, July 5, 1916; Attached to Depot, Ayr, Sept. 13, 1916; Returned to British Expeditionary Force, Nov. 6, 1917; Rejoined Battalion, Nov. 14, 1917; Wounded, Marcoing, Nov. 20, 1917; Invalided to England, Nov. 28, 1917; Attached to Depot, Ayr, Dec. 27, 1917; Lance Corporal, March 11, 1918; Corporal, May 13, 1918; Embarked for Newfoundland, furlough, July 21, 1918; Demobilized, St. John's, Feb. 25, 1919.

JOHN JOSEPH SHEEHAN   Reg. No. 35

Enlisted, Sept. 2, 1914; British Mediterranean Expeditionary Force, Aug. 20, 1915; British Expeditionary Force, March 14, 1916; Wounded, Beaumont Hamel, July 1, 1916; Invalided to England, July 5, 1916; Lance Corporal, Oct. 27, 1916; Returned to British Expeditionary Force, Dec. 30, 1916; Corporal, Feb. 9, 1917; Wounded, Sailly-Saillisel, Feb. 24, 1917; Discharged, medically unfit, Dec. 8, 1917; Enlisted Newfoundland Forestry Battalion, Dec. 11, 1917; Sergeant, Dec. 12, 1917; Embarked for United Kingdom, Dec. 21, 1917; Died of pneumonia, Dec. 28, 1917.

RICHARD JOHN SHEPPARD   Reg. No. 282

Enlisted, Sept. 8, 1914; Lance Corporal, Sept. 21, 1914; Corporal, Oct. 3, 1914; Sergeant, Feb. 6, 1915; 2nd Lieutenant, April 22, 1915; British Mediterranean Expeditionary Force, Aug. 20, 1915; Lieutenant, Oct. 15, 1915; Evacuated from Suvla, Nov. 26, 1915; Admitted Hospital, Malta, Dec. 29, 1915; Discharged to duty, April 1, 1916; British Expeditionary Force, April 24, 1916; Admitted to Hospital, Rouen, April 29, 1916; Invalided to England, June 11, 1916; Attached to Depot, Ayr, Aug. 4, 1916; Returned to British Expeditionary Force, Sept. 5, 1916; Detached for duty, Divisional Headquarters, July 21, 1917; Evacuated to Hospital, Rouen, May 23, 1918; Invalided to England, July 28, 1918; Embarked for Newfoundland, furlough, Aug. 24, 1918; Returned to United Kingdom, Nov. 18, 1918; Attached to Depot, Winchester, Dec. 6, 1918; Retired, United Kingdom, May 24, 1919.

ROBERT C. SHEPPARD   Reg. No. 473

Enlisted, Sept. 8, 1914; British Mediterranean Expeditionary Force, Aug. 20, 1915; Evacuated from Suvla, Dec. 13, 1915; Admitted to Hospital, Malta, Dec. 17, 1915; Discharged to duty, March 4, 1916; British Expeditionary Force, March 18, 1916; Wounded slightly, remained on duty, May 22, 1916; Wounded, Beaumont Hamel, July 1, 1916; Invalided to England, July 4, 1916; Attached to Depot, Ayr, Sept. 28, 1916; Embarked for Newfoundland, Oct. 10, 1916; Discharged, St. John's, medically unfit, March 28, 1917.

GEORGE SHIRRAN   Reg. No. 493

Enlisted, Sept. 11, 1914; British Mediterranean Expeditionary Force, Nov. 14, 1915; British Expeditionary Force, March 14, 1916; Wounded, Beaumont Hamel, July 1, 1916; Invalided to England, July 4, 1916; Attached to Depot, Ayr, Nov. 4, 1916; Returned to British Expeditionary Force, Sept. 7, 1917; Evacuated to Hospital, Dec. 27, 1917; Invalided to England, Jan. 10, 1918; Attached to Depot, Winchester, May 4, 1918; Demobilized, United Kingdom, March 7, 1919.

RICHARD A. SHORTALL   Reg. No. 395

Enlisted, Sept. 5, 1914; Lance Corporal, Sept. 21, 1914; Corporal, March 11, 1915; 2nd Lieutenant, April 22, 1915; British Mediterranean Expeditionary Force, Aug. 20, 1915; Wounded, Suvla, Nov. 26, 1915; Admitted Hospital, Mudros, Nov. 30, 1915; Lieutenant, Jan. 1, 1916; Transferred to Malta, Jan. 18, 1916; Rejoined Battalion, Suez, March 7, 1916; British Expeditionary Force, March 14, 1916; Killed in action, Beaumont Hamel, July 1, 1916.

WILLIAM T. SIMMONDS   Reg. No. 349

Enlisted, Sept. 7, 1914; Lance Corporal, Sept. 21, 1914; Corporal, July 2, 1915; British Mediterranean Expeditionary Force, Aug. 20, 1915; Evacuated from Suvla, Nov. 26, 1915; Invalided to England, Feb. 19, 1916; Attached to Depot, Ayr, March 13, 1916; Sergeant, April 20, 1916; British Expeditionary Force, March 1, 1918; Killed in action, De Broeken, April 13, 1918.

JOHN HENRY SIMMS   Reg. No. 88

Enlisted, Sept. 2, 1914; British Mediterranean Expeditionary Force, Aug. 20, 1915; British Expeditionary Force, March 14, 1916; Wounded, Steenbeke, Aug. 16, 1917; Died of Wounds Aug. 17, 1917; Awarded Military Medal, Oct. 18, 1917.

ROBERT RONALD SIMMS   Reg. No. 576

Enlisted, Sept. 22, 1914; British Mediterranean Expeditionary Force Aug. 20, 1915; British Expeditionary Force, March 14, 1916; Killed in action, Beaumont Hamel, July 1, 1916.

Sydney Bemister Skeffington   Reg. No. 59

Enlisted, Sept. 2, 1914; British Mediterranean Expeditionary Force
Aug. 20, 1915; British Expeditionary Force, March 2, 1916; Lance Corporal, Dec. 26, 1917; Returned to Newfoundland, furlough, July 24,
1918; Demobilized, St. John's, Feb. 15, 1919.

Arthur John Skinner   Reg. No. 202

Enlisted, Sept. 4, 1914; Struck off Strength, Newton-on-Ayr, Oct. 15
1915; Enlisted with Newfoundland Royal Naval Reserve.

Albert Ernest Slade   Reg. No. 273

Enlisted, Sept. 2, 1914; British Mediterranean Expeditionary Force
Aug. 20, 1915; Wounded, Suvla, Nov. 1, 1915; Admitted to Hospital,
Malta, Nov. 7, 1915; Rejoined Battalion, Suez, Jan. 26, 1916; British
Expeditionary Force, March 14, 1916; Embarked for Newfoundland,
furlough, July 27, 1918; Demobilized, St. John's, Feb. 15, 1919.

HARVEY HAYNES SMALL   Reg. No. 302

Enlisted, Sept. 14, 1914; British Mediterranean Expeditionary Force, Aug. 20, 1915; Wounded, Suvla, Nov. 8, 1915; Admitted to Hospital, Cairo, Nov. 13, 1915; Rejoined Battalion, Suez, Jan. 31, 1916; Lance Corporal, Feb. 27, 1916; British Expeditionary Force, March 14, 1916, Wounded, Beaumont Hamel, July 1, 1916; Invalided to England, July 3, 1916; Attached to Depot, Ayr, Aug. 21, 1916; Returned to Newfoundland, furlough, Sept. 27, 1916; Second Lieutenant, May 16, 1917; Embarked for United Kingdom, May 18, 1917; Returned to British Expeditionary Force, Jan. 5, 1918; Embarked for Newfoundland on special duty, July 21, 1918; Returned to United Kingdom, Nov. 27, 1918; Attached to Depot, Winchester, Dec. 4, 1918; Embarked for Newfoundland, Jan. 30, 1919; Retired and placed on Reserve of Officers, Feb. 25, 1919.

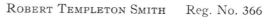

WILLIAM A. SMALL   Reg. No. 614

Enlisted, Sept. 4, 1914; British Mediterranean Expeditionary Force, Aug. 20, 1915; Evacuated from Suvla, Jan. 1, 1916; Admitted to Hospital, Malta, Jan. 17, 1916; Discharged to duty, Feb. 13, 1916; British Expeditionary Force, March 18, 1916; Wounded, Beaumont Hamel, July 1, 1916; Invalided to England, July 4, 1916; Attached to Depot, Ayr, Sept. 5, 1916; Returned to British Expeditionary Force, June 3, 1917; Rejoined Battalion, June 19, 1917; Wounded, Steenbeke, Aug. 16, 1917; Discharged to duty, Aug. 27, 1917; Evacuated to Hospital, Jan. 18, 1918; Invalided to England, Feb. 18, 1918; Repatriated to Newfoundland, April 24, 1918; Discharged, St. John's, medically unfit, May 25, 1918.

ROBERT TEMPLETON SMITH   Reg. No. 366

Enlisted, Sept. 4, 1914; Second Lieutenant, Seaforth Highlanders, and Struck off Strength, Oct. 24, 1915.

Roy Archibald Smith   Reg. No. 379

Enlisted, Sept. 8, 1914; British Mediterranean Expeditionary Force, Aug. 20, 1915; Evacuated from Suvla, Oct. 9, 1915; Invalided to England, Nov. 30, 1915; Attached to Depot, Ayr, April 3, 1916; British Expeditionary Force, March 25, 1917; Rejoined Battalion, April 18, 1917; Lance Corporal, Sept. 17, 1917; Wounded, Mesnieres, Dec. 2, 1917; Invalided to England, Dec. 5, 1917; Attached to Depot, Winchester, June 2, 1918; Acting Corporal, July 16, 1918; Embarked for Newfoundland, July 21, 1918; Demobilized, St. John's, March 19, 1919.

Walter Smith   Reg. No. 478

Enlisted, Sept. 9, 1914; Struck off Strength, Newton-on-Ayr, medically unfit, May 26, 1915.

Michael Frank Smyth   Reg. No. 512

Enlisted, Sept. 15, 1914; British Mediterranean Expeditionary Force, Aug. 20, 1915; British Expeditionary Force, March 18, 1916; Lance Corporal, Dec. 11, 1917; Corporal, July 17, 1918; Embarked for Newfoundland, furlough, July 21, 1918; Demobilized, St. John's, Feb. 15, 1919.

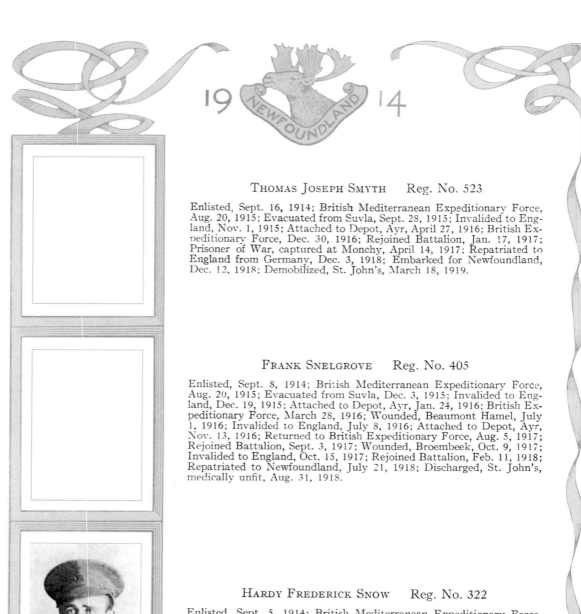

THOMAS JOSEPH SMYTH   Reg. No. 523

Enlisted, Sept. 16, 1914; British Mediterranean Expeditionary Force, Aug. 20, 1915; Evacuated from Suvla, Sept. 28, 1915; Invalided to England, Nov. 1, 1915; Attached to Depot, Ayr, April 27, 1916; British Expeditionary Force, Dec. 30, 1916; Rejoined Battalion, Jan. 17, 1917; Prisoner of War, captured at Monchy, April 14, 1917; Repatriated to England from Germany, Dec. 3, 1918; Embarked for Newfoundland, Dec. 12, 1918; Demobilized, St. John's, March 18, 1919.

FRANK SNELGROVE   Reg. No. 405

Enlisted, Sept. 8, 1914; British Mediterranean Expeditionary Force, Aug. 20, 1915; Evacuated from Suvla, Dec. 3, 1915; Invalided to England, Dec. 19, 1915; Attached to Depot, Ayr, Jan. 24, 1916; British Expeditionary Force, March 28, 1916; Wounded, Beaumont Hamel, July 1, 1916; Invalided to England, July 8, 1916; Attached to Depot, Ayr, Nov. 13, 1916; Returned to British Expeditionary Force, Aug. 5, 1917; Rejoined Battalion, Sept. 3, 1917; Wounded, Broembeek, Oct. 9, 1917; Invalided to England, Oct. 15, 1917; Rejoined Battalion, Feb. 11, 1918; Repatriated to Newfoundland, July 21, 1918; Discharged, St. John's, medically unfit, Aug. 31, 1918.

HARDY FREDERICK SNOW   Reg. No. 322

Enlisted, Sept. 5, 1914; British Mediterranean Expeditionary Force, Aug. 20, 1915; British Expeditionary Force, March 14, 1916; Evacuated to Hospital, May 3, 1916; Rejoined Battalion, July 27, 1916; Lance Corporal, Aug. 11, 1916; Killed in action, Gueudecourt, Oct. 12, 1916.

James Snow   Reg. No. 433

Enlisted, Sept. 2, 1914; British Mediterranean Expeditionary Force, Aug. 20, 1915; Wounded, Suvla, Nov. 1, 1915; Invalided to England, Dec. 5, 1915; Attached to Depot, Feb. 5, 1916; British Expeditionary Force, March 1, 1917; Returned to Depot, April 18, 1917; Returned to British Expeditionary Force, July 1, 1918; Embarked for Newfoundland, furlough, July 27, 1918; Demobilized, St. John's, Feb. 15, 1919.

Joseph Henry Snow   Reg. No. 74

Enlisted, Sept. 2, 1914; Sergeant, Sept. 21, 1914; British Mediterranean Expeditionary Force, Aug. 20, 1915; British Expeditionary Force, March 14, 1916; Second Lieutenant, June 5, 1916; Returned to Newfoundland for duty, July 11, 1916; Embarked for United Kingdom, Aug. 28, 1916; Returned to British Expeditionary Force, Oct. 27, 1916; Lieutenant, Nov. 1, 1917; Embarked for Newfoundland, furlough, July 21, 1918; Attached for duty to Depot, St. John's, Sept. 8, 1918; Acting Captain, April 12, 1919; Retired and placed on Reserve of Officers, Oct. 13, 1919.

William James Somerton   Reg. No. 265

Enlisted Sept. 2, 1914; British Mediterranean Expeditionary Force, Aug. 20, 1915; Wounded, Suvla, Oct. 17, 1915; Discharged to duty, Jan. 30, 1916; British Expeditionary Force, March 14, 1916; Wounded Beaumont Hamel, July 1, 1916; Invalided to England, July 3, 1916; Attached to Depot, Ayr, Dec. 11, 1916; Repatriated to Newfoundland, Feb. 23, 1916; Discharged, St. John's, medically unfit, Jan. 24, 1917.

19 14

GEORGE SPARKES   Reg. No. 253

Enlisted, Sept. 2, 1914; British Mediterranean Expeditionary Force, Aug. 20, 1915; Evacuated from Suvla, Dec. 5, 1915; Rejoined Battalion, Suez, March 7, 1916; British Expeditionary Force, March 14, 1916; Killed in action, Beaumont Hamel, July 1, 1916.

JOHN SPOONER   Reg. No. 498

Enlisted, Sept. 14, 1914; Lance Corporal, June 14, 1915; British Mediterranean Expeditionary Force, Aug. 20, 1915; Evacuated from Suvla Nov. 17, 1915; Admitted to Hospital, Malta, Nov. 26, 1915; Invalided to England, Jan. 25, 1916; Attached to Depot, Ayr, April 5, 1916; Second Lieutenant, July 12, 1916; British Expeditionary Force, Oct. 27, 1916; Evacuated to Hospital, March 25, 1917; Invalided to England, April 17, 1917; Embarked for Newfoundland, furlough, June 22, 1917; Retired, St. John's, medically unfit, Dec. 11, 1917.

HERBERT SPRY   Reg. No. 275

Enlisted, Sept. 3, 1914; British Mediterranean Expeditionary Force, Aug. 20, 1915; Evacuated from Suvla, Oct. 10, 1915; Rejoined Battalion, Suez, Jan. 26, 1916; British Expeditionary Force, March 14, 1916; Wounded, Beaumont Hamel, July 1, 1916; Invalided to England, July 9, 1916; Returned to British Expeditionary Force, Nov. 6, 1917; Wounded, Marcoing, Nov. 20, 1917; Invalided to England, Nov. 24, 1917; Attached to Depot, Ayr, Feb. 22, 1918; Embarked for Newfoundland, furlough, July 27, 1918; Demobilized, St. John's, Feb. 15, 1919.

Page Two Hundred Ninety

CHARLES PATRICK SPURRELL   Reg. No. 378

Enlisted, Sept. 5, 1914; British Mediterranean Expeditionary Force, Aug. 20, 1915; British Expeditionary Force, March 14, 1916; Evacuated to Hospital, June 28, 1916; Discharged to duty, July 1, 1916; Lance Corporal, Aug. 11, 1916; Wounded, Gueudecourt, Oct. 12, 1916; Invalided to England, Oct. 15, 1916; Attached to Depot, Ayr, Nov. 29, 1916; Acting Corporal, Jan. 17, 1917; Confirmed to rank, March 23, 1917; Sergeant, June 10, 1917; British Expeditionary Force, June 11, 1917; Awarded Distinguished Conduct Medal, Oct. 9, 1917; Wounded, Marcoing, Nov. 20, 1917; Invalided to England, Nov. 30, 1917; Attached to Depot, Winchester, April 22, 1918; Embarked for Newfoundland for Special Duty, May 13, 1918; Demobilized, St. John's, April 28, 1919.

JOSIAH SQUIBB   Reg. No. 243

Enlisted, Sept. 2, 1914; British Mediterranean Expeditionary Force, Aug. 20, 1915; Killed in action, Suvla, Oct. 19, 1915.

JACK SQUIRES   Reg. No. 367

Enlisted, Sept. 5, 1914; British Mediterranean Expeditionary Force, Aug. 20, 1915; Evacuated from Suvla, Dec. 1, 1915; Invalided to England, Jan. 28, 1916; Attached to Depot, Ayr, March 13, 1916; British Expeditionary Force, April 13, 1916; Wounded, Beaumont Hamel, July 1, 1916; Invalided to England, July 3, 1916; Attached to Depot, Ayr, Aug. 25, 1916; Returned to British Expeditionary Force, Oct. 3, 1916; Prisoner of War, captured at Monchy, April 14, 1917; Repatriated to England, Jan. 1, 1919; Embarked for Newfoundland, Jan. 30, 1919; Demobilized, St. John's, March 18, 1919.

Anthony James Stacey   Reg. No. 466

Enlisted, Sept. 12, 1914; British Mediterranean Expeditionary Force, Nov. 14, 1915; British Expeditionary Force, March 14, 1916; Lance Corporal, Oct. 22, 1916; Corporal, June 14, 1917; Acting Sergeant Dec. 26, 1917; Sergeant, July 24, 1918; Embarked for Newfoundland, furlough, July 27, 1918; Demobilized, St. John's, Feb. 15, 1919.

Owen William Steele   Reg. No. 326

Enlisted, Sept. 13, 1914; Sergeant, Sept. 21, 1914; Color Sergeant, Oct. 3, 1914; Second Lieutenant, April 22, 1915; British Mediterranean Expeditionary Force, Aug. 20, 1915; Lieutenant, Oct. 15, 1915; British Expeditionary Force, March 14, 1916; Wounded, July 7, 1916; Died of wounds, 87th Field Ambulance Station, July 8, 1916.

Wilfred Down Stenlake   Reg. No. 415

Enlisted, Sept. 9, 1914; British Mediterranean Expeditionary Force, Aug. 20, 1915; Evacuated from Suvla, Nov. 26, 1915; Invalided to England, Jan. 3, 1916; Attached to Depot, Ayr, May 15, 1916; Repatriated to Newfoundland, July 20, 1916; Discharged, St. John's, medically unfit Sept. 12, 1916.

19 14

John Sydney Stevenson   Reg. No. 32

Enlisted, Sept. 2, 1914; Lance Corporal, July 14, 1915; British Mediterranean Expeditionary Force, Aug. 20, 1915; Corporal, Nov. 20, 1915; Sergeant, Feb. 27, 1916; British Expeditionary Force, March 14, 1916; Second Lieutenant, July 1, 1916; Killed in action, Monchy, April 14, 1917.

Leonard Tretheway Stick   Reg. No. 1

Enlisted, Sept. 5, 1914; Sergeant, Sept. 21, 1914; British Mediterranean Expeditionary Force, Aug. 20, 1915; British Expeditionary Force, March 14, 1916; Wounded, Beaumont Hamel, July 1, 1916; Second Lieutenant, July 1, 1916; Transferred to Indian Army, Oct. 11, 1917.

Robin Stick   Reg. No. 46

Enlisted, Sept. 2, 1914; Lance Corporal, Nov. 13, 1914; Corporal, April 7, 1915; Sergeant, June 14, 1915; Second Lieutenant, July 29, 1915; British Mediterranean Expeditionary Force, Aug. 20, 1916; British Expeditionary Force, March 14, 1916; Wounded, Beaumont Hamel, July 1, 1916; Invalided to England, July 4, 1916; Attached to Depot, Ayr, Oct. 17, 1916; Returned to British Expeditionary Force, March 12, 1917; Captain, Aug. 6, 1917; Wounded, Marcoing, Nov. 20, 1917; Discharged to duty, Nov. 30, 1917; Embarked for Newfoundland, furlough, July 24, 1918; Returned to United Kingdom, Oct. 19, 1918; Returned to British Expeditionary Force, Nov. 4, 1918; Embarked for Newfoundland, May 22, 1919; Retired and placed on Reserve of Officers, June 6, 1919.

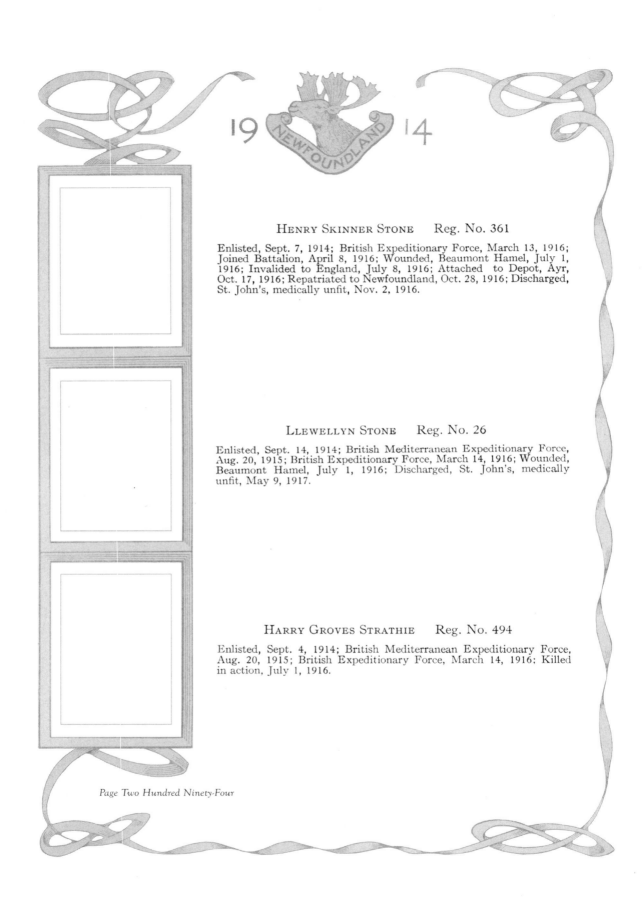

HENRY SKINNER STONE   Reg. No. 361

Enlisted, Sept. 7, 1914; British Expeditionary Force, March 13, 1916; Joined Battalion, April 8, 1916; Wounded, Beaumont Hamel, July 1, 1916; Invalided to England, July 8, 1916; Attached to Depot, Ayr, Oct. 17, 1916; Repatriated to Newfoundland, Oct. 28, 1916; Discharged, St. John's, medically unfit, Nov. 2, 1916.

LLEWELLYN STONE   Reg. No. 26

Enlisted, Sept. 14, 1914; British Mediterranean Expeditionary Force, Aug. 20, 1915; British Expeditionary Force, March 14, 1916; Wounded, Beaumont Hamel, July 1, 1916; Discharged, St. John's, medically unfit, May 9, 1917.

HARRY GROVES STRATHIE   Reg. No. 494

Enlisted, Sept. 4, 1914; British Mediterranean Expeditionary Force, Aug. 20, 1915; British Expeditionary Force, March 14, 1916; Killed in action, July 1, 1916.

1914

Charles St. Clair Strong   Reg. No. 30

Enlisted, Sept. 2, 1914; Sergeant, Sept. 21, 1914; Color Sergeant, Oct. 3, 1914; Company Sergeant Major, May 6, 1915; Wounded, Somme Raid, June 28, 1916; Second Lieutenant, Oct. 9, 1915; Lieutenant, Oct. 9, 1916; Captain, Aug. 16, 1917; Wounded, Neuve Eglise, April 12, 1918; Died of Wounds, April 13, 1918.

Augustus Leo Summers   Reg. No. 93

Enlisted, Sept. 2, 1914; Lance Corporal, Nov. 12, 1915; 2nd Lieutenant, Nov. 27, 1915; British Expeditionary Force, Nov. 17, 1916; Lieutenant, Aug. 1, 1917; Embarked for Newfoundland for special duty, May 22, 1918; Returned to United Kingdom, Oct. 12, 1918; Returned to British Expeditionary Force, Nov. 19, 1918; Embarked for Newfoundland, Jan. 30, 1919; Retired, Feb. 25, 1919.

Charles F. Taylor   Reg. No. 293

Enlisted, Sept. 9, 1914; British Mediterranean Expeditionary Force, Aug. 20, 1915; Admitted to Hospital, Mudros, Sept. 20, 1915; Discharged to duty, Oct. 4, 1915; Admitted to Hospital, Malta, Oct. 30, 1915; Rejoined Battalion, Suez, March 7, 1916; British Expeditionary Force, March 14, 1916; Killed in action, Beaumont Hamel, July 1, 1916.

George Hayward Taylor   Reg. No. 28

Enlisted, Sept. 2, 1914; Sergeant, Sept. 21, 1914; Color Sergeant, Oct. 3, 1914; Company Quartermaster Sergeant, Oct. 29, 1914; Company, Sergeant Major, July 31, 1915; 2nd Lieutenant, Oct. 9, 1915; British Mediterranean Expeditionary Force, Nov. 14, 1915; British Expeditionary Force, March 14, 1916; Killed in action, Beaumont Hamel, July 1, 1916.

Herbert Taylor   Reg. No. 7

Enlisted, Sept. 2, 1914; Lance Corporal, Oct. 30, 1915; British Mediterranean Expeditionary Force, Nov. 14, 1915; British Expeditionary Force, March 14, 1916; Wounded, Beaumont Hamel, July 1, 1916; Discharged, St. John's, medically unfit, Aug. 7, 1917.

Victor S. Taylor   Reg. No. 111

Enlisted, Sept. 2, 1914; British Mediterranean Expeditionary Force, Aug. 20, 1915; British Expeditionary Force, March 14, 1916; Lance Corporal, Aug. 8, 1916; Acting Company Quartermaster Sergeant, Feb. 1, 1917; Confirmed to Rank, June 14, 1917; Embarked for Newfoundland, furlough, July 27, 1918; Demobilized, St. John's, Feb. 15, 1919.

1914

Walter Cameron Taylor   Reg. No. 452

Enlisted, Sept. 8, 1914; British Mediterranean Expeditionary Force, Aug. 20, 1915; Evacuated from Suvla, Dec. 3, 1915; Joined Base Depot, Alexandria, March 15, 1916; British Expeditionary Force, March 18, 1916; Wounded, Beaumont Hamel, July 1, 1916; Invalided to England, July 3, 1916; Attached to Depot, Ayr, Sept. 13, 1916; Returned to British Expeditionary Force, Aug. 5, 1917; Admitted to Hospital, Rouen, Aug. 23, 1917; Acting Corporal, Dec. 26, 1917; Rejoined Battalion, Dec. 30, 1917; Confirmed to Rank, April 25, 1918; Sergeant July 24, 1918; Embarked for Newfoundland, July 27, 1918; Demobilized, St. John's, Feb. 15, 1919.

John Vincent Temple   Reg. No. 232

Enlisted, Sept. 2, 1914; Lance Corporal, July 26, 1915; British Mediterranean Expeditionary Force, Aug. 20, 1915; Evacuated from Suvla, Dec. 16, 1915; Rejoined Battalion, Dec. 30, 1915; British Expeditionary Force, March 14, 1916; Wounded, Beaumont Hamel, July 1, 1916; Invalided to England, July 6, 1916; Attached to Depot, Ayr, Oct. 3, 1916; Returned to Newfoundland, furlough, Oct. 28, 1916; Discharged, St. John's, medically unfit, March 7, 1917.

Robert Tetford   Reg. No. 277

Enlisted, Sept. 3, 1914; British Mediterranean Expeditionary Force, Aug. 20, 1915; Evacuated from Suvla, Nov. 2, 1915; Admitted to Hospital, Malta, Dec. 9, 1915; Rejoined Battalion, Suez, March 1, 1916; British Expeditionary Force, March 14, 1916; Wounded, Beaumont Hamel, July 1, 1916; Invalided to England, July 6, 1916; Returned to Newfoundland, furlough, Sept. 27, 1916; Discharged, St. John's, medically unfit, Jan. 31, 1917.

19 NEWFOUNDLAND 14

WALTER LESLIE THISTLE   Reg. No. 215

Enlisted, Sept. 4, 1914; British Mediterranean Expeditionary Force, Aug. 20, 1915; British Expeditionary Force, March 14, 1916; Lance Corporal, July 12, 1916; Wounded, Gueudecourt, Oct. 12, 1916; Invalided to England, Oct. 14, 1916; Acting Corporal, Jan. 17, 1917; Confirmed to Rank, April 24, 1917; Returned to British Expeditionary Force, April 28, 1917; Rejoined Battalion, June 14, 1917; Prisoner of War, captured at Mesnieres, Dec. 3, 1917; Repatriated to England, Dec. 25, 1918; Returned to Newfoundland, Jan. 3, 1919; Demobilized, St. John's, April 7, 1919.

JAMES ELLIOTT THOMPSON   Reg. No. 61

Enlisted, Sept. 2, 1914; British Mediterranean Expeditionary Force, Aug. 20, 1915; Corporal, Feb. 27, 1916; British Expeditionary Force, March 14, 1916; 2nd Lieutenant, June 5, 1916; Killed in action, Sailly-Saillisel, March 3, 1917.

JOHN THOMPSON   Reg. No. 139

Enlisted, Sept. 5, 1914; British Mediterranean Expeditionary Force, Aug. 20, 1915; British Expeditionary Force, March 14, 1916; Wounded accidently, Belgium, Sept. 9, 1916; Rejoined Battalion, Oct. 12, 1916; Prisoner of War, captured at Monchy, April 14, 1917; Repatriated to England, Dec. 25, 1918; Returned to Newfoundland, Jan. 30, 1919; Demobilized, St. John's, March 23, 1919.

19 NEWFOUNDLAND 14

WALTER THOMPSON   Reg. No. 138

Enlisted, Sept. 4, 1914; British Mediterranean Expeditionary Force, Aug. 20, 1915; British Expeditionary Force, March 18, 1916; Wounded, Beaumont Hamel, July 1, 1916; Rejoined Battalion, July 21, 1916; Wounded, LesFosses Farm, April 23, 1917; Evacuated to England, April 28, 1917; Repatriated to Newfoundland, Feb. 23, 1918; Discharged, St. John's, medically unfit, April 11, 1918.

HENRY TILLEY   Reg. No. 307

Enlisted, Sept. 8, 1914; British Mediterranean Expeditionary Force, Aug. 20, 1915; Admitted to Hospital, Lemnos, Sept. 20, 1915; Invalided to England, Oct. 27, 1915; Attached to Depot, Ayr, Nov. 22, 1915; Lance Corporal, Dec. 5, 1915; British Expeditionary Force, Jan. 31, 1917; Killed in action, Monchy, April 14, 1917.

RICHARD TILLEY   Reg. No. 21

Enlisted, Sept. 3, 1914; British Mediterranean Expeditionary Force, Aug. 20, 1915; British Expeditionary Force, March 14, 1916; Wounded, Beaumont Hamel, July 1, 1916; Discharged, medically unfit, Aug. 28, 1917; Reattested, Oct. 20, 1917; Lance Corporal, Jan. 15, 1918; Corporal, Oct. 15, 1918; Acting Sergeant, March 1, 1919; Discharged, St. John's, Nov. 3, 1919.

1914

AUSTIN GERALD TIPPLE   Reg. No. 583

Enlisted, Sept. 22, 1914; British Mediterranean Expeditionary Force, Aug. 20, 1915; British Expeditionary Force, March 14, 1916; Wounded, Beaumont Hamel, July 1, 1916; Invalided to England, July 6, 1916; Admitted 3rd London General Hospital, Wandsworth, July 6, 1916; Discharged from Hospital, Jan. 24, 1917; Repatriated to Newfoundland, Feb. 2, 1917; Discharged, St. John's, medically unfit, March 7, 1917.

JAMES JOHN TOBIN   Reg. No. 69

Enlisted, Sept. 2, 1914; British Mediterranean Expeditionary Force, Aug. 20, 1915; Returned to Newfoundland, furlough, May 30, 1916; Embarked for United Kingdom, July 19, 1916; Acting Corporal, Sept. 9, 1916; 2nd Lieutenant, Nov. 1, 1916; British Expeditionary Force, May 4, 1917; Killed in action, Marcoing, Nov. 20, 1917.

HARRY ALEXANDER TOMPKINSON   Reg. No. 298

Enlisted, Sept. 5, 1914; British Mediterranean Expeditionary Force, Aug. 20, 1915; Wounded, Suvla, Nov. 30, 1915; Evacuated to Hospital, Malta, Dec. 7, 1915; Joined Base Depot, Alexandria, March 4, 1916; British Expeditionary Force, March 18, 1916; Admitted to Hospital, Rouen, March 30, 1916; Transferred to England, April 27, 1916; Attached to Depot, Ayr, May 2, 1916; Repatriated to Newfoundland, July 20, 1916; Discharged, St. John's, medically unfit, Sept. 12, 1916.

19 NEWFOUNDLAND 14

WILLIAM TREBBLE   Reg. No. 18

Enlisted, Sept. 7, 1914; British Mediterranean Expeditionary Force, Aug. 20, 1915; Lance Corporal, Oct. 6, 1915; Corporal, Feb. 27, 1916; British Expeditionary Force, March 14, 1916; Wounded, Beaumont Hamel, July 1, 1916; Discharged, St. John's, medically unfit, Oct. 19, 1917.

GEORGE BEVERLEY TUFF   Reg. No. 2

Enlisted, Sept. 2, 1914; British Mediterranean Expeditionary Force, Aug. 20, 1915; British Expeditionary Force, March 14, 1916; Wounded, Beaumont Hamel, July 1, 1916; Lance Corporal, Nov. 6, 1916; Acting Corporal, Jan. 17, 1917; Acting Sergeant, June 19, 1917; Confirmed to Corporal Rank, April 27, 1918; Confirmed to Sergeant Rank, Feb. 12, 1919; Demobilized, St. John's, June 29, 1919.

JAMES ROY TUFF   Reg. No. 23

Enlisted, Sept. 2, 1914; British Mediterranean Expeditionary Force, Aug. 20, 1915; British Expeditionary Force, March 14, 1916; Lance Corporal, Aug. 8, 1916; Corporal, Nov. 23, 1916; Wounded, Monchy, April 14, 1917; Died of Wounds, April 28, 1917.

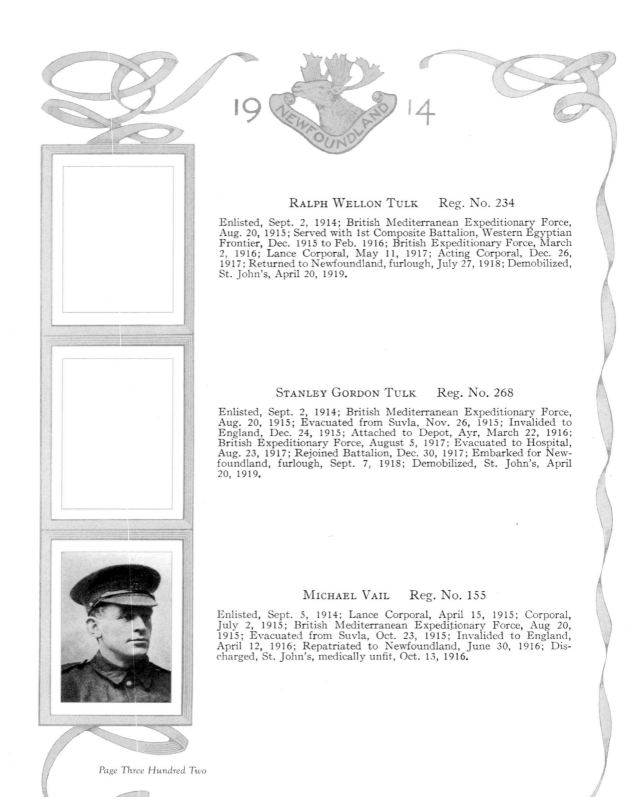

RALPH WELLON TULK   Reg. No. 234

Enlisted, Sept. 2, 1914; British Mediterranean Expeditionary Force, Aug. 20, 1915; Served with 1st Composite Battalion, Western Egyptian Frontier, Dec. 1915 to Feb. 1916; British Expeditionary Force, March 2, 1916; Lance Corporal, May 11, 1917; Acting Corporal, Dec. 26, 1917; Returned to Newfoundland, furlough, July 27, 1918; Demobilized, St. John's, April 20, 1919.

STANLEY GORDON TULK   Reg. No. 268

Enlisted, Sept. 2, 1914; British Mediterranean Expeditionary Force, Aug. 20, 1915; Evacuated from Suvla, Nov. 26, 1915; Invalided to England, Dec. 24, 1915; Attached to Depot, Ayr, March 22, 1916; British Expeditionary Force, August 5, 1917; Evacuated to Hospital, Aug. 23, 1917; Rejoined Battalion, Dec. 30, 1917; Embarked for Newfoundland, furlough, Sept. 7, 1918; Demobilized, St. John's, April 20, 1919.

MICHAEL VAIL   Reg. No. 155

Enlisted, Sept. 5, 1914; Lance Corporal, April 15, 1915; Corporal, July 2, 1915; British Mediterranean Expeditionary Force, Aug 20, 1915; Evacuated from Suvla, Oct. 23, 1915; Invalided to England, April 12, 1916; Repatriated to Newfoundland, June 30, 1916; Discharged, St. John's, medically unfit, Oct. 13, 1916.

FRANCIS J. VAUGHAN   Reg. No. 481

Enlisted, Sept. 9, 1914; Lance Corporal, Sept. 18, 1915; Corporal, Oct. 12, 1916; Acting Sergeant, Nov. 29, 1916; Embarked for Newfoundland, June 15, 1917; Attached to Headquarters, St. John's, May 18, 1918; Died at General Hospital, St. John's, May 22, 1918.

OSCAR AUGUSTUS VAUGHAN   Reg. No. 337

Enlisted, Sept, 7, 1914; Lance Corporal, July 29, 1915; British Mediterranean Expeditionary Force, Aug. 20, 1915; Evacuated from Suvla, Dec. 16, 1915; Invalided to England, Dec. 26, 1915; Attached to Depot, Ayr, Jan. 28, 1916; Embarked for Newfoundland, furlough, June 6, 1917; Died at Jensen Camp, St. John's, July 4, 1917.

RICHARD H. VOISEY   Reg. No. 152

Enlisted, Sept. 4, 1914; British Mediterranean Expeditionary Force, Aug. 20, 1915; Served with 1st Composite Battalion, Western Egyptian Frontier, Dec. 1915, to Feb. 1916; British Expeditionary Force, March 2, 1916; Lance Corporal Aug. 11, 1916; Wounded, Gueudecourt, Oct. 12, 1916; Repatriated to Newfoundland, June 6, 1917; Discharged, St. John's, medically unfit, June 11, 1917; Reattested for duty at Depot, St. John's, Dec. 9, 1917; Acting Corporal, May 31, 1918; Acting Sergeant, Nov. 18, 1918; Demobilized, St. John's, Sept. 1, 1919.

Frank Walsh   Reg. No. 161

Enlisted, Sept. 5, 1914; British Mediterranean Expeditionary Force, Aug. 20, 1915; Lance Corporal, Oct. 25, 1915; Corporal, Feb. 27, 1916; British Expeditionary Force, March 14, 1916; Wounded, Beaumont Hamel, July 1, 1916; Invalided to England, July 4, 1916; Acting Sergeant, Sept. 12, 1916; Returned to British Expeditionary Force, Dec. 12, 1916; Acting Company Quartermaster Sergeant, Jan. 28, 1917; Confirmed to Rank, June 14, 1917; Returned to Newfoundland, furlough, July 27, 1918; Demobilized, St. John's, Feb. 15, 1919.

George Edward Walsh   Reg. No. 506

Enlisted, Sept. 16, 1914; British Mediterranean Expeditionary Force, Aug. 20, 1915; Evacuated from Suvla, Sept. 20, 1915; Rejoined Battalion, Suez, Jan. 16, 1916; British Expeditionary Force, March 14, 1916; Embarked for Newfoundland, furlough, July 27, 1918; Demobilized, St. John's, Feb. 15, 1919.

Michael Francis Walsh   Reg. No. 399

Enlisted, Sept. 5, 1914; British Mediterranean Expeditionary Force, Aug. 20 1915; Evacuated from Suvla, Nov. 30, 1915; Discharged to duty, Jan. 7, 1916; British Expeditionary Force, March 18, 1916; Killed in action, Beaumont Hamel, July 1, 1916.

PATRICK JOSEPH WALSH   Reg. No. 286

Enlisted, Sept. 5, 1914; British Mediterranean Expeditionary Force, Aug. 20, 1915; Evacuated from Suvla, Oct. 21, 1915; Invalided to England, Nov. 6, 1915; Attached to Depot, Ayr, Jan. 11, 1916; Lance Corporal, Jan. 29, 1916; Acting Corporal, April 20, 1916; Acting Sergeant, May 30, 1916; British Expeditionary Force, Jan. 31, 1917; Wounded, LesFosses Farm, April 23, 1917; Invalided to England, May 15, 1917; Attached to Depot, Ayr, Sept. 6, 1917; Confirmed to Rank of Sergeant, April 27, 1918; Acting Company Sergeant Major, July 4, 1918; Confirmed to Rank, Dec. 20, 1918; Embarked for Newfoundland, April 2, 1919; Demobilized, St. John's, May 16, 1919.

FREDERICK WALTER WATERMAN   Reg. No. 441

Enlisted, Sept. 8, 1914; British Mediterranean Expeditionary Force, August 20, 1915; Lance Corporal, Sept. 20, 1915; Evacuated from Suvla, Dec. 16, 1915; Rejoined Battalion, Suez, Jan. 16, 1916; British Expeditionary Force, March 14, 1916; Wounded, Beaumont Hamel, July 1, 1916; Invalided to England, July 3, 1916; Attached to Depot, Ayr, Sept. 5, 1916; Acting Corporal, Jan. 17, 1917; Returned to British Expeditionary Force, Feb. 10, 1917; Sergeant, March 14, 1917; 2d Lieutenant, May 1, 1917; Mentioned in despatches, April 7, 1918; Embarked for Newfoundland, July 27, 1918; Returned to United Kingdom, Oct. 12, 1918; Lieutenant, Nov. 1, 1918; British Expeditionary Force, Nov. 24, 1918; Assistant Adjutant, Jan. 16, 1919; Adjutant, April 29, 1919; Embarked for Newfoundland, May 22, 1919; Awarded Military Cross, June 3, 1919; Retired, St. John's, June 14, 1919.

FRANCIS EMILIE WATTS   Reg. No. 71

Enlisted, Sept. 2, 1914; Lance Corporal, July 30, 1917; Discharged, St. John's, medically unfit, Dec. 7, 1918.

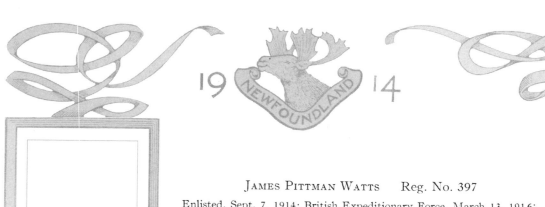

James Pittman Watts   Reg. No. 397

Enlisted, Sept. 7, 1914; British Expeditionary Force, March 13, 1916; Joined Battalion in France, April 8, 1916; Admitted to Hospital, July 21, 1916; Rejoined Battalion, Sept. 1, 1916; Killed in action, Gueudecourt, Oct. 12, 1916.

Rupert King Watts   Reg. No. 276

Enlisted, Sept. 3, 1914; Lance Corporal, June 14, 1915; British Mediterranean Expeditionary Force, Aug. 20, 1915; Evacuated to Hospital, Sept. 27, 1915; Died at 1st Australian Hospital, Mudros, Sept. 27, 1915.

Arthur Webber   Reg. No. 236

Enlisted, Sept. 2, 1914; British Mediterranean Expeditionary Force, Aug. 20, 1915; Evacuated from Suvla, Oct. 26, 1915; Discharged from Hospital, Dec. 10, 1915; British Expeditionary Force, March 18, 1916; Joined Battalion, April 15, 1916; Lance Corporal, July 12, 1916; Corporal, Sept. 14, 1916; Sergeant, Nov. 23, 1916; Awarded Military Medal, Jan. 6, 1917; Wounded, Monchy, April 14, 1917; Invalided to England, April 21, 1917; Italian Bronze Medal, May 24, 1917; Repatriated to Newfoundland, March 12, 1918; Discharged, St. John's, medically unfit, April 18, 1918

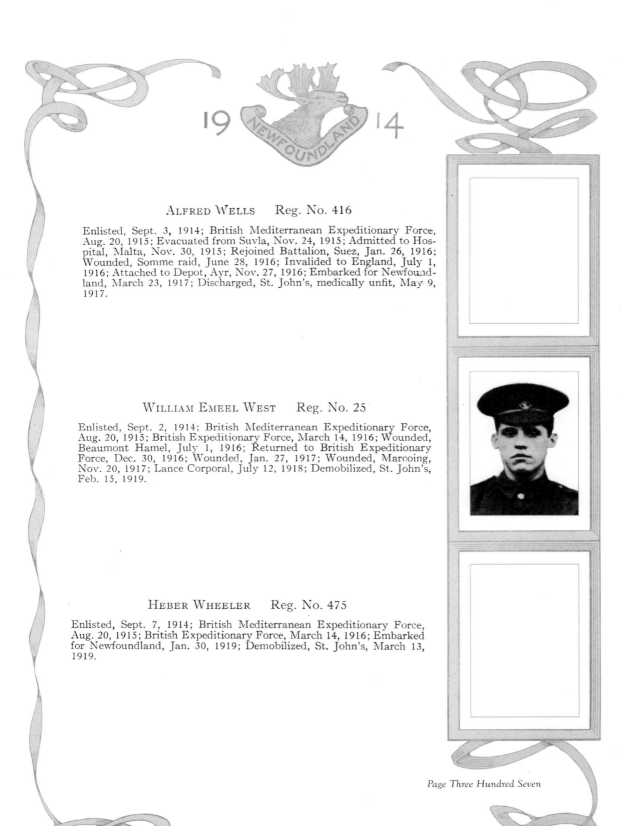

ALFRED WELLS   Reg. No. 416

Enlisted, Sept. 3, 1914; British Mediterranean Expeditionary Force, Aug. 20, 1915; Evacuated from Suvla, Nov. 24, 1915; Admitted to Hospital, Malta, Nov. 30, 1915; Rejoined Battalion, Suez, Jan. 26, 1916; Wounded, Somme raid, June 28, 1916; Invalided to England, July 1, 1916; Attached to Depot, Ayr, Nov. 27, 1916; Embarked for Newfoundland, March 23, 1917; Discharged, St. John's, medically unfit, May 9, 1917.

WILLIAM EMEEL WEST   Reg. No. 25

Enlisted, Sept. 2, 1914; British Mediterranean Expeditionary Force, Aug. 20, 1915; British Expeditionary Force, March 14, 1916; Wounded, Beaumont Hamel, July 1, 1916; Returned to British Expeditionary Force, Dec. 30, 1916; Wounded, Jan. 27, 1917; Wounded, Marcoing, Nov. 20, 1917; Lance Corporal, July 12, 1918; Demobilized, St. John's, Feb. 15, 1919.

HEBER WHEELER   Reg. No. 475

Enlisted, Sept. 7, 1914; British Mediterranean Expeditionary Force, Aug. 20, 1915; British Expeditionary Force, March 14, 1916; Embarked for Newfoundland, Jan. 30, 1919; Demobilized, St. John's, March 13, 1919.

John Joseph Whelan Reg. No. 169

Enlisted, Sept. 4, 1914; British Mediterranean Expeditionary Force, Aug. 20, 1915; Lance Corporal, Oct. 25, 1915; Evacuated from Suvla, Dec. 22, 1915; Invalided to England, Jan. 2, 1916; Corporal, Feb. 15, 1916; Acting Sergeant, March 30, 1916; British Expeditionary Force, Oct. 3, 1916; Wounded, LesFosses Farm, April 23, 1917; Invalided to England, May 1, 1917; Repatriated to Newfoundland, Feb. 23, 1918; Discharged, St. John's, medically unfit, Oct. 7, 1918.

Michael Thomas Whelan Reg. No. 432

Enlisted, Sept. 8, 1914; British Mediterranean Expeditionary Force, Aug. 20, 1915; Evacuated from Suvla, Oct. 12, 1915; Invalided to England, Feb. 11, 1916; Attached to Depot, Ayr, May 20, 1916; British Expeditionary Force, Aug. 24, 1916; Wounded, Gueudecourt, Oct. 12, 1916; Invalided to England, Oct. 19, 1916; Attached to Depot, Ayr, Dec. 13, 1916; Repatriated to Newfoundland, Sept. 13, 1917; Discharged, St. John's, medically unfit, Feb. 5, 1918.

Charles Edward White Reg. No. 171

Enlisted, Sept. 4, 1914; British Mediterranean Expeditionary Force, Aug. 20, 1915; Lance Corporal, Oct. 6, 1915; Evacuated from Suvla, Nov. 17, 1915; Invalided to England, Jan. 16, 1916; Acting Corporal, March 30, 1916; Acting Sergeant, May 2, 1916; Acting Company Sergeant Major, Oct. 9, 1916; British Expeditionary Force, Oct. 11, 1916; Acting Company Sergeant Major, Dec. 5, 1916; Confirmed to Rank of Company Sergeant Major, Dec. 5, 1916; Confirmed to Rank of Regimental Sergeant Major, Dec. 5, 1916; Wounded, Monchy, April 14, 1917; Invalided to England, April 18, 1917; Returned to British Expeditionary Force, March 27, 1918; Acting Regimental Sergeant Major, May 3, 1918; Confirmed to Rank of Regimental Sergeant Major, June 30, 1918; Returned to Newfoundland, furlough, July 27, 1918; Awarded Meritorious Service Medal, Jan. 18, 1919; Honorary 2nd Lieutenant, Feb. 15, 1919; Retired, St. John's, Feb. 15, 1919.

19 14

DOUGALD WHITE   Reg. No. 37

Enlisted, Sept. 2, 1914; British Mediterranean Expeditionary Force, Nov. 14, 1915; British Expeditionary Force, March 14, 1916; Transferred to Depot, classified "Permanent Base," Dec. 30, 1916; Discharged, St. John's, medically unfit, Dec. 21, 1918.

EDWARD WHITE   Reg. No. 486

Enlisted, Sept. 11, 1914; British Mediterranean Expeditionary Force, Aug. 20, 1915; Evacuated from Suvla, Nov. 7, 1915; Invalided to England, Jan. 14, 1916; Attached to Depot, Ayr, May 2, 1916; British Expeditionary Force, Jan. 31, 1917; Admitted to Hospital, Rouen, Feb. 3, 1917; Rejoined Battalion, Sept. 9, 1917; Admitted to Hospital, Sept. 27, 1917; Invalided to England, Oct. 24, 1917; Attached to Depot, Ayr, Nov. 29, 1917; Embarked for Newfoundland, furlough, July 21, 1918; Demobilized, St. John's, Feb. 15, 1919.

WILLIAM WHITE   Reg. No. 345

Enlisted, Sept. 2, 1914; British Mediterranean Expeditionary Force, Aug. 20, 1915; British Expeditionary Force, March 14, 1916; Killed in action, Beaumont Hamel, July 1, 1916.

John Williams   Reg. No. 5

Enlisted, Sept. 2, 1914; Lance Corporal, Sept. 21, 1914; Corporal, Nov. 12, 1914; Sergeant, April 23, 1915; British Mediterranean Expeditionary Force, Aug. 20, 1915; Evacuated from Suvla, Dec. 2, 1915; Invalided to England, Dec. 20, 1915; Attached to Depot, Ayr, Feb. 5, 1916; 2nd Lieutenant, July 12, 1916; British Expeditionary Force, Oct. 8, 1916; Evacuated to Hospital, April 3, 1917; Invalided to England, May 8, 1917; Attached to Depot, Ayr, July 14, 1917; Lieutenant, Jan. 12, 1918; Returned to British Expeditionary Force, Aug. 26, 1918; Rejoined Battalion, Aug. 28, 1918; Evacuated to Hospital, Sept. 13, 1918; Transferred to United Kingdom, April 23, 1919; Embarked for Newfoundland, June 24, 1919; Retired, July 17, 1919.

Roland Williams   Reg. No. 10

Enlisted, Sept. 2, 1914; Lance Corporal, April 21, 1915; British Mediterranean Expeditionary Force, Aug. 20, 1915; Corporal, Nov. 14, 1915; Evacuated from Suvla, Dec. 1, 1915; Invalided to England, Dec. 19, 1915; Attached to Depot, Ayr, April 8, 1916; Sergeant, Oct. 27, 1916; Embarked for Newfoundland, furlough, July 21, 1918; Demobilized, St. John's, Feb. 15, 1919.

Henry Kelso Wilson   Reg. No. 305

Enlisted, Sept. 7, 1914; British Mediterranean Expeditionary Force, Aug. 20, 1915; British Expeditionary Force, March 14, 1916; Evacuated to Hospital, March 30, 1916; Discharged to Base, April 26, 1916; Admitted to Hospital, Rouen, May 21, 1916; Invalided to England, June 1, 1916; Attached to Depot, Ayr, June 25, 1916; Embarked for Newfoundland, furlough, July 21, 1918; Demobilized, St. John's, Feb. 15, 1919.

19 14

GEORGE JOSEPH WINSLOW   Reg. No. 317

Enlisted, Sept. 7, 1914; Lance Corporal, Dec. 8, 1914; Armourer, Dec. 18, 1914; Corporal, June 14, 1915; British Mediterranean Expeditionary Force, Aug. 20, 1915; Evacuated from Suvla, Sept. 29, 1915; Armourer Sergeant, Nov. 14, 1915; Joined Battalion, Jan. 15, 1916; Admitted to Hospital, Suez, March 7, 1916; Discharged to duty, May 14, 1916; Discharged to Marseilles from Egypt, May 27, 1916; Rejoined Battalion, June 30, 1916; Wounded, Beaumont Hamel, July 1, 1916; Invalided to England, July 3, 1916; Attached to Depot, Ayr, Oct. 7, 1916; Embarked for Newfoundland, May 18, 1917; Attached for duty at Depot, St. John's, June 1, 1917; Demobilized St. John's, Feb. 8, 1919.

EDGAR WINDSOR   Reg. No. 472

Enlisted, Sept. 8, 1914; British Mediterranean Expeditionary Force, Aug. 20, 1915; Evacuated from Suvla, Oct. 13, 1915; Invalided to England, Oct. 27, 1915; Attached to Depot, Ayr, Nov. 22, 1915; Lance Corporal, Dec. 5, 1915; Corporal, April 20, 1916; Acting Sergeant, Dec. 19, 1916; British Expeditionary Force, Aug. 5, 1917; Joined Battalion, Aug. 28, 1917; Killed in action, Broembeek, Oct. 9, 1917.

STANLEY CHARLES WINDSOR   Reg. No. 301

Enlisted, Sept. 8, 1914; British Mediterranean Expeditionary Force, Aug. 20, 1915; Evacuated from Suvla, Dec. 14, 1915; Admitted to Hospital, Malta, Dec. 17, 1915; Invalided to England, March 29, 1916; Attached to Depot, Ayr, April 27, 1916; Lance Corporal, Oct. 13, 1916; British Expeditionary Force, Oct. 24, 1916; Rejoined Battalion, Nov. 18, 1916; Wounded, Steenbeke, Aug. 20, 1917; Invalided to England, Aug. 31, 1917; Attached to Depot, Ayr, Dec. 12, 1917; Acting Corporal, May 20, 1918; Returned to Newfoundland, furlough, Aug. 21, 1918; Discharged, St. John's, medically unfit, Oct. 26, 1918.

1914

ERNEST WOOD   Reg. No. 29

Enlisted, Sept. 2, 1914; British Mediterranean Expeditionary Force, Aug. 20, 1915; Served with 1st Composite Battalion, Western Egyptian Frontier, Nov. 1915, to Feb. 1916; British Expeditionary Force, March 2, 1916; Demobilized, St. John's, Feb. 15, 1919.

FRANK WOODFORD   Reg. No. 364

Enlisted, Sept. 5, 1914; British Mediterranean Expeditionary Force, Aug. 20, 1915; British Expeditionary Force, March 14, 1916; Evacuated to Hospital, May 4, 1916; Rejoined Battalion, June 30, 1916; Killed in action, Beaumont Hamel, July 1, 1916.

EDWARD WYATT   Reg. No. 371

Enlisted, Sept. 5, 1914; British Mediterranean Expeditionary Force, Aug. 20, 1915; British Expeditionary Force, March 14, 1916; Transferred to 168th Machine Gun Company, Belgium, Sept. 2, 1916; Embarked for Newfoundland, furlough, Sept. 23, 1918; Demobilized, St. John's, Feb. 25, 1919.

1914

Thomas Walter Wyatt   Reg. No. 386

Enlisted, Sept. 7, 1914; British Mediterranean Expeditionary Force, Aug. 20, 1915; Admitted to Hospital, Mudros, Oct. 25, 1915; Discharged to duty, Jan. 10, 1916; British Expeditionary Force, March 14, 1916; Wounded, Beaumont Hamel, July 1, 1916; Invalided to England, July 4, 1916; Attached to Depot, Ayr, Oct. 3, 1916; Embarked for Newfoundland furlough, July 21, 1918; Discharged, St John's, medically unfit, Nov. 25, 1918.

Gordon Bemister Yates   Reg. No. 570

Enlisted, Sept. 17, 1914; British Mediterranean Expeditionary Force, Aug. 20, 1915; Evacuated from Suvla, Oct. 1, 1915; Admitted to Hospital, Cairo, Oct. 5, 1915; Rejoined Battalion, Suez, March 1, 1916; British Expeditionary Force, March 14, 1916; Wounded, Beaumont Hamel, July 1, 1916; Invalided to England, July 4, 1916; Attached to Depot, Ayr, Aug. 29, 1916; Embarked for Newfoundland, Sept. 27, 1916; Discharged, St. John's, medically unfit, Jan. 26, 1917.

Andrew Yetman   Reg. No. 43

Enlisted, Sept. 16, 1914; British Mediterranean Expeditionary Force; Aug. 20, 1915; British Expeditionary Force, March 14, 1916; Wounded, Beaumont Hamel, July 1, 1916; Invalided to England, July 3, 1916 Repatriated to Newfoundland, July 10, 1917; Discharged, St. John's, medically unfit, June 14, 1918.

NEWFOUNDLAND

WILLIAM YETMAN   Reg. No. 610

Enlisted, Sept. 28, 1914; British Mediterranean Expeditionary Force, Aug. 20, 1915; British Expeditionary Force, March 14, 1916; Wounded, Beaumont Hamel, July 1, 1916; Invalided to England, July 3, 1916; Attached to Depot, Ayr, Aug. 8, 1916; Returned to British Expeditionary Force, April 25, 1917; Rejoined Battalion, July 7, 1917; Evacuated to Hospital, Jan. 9, 1918; Discharged to Base Depot, Aug. 25, 1918; Transferred to England, Sept. 2, 1918; Embarked for Newfoundland, furlough, Sept. 7, 1918; Demobilized, St. John's, Feb. 25, 1919.

19 NEWFOUNDLAND 14

The Editor desires to extend his heartiest thanks to all those who have assisted in any way in the publication of this volume, and in particular to:

J. A. Clift, Esq., K. C.
Lt.-Col. George Carty
George Langmead, Sr., Esq.
S. O. Steele, Esq.
Lieut. H. C. Janes
J. C. Parsons, Esq., Photographer
H. S. Parsons, Esq. Photographer
David A. Grant, Esq., Photographer
Funk & Wagnalls Co. (The Literary Digest)
C. F. Williams & Son, Inc.

The Editor considers it very unfortunate that all the photographs of the men who formed the First Contingent of Newfoundland's Fighting Battalion were not obtainable. Where the photographs were not obtained, a space has been left so that anyone interested in a particular soldier, whose photograph does not accompany his military record, can have a photograph made the uniform size and pasted in the space provided for that purpose.